Conflict Regulation

Other Titles of Interest

Westview Special Studies in Peace, Conflict, and Conflict Resolution

Conflict Regulation
Paul Wehr

This volume examines conflict and conflict regulation processes. The author reviews theories of conflict and techniques of conflict management and then presents case studies of self-limiting conflict in Gandhi's India, Nazi-occupied Norway, and at a nuclear weapons plant in Colorado to illustrate unconventional approaches to conflict regulation. He also discusses the emergence and resolution of environmental and resource conflicts in Colorado's mountain communities. The material was originally prepared for an American Association for the Advancement of Science short course for college teachers. Interdisciplinary in perspective, with emphasis on recent developments, it should be useful in teaching and as a general introduction to the field of conflict regulation.

Paul Wehr is associate professor of sociology and director of the Environmental Conciliation Project in the Institute of Behavioral Science, University of Colorado, Boulder. Professor Wehr is coauthor of *Peace and World Order Systems*.

Conflict Regulation

Paul Wehr

Foreword by Kenneth E. Boulding

Westview Press / Boulder, Colorado

Westview Special Studies in Peace, Conflict, and Conflict Resolution

Copyright © 1979 by Westview Press, Inc.

Published in 1979 in the United States of America by
  Westview Press, Inc.
  5500 Central Avenue
  Boulder, Colorado 80301
  Frederick A. Praeger, Publisher

Library of Congress Cataloging in Publication Data:
Wehr, Paul.
  Conflict regulation.
  (Westview special studies in peace, conflict, and conflict resolution)
  Bibliography: p.
  1. Social conflict. 2. Social conflict—Case studies. 3. War and society. 4. Peace.
I. Title. II. Series.
HM281.W42   301.6'3   78-14588
ISBN 0-89158-351-3
ISBN 0-89158-352-1 pbk.

Printed and bound in the United States of America

To my parents,
who taught me much about peacemaking

Contents

Figures and Tables

Foreword

The past thirty years have seen the emergence of a new discipline (or perhaps we should call it an "interdiscipline") in the social sciences that goes by a variety of names in the general field of the study of conflict. The French called it *polemologie*; it has been called peace and conflict studies, peace science, peace research, and so on. These different names reflect slightly different definitions of the field, different divisions between the pure and the applied. But there is still a large area of overlap. The study has its pure aspect in that it takes the phenomenon of conflict, which is a property of virtually all social systems, and abstracts it from the larger social system very much as economics abstracts the concept of exchange. Thus, pure "conflict science" examines both the general patterns and the particular forms of conflict, both analytically and descriptively. On the applied side there is peace research, or peace science as Walter Isard calls it, which is concerned with the application of the general study of conflict to its peaceful management. At the other end of the scale we have the strategic sciences, which are more concerned with winning conflicts than with moderating them. The distinction between pure and applied is one of emphasis and there is, again, a good deal of overlap simply because, whatever its objective, the applied field must take account of the real world of conflict dynamics and patterns.

One can perhaps distinguish three stages in the development of a discipline. The first is the bibliographical stage, in which there is a growing bibliography, beginning with the pioneers and often expanding almost exponentially. In the second stage

xiii

the discipline develops journals that further expand the specialized bibliography. In this stage the discipline usually begins to be taught in a somewhat irregular and casual way, later moving into regular programs, like the conflict and peace studies programs that now can be found at many colleges and universities. In the third stage textbooks appear and the materials of the bibliography are condensed and abstracted into a coherent body of thought that tends to be perpetuated from one textbook to the next.

I suspect that "conflict science," both pure and applied, is very close to the third stage, and Paul Wehr's useful and stimulating volume may well signal the approach to it, even though it is designed not as a textbook but as a guide to the literature and as a case study of several applied fields. The first part of the book is an especially useful discussion of the literature of conflict studies. The second part applies principles to the somewhat unusual but extremely interesting case of local conflict related to environmental and developmental problems. It is a powerful demonstration of the principle that there is a discipline of conflict science with application in many different fields—not only in the more conventional areas of international relations and war and peace, but also at many other levels in social systems. This is not—and is not intended be—the definitive and complete textbook that we are waiting for, yet it is an important step towards it; teachers, students, and general readers will all find it helpful.

Kenneth E. Boulding

Preface

Humankind has been regulating conflict for centuries. The political treatises of Hobbes, Locke, Rousseau, Plato, and Ibn Khaldun dealt largely with the problems of regulating conflict within and between societies. Galtung (1965) traces the development of institutionalized conflict resolution from the medieval period. The use of oracles, trial by ordeal, regulated warfare, private and judicial duels, and arbitration were prominent techniques in that development.

Nevertheless, fighting has been more visible than peace-making and peacekeeping, and there is little doubt that considerably more energy has been invested in creating new methods for waging conflict than for regulating and resolving it. This imbalance in investment has been reinforced by modern historians and social theorists who, by oversight or by design, have consistently slighted the processes of conflict regulation. Wars, for example, normally terminate in negotiation, peace settlements, reconstruction, and reestablishment of peaceful relations. Historians, however, normally devote chapters to the fighting stages of the war and paragraphs to the termination process. There has also been a noticeable lack of scholarly interest in nonviolent resistance to tyranny, aggression, and conscription for war. Only recently with the research of Sharp (1973), Brock (1968), Lynd (1966), and others, has this important method of conflict regulation entered the mainstream of academic scholarship.

Fortunately, increasing numbers of scholars, industrial and community leaders, government officials at all levels, and students have shown interest in conflict regulation in recent years. As the destructive potential and accessibility of weapons increases, so does the urgency of developing means of regulating conflict and minimizing its violence. Conflict regulation can be both a science and a craft. In either case it is learned—through research, study, training, and experience. In the past decade a number of programs have been established to train persons in conflict regulation and dispute settlement (see Appendix A). Academic centers have also been created to study conflict and peace processes (see Appendix B). Though the researcher and the practitioner do not yet interact sufficiently, their collaboration grows steadily more productive.

As conflict regulation becomes a more significant concern for academicians, policymakers, and leaders of social change movements, we shall see it take shape as both an academic and a professional specialization. More faculty will teach and research it, and more students will study and practice it and then move into professional peacemaking roles. Education, business, government, public interest organizations—every important field will see increasing need for professional help in conflict regulation.

As a rapidly expanding field, conflict regulation desperately needs a literature of its own. There now exists substantial published work in conflict analysis, conflict resolution, and justice theory. This essential material lies scattered throughout the disciplines, and little has been done to integrate it or to use it in practice. With this book I seek to interconnect some of the scattered material, to encourage its practical application, and to stimulate more teaching and research.

The emphases of this book are dictated by the nature of the topic. First, the study of conflict regulation is transdisciplinary. Each discipline has its contribution to make. A topical field such as this lends itself not at all to discipline-bound investigation—in fact, does any problem worthy of intensive study?

This book also looks at conflict and conflict regulation at different levels of human interaction. Does conflict exhibit common properties across the interpersonal, the intergroup, the interorganizational, and the international levels? If it does, so should the methods of regulating it. I believe there is more cross-level commonality in the origins, dynamics, and regulation of conflict than we have been aware of in the past.

As I treat it here, conflict regulation is a good deal broader than normally defined. It is concerned with the management and resolution of overt conflict and disputes, of course. But anticipation and prevention of conflict is also a part of the regulation process. So is the invention of new styles of waging nonviolent conflict by groups and nations struggling against external domination and social injustice. All of these are means by which conflict can be kept within acceptable bounds and moving toward creative outcomes.

I have written this book primarily for teachers and their students. It has a decided bias in favor of the mixing of reflection and action in a student's learning experience. The interaction of the two is at the core of conflict studies. Without this interaction one can perhaps learn about conflict regulation but never know how to go about it. I am, in this book, encouraging certain learning styles: problem-centered, practice-linked, change-directed, future-oriented, self-taught. All of these combined characterize what I call active learning.

I begin with a review of theoretical approaches to the analysis of conflict, its origins, and dynamics. This is an extensive rather than an intensive review—an overview, at best. It leads into a discussion of the major types of regulation modes and some specific innovative methods developed in recent years. Finally, I present several case studies from my own research to illustrate how certain conflict regulation principles are applied to problems beyond the range one usually associates with conflict resolution and peacemaking. In one sense the book is a primer. It is designed not to give the last word, but to stimulate others to further explore the field and to experiment with it. At the end of some chapters I have suggested in- and out-of-class conflict learning exercises—the complete exercises are included as appendixes.

When I introduce my students to the field of conflict regulation, I attempt to help them assess their initial knowledge and competence. What personal knowledge of conflict and conflict regulation does each student have? Most students in my classes are unaware initially that their personal histories can teach them much about conflict and its regulation. Students can also learn a great deal by sharing these histories with one another. I have found three exercises to be particularly useful for knowledge assessment: family past-imaging (Appendix C); conflict waging and regulation styles (Appendix D); and a personal conflict impact essay (Appendix E).

Paul Wehr

Acknowledgments

This book is a collection of studies I have done over the past seven years. Each has been facilitated by research funds from private and public sources and enriched by the critical review and encouragement of many colleagues and friends.

The Short Courses for College Teachers program of the American Association for the Advancement of Science, the National Endowment for the Humanities, the Ford and Rockefeller foundations, and the North Atlantic Treaty Organization all funded parts of the research and writing. These organizations deserve special credit for supporting peace research at a time when it was regarded as a high-risk venture. The Consortium on Peace Research, Education and Development, the Institute for World Order, and the International Peace Research Association provided networks of colleagues for testing and revising conclusions. A grant from the Committee on University Scholarly Publications at the University of Colorado has made possible the publication of this book.

Among my University of Colorado colleagues, Elise and Kenneth Boulding have greatly enriched my understanding of conflict and peace processes. My fellow members of the university Conflict and Peace Studies Committee have been congenial partners in the search for more effective approaches to teaching and research in practical application of what Kenneth Boulding has called conflict science. Otomar Bartos, himself a student of conflict resolution, has shed new light on this problem for me. Gilbert White has been a continuing source of encouragement and incisive critique. The members of my graduate seminar in conflict management have made helpful comments on the manuscript as have my colleagues Susan Carpenter and John Shippee.

In the past, my research on nonviolent collective behavior has benefited greatly from my work with A. Paul Hare, whose pioneering efforts to vigorously apply social theory to nonviolent action are well known. It was theorist Philip Rieff who first impressed upon me the value of multiple analytic perspectives and thus committed me to drawing upon multiple theoretical schools for my own image of social reality, a commitment that I have valued highly.

I am indebted to Gloria Lund for her patient and skillful typing of this manuscript, to Robin Crews for his preparation of the figures and tables, and to my editors Lynne Rienner, Lynn Lloyd, and Douglas Beall for their untiring work with me and their faith in the final product.

Finally, my daughter Kirsten, who at the tender age of eleven is already wise and skilled in the ways of interpersonal peacemaking, has challenged me to meld theory and practice more effectively and has forced me to keep at the task of making conflict, wherever it is inevitable, more creative in both process and outcome.

Paul Wehr

Conflict Regulation

1. Conflict Analysis

To effectively intervene in a conflict to resolve it, one must be able to analyze it properly. There are two levels of analysis that students of conflict regulation must master. At the macro level, we know much about the origins and dynamics of social and international conflict and about the relationship of conflict to violence. There is, however, no general theory of these processes nor is there agreement across or within disciplines. At this point in the development of the field, the best we can do is present a number of analytical frameworks to draw upon when analyzing a particular conflict case. Later in this chapter, an approach to microanalysis will also be presented.

Origins

Why does social and international conflict occur? Theoretical debates of the past two decades and the paradigms emerging from them suggest a number of propositions.

1. *Conflict and fighting is innate in all social animals including man.* This view is most clearly presented by ethologist Konrad Lorenz (1969). Its characterization of human conflict relies heavily on instinctual theories of aggression, competition for territorial space (Ardrey, 1966), and other parallels drawn between human conflict and conflictual interaction in lower animals. According to this approach, humans differ from the lower animals in their fighting habits primarily in that (1) humans have no natural weapons and have used their

superior intelligence to create overly destructive ones, and (2) humans lack the inhibition against intraspecific killing that protects the survival of other species. Lorenz's proposals for regulation of conflict and fighting among humans concentrate on sublimation and displacement processes whereby destructive impulses are channeled into more or less constructive forms of fighting such as sports contests.

The response to this instinctual theory has been sharp and critical from some behavioral scientists (Montague, 1968; Gorney, 1973) and supportive from others (Storr, 1968). The major counterargument seems to be that the gap between human behavior and that of lower animals is too great to permit drawing the parallels ethologists do. As Kenneth Boulding puts it,

> if displaced aggression in the goose leads to love, as Lorenz says it does, or if territoriality is a characteristic of the Uganda Kob, as Ardrey describes, does this mean either that man's ancestors possessed these qualities and attributes or that man today does? It is clear that a great leap has been made in the dark but it is by no means clear that our feet have landed on firm ground. (Montague, 1968:86)

Moreover, recent research by Leakey (1977) suggests that early man, more like lower animals in biological evolutionary terms, was a relatively pacific being. Although I tend not to accept the existence of a fighting instinct among humans, this idea does present an interesting challenge to social scientific conflict theory and should be part of a theoretical review of the field. The theory may have political importance as well. There is the possibility of a popularized form of the proposition becoming a self-fulfilling prophecy. If humans are genetically programmed to fight over territory and other values, then war is imbued with a certain inevitability, a "cosmic legitimacy" it otherwise lacks, and efforts to regulate conflict make less sense. This is not, of course, what Lorenz is saying, but when Ardrey popularized his territoriality concept at the height of the Vietnam War, the territoriality/fighting theory was cleverly woven into official justification of the war. In a Gallup poll of the late sixties, a large proportion of the respondents felt that war is an inevitable consequence of human nature and that efforts to do away with it are futile.

2. *Social conflict originates in the nature of certain societies and how they are structured.* This proposition is suggested by what are known as *coercion theorists.* Karl Marx is the most influential of the group, which views capitalist society as a highly stratified structure within which coherence is maintained through coercion of some groups or classes by others. This image of society and conflict origin implies an inevitable class-oriented conflict of interests—built-in latent conflict that must ultimately become manifest. Marcuse (1968) and C. Wright Mills (1959) provide variations on the basic theme that views conflict not as a random occurrence, but as the product of a capitalist social and economic structure.

Coercion theory implies that a conflict of interests within society is not permanent and that a consensual model of a classless society emerges from revolutionary social conflict. Various ideologues such as Lenin, Mao Tse-tung, and Fanon are contributers to this body of theory.

Other conflict theorists see social conflict emerging from control of some groups by others, but they do not relate that control necessarily to Marx's concept of social class. Dahrendorf (1959) sees an inevitable conflict of interests in society, but not between Marxist-type classes. According to Dahrendorf, authority, not property, is the prime source of social conflict. What he terms *conflict groups* are the agents of conflict. Social conflict centers around access to authority, and as "quasi-groups" such as laborers become aware of differential access to that authority, their latent interests become manifest, and conflict increases. Examples of conflict groups in American society would be labor unions and minority equal-rights organizations.

3. *Conflict is an aberration, a dysfunctional process in social systems.* This proposition is reflected in the theory of the *consensus* or integration school. Theorists such as Parsons (1951) and Smelser (1962) view society as a system cohering around normative consensus. Societal coherence is rooted in the legitimacy of both the social system and the roles and statuses within it as perceived by its members. The social order need not, according to this view, be imposed by groups with pre-

dominant power, because it is perceived legitimacy that sustains it. When and where conflict occurs, it is a random, almost incidental process and reflects a pathological strain in the system—a threat to systemic equilibrium. If the strain becomes too great, political revolution may occur as system legitimacy disintegrates (Johnson, 1966). These theorists see cooperation as the normal state of interpersonal and inter-group relations in any society, and it seems difficult for them to deal with the processes of conflict and change within a society—particularly the important reciprocal relationship between those processes.

Although the coercion and consensus explanations of social conflict have battled it out over the past two decades, Dahrendorf observes that

> a decision which accepts one of these theories and rejects the other is neither necessary nor desirable. There are sociological problems for the explanation of which the integration theory of society provides adequate assumptions; there are other problems which can be explained only in terms of the coercion theory of society; there are finally, problems for which both theories appear adequate. For sociological analysis, society is Janus-headed, and its two faces are equivalent aspects of the same reality. (1959:159)

He goes on to suggest how the coercion and consensus views might be compatible in a general theory of conflict. His own conflict/integration model gives equal weight to the stable and the changing aspects of society—its recurring, conserving elements and its innovative, discontinuous ones.

Dahrendorf categorizes conflict as legitimate and routinized or illegitimate and uncontrolled, as interest groups develop and begin to conflict with those having exclusive access to authority. The challenging groups engage in illegitimate or encapsulated conflict, since they are not initially accorded legitimacy by dominant groups. The past century of American history reflects the repressive response of existing authority structures to the challenges of the labor movement, racial and ethnic minorities, and women (Gurr and Graham, 1970). Until recently the United Farm Worker movement was denied the right to conflict by farm management, state governments, and in many instances even the judiciary.

Once conflict groups have attained the right to conflict, and acceptable arenas and appropriate means of conflicting over access to authority have been determined, conflict becomes routinized and conflict management can occur within recognized bounds—by the rules, so to speak. Gamson (1975) has identified various means by which challenging groups in American history have achieved this right to conflict. Before a struggling group is recognized as a legitimate conflict agent, the conflict may be violent, with structural changes resisted in every possible way by groups having dominant access to authority. When legitimacy is recognized, however, the possibilities for regulation of conflict through institutionalization are greatly improved.

Dahrendorf's integrative theory of conflict encourages the formulation of composite theoretical frameworks for clarifying the origins of conflict. There are no general theories, and one should piece together a coherent framework for oneself.

4. *Conflict occurs because it is functional for social systems.* Conflict is not inherently pathological or necessarily dysfunctional. Coser (1956) illustrates through testable propositions how societies can be strengthened internally, relations between societies maintained and reinforced, and social pathology reduced—all through conflict. Oberschall (1973) sees the conflict associated with social movements as potentially functional for social systems. The functionality of conflict is, however, heavily dependent on the reference unit. War with another nation may bring coherence and internal strength to a society and may therefore be functional for that society. At the same time, however, it may also be dysfunctional for the regional and international systems that society is part of. It is important to distinguish between short- and long-run functionality. An external threat that pulls a society together may permit short-range survival, but over long periods may bring about deterioration through attrition. Israel could be a case in point.

Ethnologists such as Bourdieu (1962) have pointed out the

functional, even indispensable role that conflict plays in certain traditional societies. Among the Berber Kabyles of North Africa, for example, balance and controlled conflict have been keystones of societal maintenance. Himes (1966) applies the functional theory of conflict to an analysis of racial conflict in the United States, where the conflict process has permitted considerable power equalization and status coordination between races, thereby strengthening the larger society.

5. *Conflict between societies occurs because each, as a nation-state, pursues often incompatible national interests.* These interests center around security, power, and prestige. Scholars and practitioners supporting this proposition see the nation-state as a totally different type of conflict unit— different primarily because of the concept of national sovereignty and the absence of enforceable constraints and sanctions on national behavior in the international system.

Competing national interests, miscalculation by leaders, the over-concentration of power in any one locus—these are the roots of war, according to this perspective. Hans Morgenthau (1967) is perhaps the most influential of these theorists, a group we might call the *realist school.* Kissinger (1964) and Knorr (1966) also take the power politics perspective in the analysis of international conflict, with the balance of power, deterrence, blocs, spheres of influence, national security, and national interest being the central concepts.

While the power politics model seems to be currently dominant in the analysis of international conflict, it is challenged by another group of theorists that sees the world as an increasingly global system in which nation-states make up only one set of actors. Their research focuses on transnational networks—legal structures, multinational corporations, voluntary associations, supranational organizations, religious bodies, and the like—that bypass or are not directly dependent on national governments and increasingly influence global processes. Kriesberg (1972), Angell (1969), Alger (1975), Judge (1972), Nye and Keohane (1971), and Falk and Mendlovitz (1966) provide a counterview to the conventional image of the international system as a jumble of power blocs, clashing national interests, and warring states. Perhaps the most accurate label for this emerging school of theory would be the *transnational interaction perspective*.

There are other challenges to the power politics view of the origins of international conflict as well. *Linkage theory* posits the existence of multiple subsystems (Singer, 1969) that facilitate the interpenetration of national systems, and it calls into serious question the classic power politics worldview. One approach sees foreign policy, including warmaking and conciliation, as at least a partial extension of domestic politics. Any thoughtful observer of the Southeast Asia policies of recent American administrations would have support for such a view.

The *Marxist model* too, is ultimately extended to an analysis of relationships between nation-states. Marxism is a general theory that characterizes a global conflict of interests as inherent in the capitalist international structure with its exploited and exploiting—the latter conflicting both with the exploited and among themselves for resources and markets. Modern interpretations of this view would include Baran and Sweezy (1968) and Galtung (1970).

Other approaches to analyzing origins of international conflict include the Correlates of War research (Singer, 1972), which seeks to identify what convergence of factors facilitates war, and *alternative world futures* (Mendlovitz, 1975), which analyzes basic global peace and world order problems and envisions alternative futures and the policies through which they would be brought about.

6. *Conflict is a consequence of poor communication, misperception, miscalculation, socialization, and other unconscious processes.* Behavioral conflict researchers hold that the incompatibility of interests between conflict parties is often illusory. They focus upon the actors in a conflict: decision-making styles of leaders, variables influencing decision making, perceptions of and communication between conflict parties, values and attitudes influencing conflictual behavior, personality variables that make for peace- or war-proneness. Behaviorists like North (1963) and Kelman (1965) see the origins of war as human miscalculation and misperception at least as much as the pursuit of competing national interests.

The misperception and mental sets of decision makers seem to have been a major factor in the involvement of the United States in Vietnam (Halberstam, 1972).

One would include in this perspective much of the research on gaming, racial and ethnic prejudice, conflict-related decision making, cognitive conflict studies, and political socialization as it relates to handling conflict. Contributions in this area include those of Burton (1969), Rapoport (1961), Elise Boulding (1972), Klineberg (1964), Eckhardt (1972), and White (1970). Decision-making analysis (Snyder, 1962) best reveals the complexity of the processes by which foreign policy decisions are made that will lead toward and away from war. This approach counters the fiction that nations themselves are actors that conflict and cooperate according to a separate set of principles beyond the understanding and influence of ordinary citizens.

7. *Conflict is a natural process common to all societies, with predictable dynamics and amenable to constructive regulation.* This proposition reflects my own strong bias. Each conflict situation can be analyzed for constructive intervention. J. S. Coleman (1957) initiated this microanalytical approach with his paradigm for community-based conflict. Kriesberg (1973), Laue and Cormick (1973), and Burton (1969) all suggest additional analytical frameworks and, in some cases, intervention techniques for treating conflict as a regulable and potentially creative process. This final proposition is essential to positions advanced later in this book.

Dynamics

Understanding the macro- and microprocesses of conflict is essential for conflict regulation. Much less work has been done by social scientists in this area than on conflict origins. There are, however, several propositions that reflect important work done in the field.

1. *Social conflict is a dialectical and phasic process in which synthesis takes place and by which society is transformed from one state to another.* Drawing upon Hegel's concept of the dialectic and applying it to historical reality, Marx saw class conflict developing in phases, with each phase unfolding from

the preceding one and leading ultimately to complete revolution. This would produce a basically conflict-free society since there would no longer be class interests.

Gandhi's conceptualization of conflict was also a dialectical one (Bondurant, 1965). His view of the movement of society from a condition of nontruth to one of social truth was not final like that of Marx. In his view, conflict will not disappear but is in itself a continual source of truth-finding. The absolute truth will never be found, as it will be for Marx, and conflict will continue. Gandhi's dialectic, as we shall discuss later, was a very personal one, resulting not in the victory of one group over another, but in a synthesis of the truths of the parties in conflict.

2. *Social conflict is primarily cyclical in its development and moves through a predictable sequence of stages.* Kriesberg (1973) provides the most comprehensive review of sociological conflict theory, but he also generates some new propositions. His mode of analysis is a cyclical one tracing the formation of objective conflict and following it through the awareness, escalation, deescalation, and termination phases to outcomes that may or may not contain the potential for a recycling of the conflict (Figure 1).

3. *Conflict progresses as oppressed groups become more aware of a conflict of interest and move to alter the situation.* Curle (1971) sees the linear sequence of this process as (1) lower awareness—as in the case of slavery where a slave knows of his status but is ignorantly passive; (2) a higher awareness of the basic conflict of interests—through education; (3) a confrontation of oppressed and oppressor—by either violent or nonviolent means; (4) conciliation and bargaining; and (5) a restructuring of the formerly unpeaceful relations (see Figure 2).

Writers like Curle, Friere (1971), and Dolci (1970), who concentrate on grossly asymmetrical conflict situations, find accomodation an inappropriate technique of conflict regulation. From their perspectives, awareness, confrontation, and restructuring of the conflict-producing relationships are essential parts of the conflict developing and regulating process. Chalmers Johnson (1966) presents the awareness/confrontation sequence in terms of systemic theory, by which endogenous and exogenous factors bring about awareness and

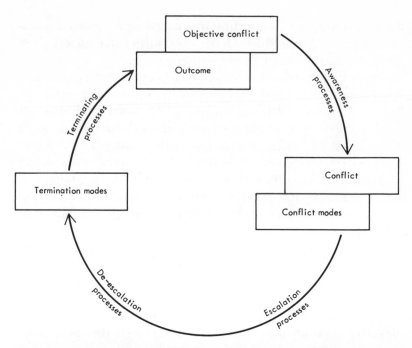

Figure 1. The cyclical path of conflict. (From Louis Kriesberg, *The Sociology of Social Conflicts,* copyright © 1973, p. 19. Reprinted by permission of Prentice-Hall, Inc., Englewood Cliffs, N.J.)

ultimately political revolution, if elites do not respond to the pressure for change in enlightened ways.

A theoretical confrontation exists between the consensualist position, represented in such works as Smelser's *Theory of Collective Behavior,* and more radical social theorists (Gamson, 1975). The former views protest movements as aberrations in the social system, as irrational signs of system stress motivated by contrived elitist ideologies. The latter sees protest movements as rational responses to coercion and intolerable social and political conditions—with quite deliberate strategies for changing those conditions. The community-organizing strategies of Saul Alinsky (1971) seem to support the rationalist theory of social protest.

Most social theorists posit a basic link between perceived legitimacy and social conflict within the social system. Where the legitimacy of a sociopolitical system is widely accepted by

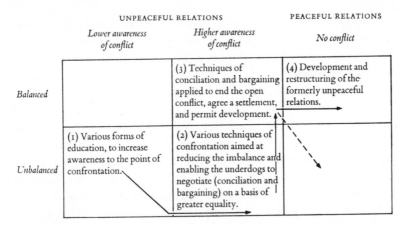

Notes: (a) The peacemaking sequence may, of course, begin at any of the stages of conflict.
(b) The broken arrow would illustrate, for example, that a minority group, having striven for greater equality, is satisfied with a measure of self-government short of independence; even so, the relationship would clearly be more peaceful than it was previously, with an acceptable degree of imbalance.

Figure 2. Peacemaking approaches appropriate for different sorts or stages of conflict. (From Adam Curle, *Making Peace*, New York: Barnes and Noble, 1971. Reprinted by permission of the author.)

its members, conflict remains controlled and at minimal levels of intensity. When awareness of inherent conflicts or contradictions increases, perceived legitimacy among the population declines and conflict is heightened. A solid example of this dynamic is the university-based protests of the late 1960s and early 1970s. Largely because of what were perceived as unethical war policies, increasingly authoritarian government, and irrelevant educational curricula and governance, large numbers of students withdrew support from the structures of American society. Conflict rapidly escalated as perceived legitimacy declined among the young and other segments of the population. This legitimacy/conflict relationship of inverse correlation seems to operate in all unequal power relationships whether between husband and wife, university and student, or master and slave.

Another major theoretical tradition in American conflict

sociology has concerned itself with culture clash. This tradition has its roots in the study of racial and ethnic conflict in
the early decades of this century by the Park/Burgess University
of Chicago School. These theorists, like the Marxists, found the
origins of social conflict in the structure of society, the differential access to societal rewards available to various ethnic and
racial groups, and the challenge response to oppressed status in
the form of both random rebellion and social movements. This
early research and theory encouraged later studies such as those
of Myrdal (1962) and Oberschall (1973), whose analytical view
of conflict strongly reflects the ethnic/racial paradigm.

4. *Conflict is essentially a dynamic of an interaction of two
or more parties moving within a field to the optimum position
(within rank-ordered sets of positions), perceived to be occupied by an opponent.* Kenneth Boulding's perception of the
conflict process centers on the behavior of each conflict party.

> The behavior of a behavior unit consists in its moving to the
> best position possible, i.e., the point within its possibility
> boundary that is higher than any other on the value ordering.
> This principle is illustrated, in terms that will be familiar to
> economists, in [Figure 3]. Here we suppose the plane of the
> paper represents the behavior space of an individual located at
> A. Each point on the paper, or *field*, represents a certain state
> of the universe that is within the purview of the individual at A.
> We neglect here the problem of the various ways in which these
> can be ordered: if there are only two variables in the behavior
> system, the plane can then express any combination of these by

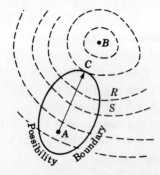

Figure 3. The conflict field. (From Kenneth Boulding, *Conflict and Defense*,
New York: Harper & Row. Reprinted by permission of Kenneth E. Boulding.)

a set of Cartesian coordinates. We do not limit ourselves to this condition, however; since there is an infinite number of points on the plane, there is no reason why each one should not represent a state of a multidimensional universe. We order the field only to the extent that we suppose a line (the heavy line in the figure) represents the boundary of possibility, so that all points inside the line represent states of the universe that are possible or available to the behavior unit at A and that all points outside the line represent states that are not. (1962:7-8)

This concept of the "conflict field" is one used also by Lewin (1948) and helps greatly to limit the complexity of analysis for any particular conflict case.

5. *Each conflict situation contains certain predictable elements and dynamics such as escalation, inhibiting and facilitating processes, and leadership change.* Coleman (1957) identifies conflict parties; intensification processes such as the operation of Gresham's law; and concepts of the escalatory spiral and its correlative dynamics such as personalization of the conflict, proliferation and generalization of issues, and reciprocal causation. All of these factors are valuable for analyzing conflicts at all levels. Heirich (1971) applies the escalatory spiral concept in his analysis of the conflict generated by the Free Speech Movement in Berkeley in the mid-sixties. The UNESCO study (Bernard, 1957) remains an extremely useful multiple perspectives analysis of intergroup and international conflict processes, as does the work of Mack and Snyder (1957).

Conflict and Violence

A third theoretical debate in conflict analysis centers about the relationship of conflict to violence—two concepts all too often perceived as identical or closely linked. Actually, much conflict occurs without violence and much violence, such as structural and criminal violence, exists without overt conflict.

Some conflict analysts are not immediately concerned with the conflict/violence relationship. Peace researchers are, however. Their interest in conflict is primarily motivated by their desire to minimize violence. Several propositions have emerged from peace-related research.

1. *There are two types of violence requiring the attention of peace researchers—behavioral and structural violence. Behavioral violence* refers to what we commonly think of as violence—that which causes apparent injury to persons and things. Wars would head the list in this category, which also includes random street violence, riots, murder, suicide, genocide, child abuse, and vandalism. It is with behavioral violence that peace research has been heretofore primarily concerned.

Collective violence has been a topic in sociological theory since Sorel (1967), who characterized violence as having a natural and even therapeutic function within the social order. Random personal violence accompanying the growth of anomie and anonymity in urbanized society has received increasing attention from modern sociologists.

Most recently, the concept of *structural violence* has been developed by Galtung (1969) and others. This approach ties behavioral violence directly to the nature of national and international stratification and the dominance/dependence relationships implied thereby. It sees social and personal violence resulting from unjust, repressive, and oppressive sociopolitical structures. Starvation and malnutrition, both of which restrict life chances, are seen as violence resulting from an inequitable world economic system and repressive regimes in various nations. Peace researchers concentrating on behavioral violence maintain that unless the acute problems of overt and organized violence (i.e., nuclear war, civil violence) are solved, we will not survive to deal with the chronic problems of structural violence. The "structuralists" respond that the roots of overt violence are in existing structures themselves and the former will not and cannot be reduced without changes in the latter.

There is also a debate within peace research concerning the role of values in research. Peace and conflict experts have differed over appropriate ideological reference points, with those principally concerned with behavioral violence maintaining that there should be none. The others argue that they are inevitable and must be recognized.[1] This internal conflict and the schism it has brought about within peace research has produced forceful, open discussion of important ideological and theoretical issues. However, it may also have retarded the growth of the field by suggesting a false incompatibility of approaches. The disarray of a behavioral violence versus structural violence argument, with the remaining group of us falling neatly into neither camp, is confusing for scholars and students entering the field.

There is room, in fact a need, for several approaches in peace and conflict research. Each contributes heuristic power and methodological tools to the study of conflict, conflict resolution, the progressive elimination of violence, and justice-producing social change. I suggest that Dahrendorf (1959) can help us out of this ideology trap that prohibits us from clearly defining parameters and basic objectives. Dahrendorf, as I have shown earlier, traces the process by which "illegitimate conflict," in which an oppressed interest group is not accorded the right to conflict, gradually becomes legitimized, routinized, and less and less violent, with the conflict parties increasingly equalized in their capacity to coerce or persuade their adversaries. He uses the legitimization and institutionalization of labor-management conflict as a case in point. Once legitimate adversary status was accorded representatives of labor, a quite different set of conflict dynamics and rules for conflict came into play. Another example might be the equal rights movement of the past century in the United States. Oppressed racial and ethnic minorities in recent years have been accorded formal bargaining status in local, regional, and national disputes over racial and economic justice. The legitimization and routinization of interracial conflict is still far behind that of labor-management conflict, but it has progressed substantially. In Dahrendorfian terms, we can categorize conflicts along a continuum stretching between two poles: (1) completely non-institutionalized, normless, violent, no-holds-barred conflict, and (2) highly ritualized, routinized, legitimized disputes. The former tend to be more violent and less desirable ways of bringing about social justice. One of the tasks of peace researchers is to develop techniques for moving more conflicts away from pole 1 and toward pole 2.

2. *Symmetry in conflict, other things being equal, reduces the violence produced in the conflict-waging process.* Parity in the nuclear deterrence process, for example, is one of the key

factors in assuring that neither side uses the tools of violence available to it. Nuclear deterrence is not in my estimation a desirable or workable policy in the long run, but if it works it does so because of symmetry and credibility.

The same holds true in lower-level conflict formations. In the Palestinian-Israeli dispute, Palestinian terrorism is partially a consequence of the asymmetry of that conflict. Palestinians are comparatively weak and desperate adversaries and are therefore willing to use ever more violent means to wage the conflict. Asymmetry pushes the weak to raise the level of violence. Israeli reprisals are likewise extremely violent and ruthless, in large measure because Israel is the dominant military power in the area and can do what she wishes. Grossly asymmetrical conflict, then, tends to raise violence levels on the part of desperate underdogs who see their options narrowed and on the part of dominant parties who see little external restraint on their use of violence.

Senghaas (1973) distinguishes between symmetrical and asymmetrical conflict formations, the former in which the parties are relatively equal in power and status, and the latter in which they are not. In the first type, conflict reduction involves association or integration between the conflicting parties. Resolution of asymmetrical conflict, on the other hand, implies a process by which the conflict becomes manifest, then polarized, and passes from asymmetry to symmetry and ultimately to a situation where justice is achieved. Peace research seeks to make conflict more symmetrical and to develop new techniques for making it less violent.

3. *Stable peace is a developmental process, not merely the absence of visible violence.* Often the absence of overt conflict in social relations denotes a state of oppression and stagnation, a state of nonpeace. Peace is in part the process of the settlement of violent and destructive disputes, but it also requires the transformation of social and political institutions that do violence to persons and groups. In short, justice insures tranquility and both are elements of stable peace.

Peace research must work in two directions: toward both associative and dissociative objectives (Galtung, 1975). The associative objective calls for research to resolve disputes, refining the techniques of regulating symmetrical conflicts with a broad range of methods. Neutral third-party intervention, training for mediation, maximizing association and accommodation among mutually hostile states, and disarmament and arms control would all be important research areas. The dissociative objective, however, requires research to bring grossly asymmetrical conflict to a point where it can be resolved nonviolently. This would involve studying and developing new forms of nonmilitary struggle by which weaker parties in an asymmetrical conflict can successfully wage conflict and achieve justive objectives without being annihilated by dominant groups or evoking armed intervention by powerful states. Some peace researchers will be ideologically and theoretically drawn toward the first area of study and others toward the second. Of course, the areas will overlap, as in community racial disputes where civil disobedience and the art of negotiation may both be called for.

4. *Order in the world depends not only on fashioning nonviolent means of resolving disputes but on collectively solving global problems.* This proposition rests on data gathered by world order researchers (Mendlovitz, 1975) and on the assumption that world order requires that we conceptualize multicultural alternative futures toward which world leaders can work. How, for example, can the problem of global poverty be resolved in isolation from that of overpopulation or the problem of violence be dealt with effectively while the problem of environmental deterioration is left untouched? Burton (1972) carries this line of thinking further and speaks of a global mentality.

5. *Violent and nonviolent behaviors are for the most part learned responses.* Social research suggests that violence is a learned response to frustration or conflict, that society (e.g., mass media, military organizations, gang socialization, literature) teaches people how to be violent and encourages them to be so. There are naturalist theories of violence (Sorel, 1967) that suggest otherwise, though the weight of social scientific evidence seems to be against them.

Although neither violence nor nonviolence may be genetically determined, there is a potential in humans for violent and cruel behavior. As Milgram's obedience experiment (1963) clearly demonstrated, rather normal humans will, under unusual circumstances, commit deliberate acts of cruelty and violence. Zimbardo's experiments (1969) with simulated prison guard roles produced similar results. Social roles (e.g., that of the constrained prison guard with ultimate authority and that of obedient subject) shape behavior in abnormal ways to produce violent behavior.

The propositions presented thus far suggest some of the major directions now being taken by conflict theorists. They are not, however, researchable propositions. What the field needs now is the formulation of precise and testable hypotheses concerning the nature of conflict and possible means of regulating it. Mack and Snyder (1957), Young (1969), and Coser (1956) have already begun this process.

There is currently a movement toward transdisciplinary and cross-level analysis of conflict. This is motivated mainly by persons who are trained or have been active in more than one discipline, such as Curle (1971) and Burton (1969). It should be noted that much of the seminal work in modern conflict analysis has been done by social theorists like Kenneth Boulding (1962) and Quincy Wright (1965), whose theoretical orientations transcend disciplinary boundaries.

Mapping Specific Conflicts

The macroscopic view of conflict emerging from this review of transdisciplinary theory is essential for students of conflict, but it is not very helpful for analyzing specific conflict situations. For that one needs a map as a framework for analysis. I have devised the following guide to conflict mapping from my own field experience.

CONFLICT MAPPING GUIDE

Mapping is a first step in intervening to manage a particular conflict. It gives both the intervenor and the conflict parties a clearer understanding of the origins, nature, dynamics, and possibilities for resolution of the conflict. Because a conflict is a social process and is continually changing, any map of it will be valid for only a certain period of time and must be periodically updated. The map should include the following information:

I. *Summary Description* (one-page maximum)

II. *Conflict History.* The origins and major events in the evolution both of the conflict and its context. It is important to make this distinction between the interactive conflict relationship among the parties, and the context within which it occurs.

III. *Conflict Context.* It is important to establish the scope and character of the context or setting within which the conflict takes place. Such dimensions are geographical boundaries; political structures, relations, and jurisdictions; communication networks and patterns; decision-making methods. Most of these are applicable to the full range of conflict types from interpersonal to international levels.

IV. *Conflict Parties.* Decisional units which are directly or indirectly involved in the conflict and have some significant stake in its outcome.

A. *Primary:* parties whose goals are, or are perceived by them to be, incompatible and who interact directly in pursuit of those respective goals. Where the conflict parties are organizations or groups, each may be composed of smaller units differing in their involvement and investment in the conflict.

B. *Secondary:* parties who have an indirect stake in the outcome of the dispute but who do not feel themselves to be directly involved. As the conflict progresses secondary parties may become primary, however, and vice-versa.

C. *Interested third parties:* those who have an interest in the successful resolution of the conflict.

Pertinent information about the parties in addition to who they are would include the nature of the power relations between/among them (e.g., symmetrical or asymmetrical); leadership; each party's main goal(s) in the conflict; potential for coalitions among parties.

V. *Issues.* Normally, a conflict will develop around one or more issues emerging from or leading to a decision. Each issue can be viewed as a point of disagreement that must be resolved. Issues can be identified and grouped according to the primary generating factor:

> A. *Facts-based:* disagreement over *what is* because of how parties perceive *what is.* Judgment and perception are the primary conflict generators here.
>
> B. *Values-based:* disagreement over *what should be* as a determinant of a policy decision, a relationship or some other source of conflict.
>
> C. *Interests-based:* disagreement over *who will get what* in the distribution of scarce resources (e.g., power, privilege, economic benefits, respect).
>
> D. *Non-realistic:* originating elsewhere than in disparate perceptions, interests, values. Style of interaction the parties use, the quality of communication between them, or aspects of the immediate physical setting such as physical discomfort are examples.

With few exceptions, any one conflict will be influenced by some disagreement emerging from each of these sources but normally one source is predominant. It is useful not only to identify each issue in this way, but to identify as well the significant disparities in perception, values, and interests motivating each party. (*Values* are here defined as beliefs that determine a party's position on any one issue [e.g., economic growth is always desirable]. *Interests* are defined as any party's desired or expected share of scarce resources [e.g., power, money, prestige, survival, respect, love]).

VI. *Dynamics.* Social conflicts have common though not always predictable dynamics that if recognized can help an intervenor find the way around a conflict. The intervenor must seek to reverse some of these and make them dynamics of regulation and resolution. They include:

A. *Precipitating events* signaling the surfacing of a dispute.

B. *Issue emergence, transformation, proliferation.* Issues change as a conflict progresses—specific issues become generalized, single issues multiply, impersonal disagreements can become personal feuds.

C. *Polarization.* As parties seek internal consistency and coalitions with allies, and leaders consolidate positions, parties in conflict tend toward bipolarization that can lead both to greater intensity and to simplification and resolution of the conflict.

D. *Spiraling.* Through a process of reciprocal causation, each party may try to increase the hostility or damage to opponents in each round, with a corresponding increase from the latter. Deescalatory spirals are also possible in which opponents reciprocally and incrementally reduce the hostility and rigidity of their interaction.

E. *Stereotyping and mirror-imaging.* Opponents often come to perceive one another as impersonal representations of the mirror-opposite of their own exemplary and benign characteristics. This process encourages rigidity on position and miscommunication and misinterpretation between conflict parties.

VII. *Alternative Routes to a Solution(s) of the Problem(s).* Each of the parties and often uninvolved observers will have suggestions for resolving the conflict. In conflicts within a formal policymaking framework, the options can be formal plans. In interpersonal conflicts, alternatives can be behavioral changes suggested to (or by) the parties. It is essential to identify as many "policies" as possible as have already surfaced in the conflict. They should be made visible for both the conflict parties and the intervenor. The intervenor may then suggest new alternatives or combinations of those already identified.

VIII. *Conflict Regulation Potential.* In and for each conflict situation are to be found resources for limiting and perhaps resolving the conflict. The mapping process notes these resources, albeit in a preliminary way. They may include:

A. *Internal limiting factors* like values and interests the conflicting parties have in common, or the intrinsic value of a relationship between them that neither wishes to destroy, or cross-pressures of multiple commitments of parties that constrain the conflict.

B. *External limiting factors* like a higher authority who could intervene and force a settlement or an intermediary from outside the conflict.

C. *Interested or neutral third parties* trusted by the parties in conflict who could facilitate communication, mediate the dispute, or locate financial resources to alleviate a scarcity problem.

D. *Techniques of conflict management,* both those familiar to the different conflict parties and third parties, and those known to have been useful elsewhere. Such methods range from the well-known mediation, conciliation, and rumor control to fractionating issues and extending the time range to encourage settlement.

IX. *Using the Map.* The conflict map is most useful (and quite essential) as the initial step in conflict intervention. Mapping permits an informed judgment about whether the intervention should continue. The map is also helpful in assisting conflict parties to move back from and make sense out of a process to which they are too close. If the mapper decides to further intervene, sharing the map can loosen up the conflict, making it easier to resolve. Finally, the map helps demystify the process of conflict that, for so many people, seems a confusing, unfathomable, inexplicable, and thoroughly frustrating phenomenon.

Conflict Analysis Exercises

1. *Adapt the conflict mapping guide* for use at different levels of conflict from the interpersonal to the international and apply it to particular cases.
2. *Personal Conflict Impact Essays* (See Appendix E). Analyze the influence conflict has had in their personal lives, how they responded to it, how they feel about it now, and how they have learned or could learn from it.
3. *Simulation and Gaming Suggestions:*
   a) Starpower (Shirts, n.d.)
   b) Inter-Nation Simulation (Guetzkow et al., 1963)
   c) Zandar Crisis (Burgess, 1973)
   d) Parker High School Exercise (See Appendix F)
4. *Attitudes Toward Conflict Survey.* Design and carry out a survey of public opinion/attitudes, on conflict and violence in their most common forms. One can learn much about conflict through how others view it.
5. *Become involved in social settings where conflict* is likely to permit your involvement. Analyze your role in it.
6. *Media Suggestions:*
   a)Film: "This Question of Violence" (National Educational Television, Indiana University, Bloomington: 59 minutes)
   b) War-Peace Film Guide (Dougall, 1973). Excellent guide to film resources, with some good films on conflict and violence.
7. *Ranking Conflict Behaviors Exercise* (See Appendix G).

2. Conflict Regulation: Models and Techniques

Sociologists have been concerned with both the creative and destructive consequences, the functional and dysfunctional aspects of social conflict for nearly a century. It is within the past three decades, however, that they and other social scientists have studied both the theory and technique of regulating conflict. One of the earliest such studies was Williams' *Reduction of Intergroup Tensions* (1947), which researched problems of ethnic, racial, and religious antagonism and formulated theoretical propositions and research possibilities. Sorokin (1957) was also a prime mover in early sociological research on the causes, dynamics, and limitation of war and civil violence.

A number of conflict regulation studies reflect attempts at applying specific theoretical constructs to the deescalation and limiting of actual intra- and international conflict cases. Osgood (1962) suggests a reciprocal concession technique for reversing the escalatory spiral characterizing international arms races. Etzioni (1964) develops the concept of *encapsulation* in which conflict parties agree on certain rules and parameters and exclude certain of the more extreme conflict forms, for use in regulating superpower hostility. Dahrendorf (1959) conceives of a process similar to encapsulation, in which groups in society conflicting over access to authority increasingly ritualize and moderate the conflicts. Coleman (1957) notes particular limiting factors, such as cross-cutting affiliations within community conflict formations, that work against escalation and intensification.

A second body of theory concerns the formal and informal

processes of conflict resolution and dispute settlement and the intervention of professional third-party actors in those processes. The dynamics of the negotiation process is one area of research. Bartos (1974), Evan and McDougall (1967), and Douglas (1962), among others, have concentrated on the structure and dynamics of negotiation. The Evan/McDougall study suggests that settlement is more easily achieved when consensus within the negotiating parties breaks down and bilateral consensus occurs. Bartos found that the "hard liner" or tough bargainer maximized gains at the expense of the "conciliator" in simulated negotiation.

Other scholars work more directly on techniques of intervention to moderate and resolve conflicts. Warren (1964) provides insight into the role of the third-party intermediary operating in a conflict intersystem—a self-sustaining conflict that is supportive of the social systems engaged in it. This unusual conflict relationship is illustrative of Coser's functional concept of conflict.

Burton's (1969) theoretical contribution is rooted in conflict intervention experiments where techniques of *controlled communication* are applied to bring leaders of warring states to a point of willingness to negotiate a settlement. Both Warren and Burton are primarily concerned with altering communication patterns and images, and both have developed their theory and technique while involved in actual international conflict situations. Skinnerian behaviorism has also developed conflict regulation concepts like counter-control.

Community disputes are a second arena in which sociologists are intervening. Laue and Cormick (1973) use the construct of *empowerment* as the base of their strategies. In disputes where power is grossly asymmetrical in its distribution, as is often the case in racial and ethnic disputes, they suggest that interventionists must help the weak parties empower themselves if meaningful negotiation and settlement is to occur.

Last, there has been substantial work done in the sociology of nonviolence. There is a tradition of nonviolent conflict that has until recently been virtually ignored by social scientists. Sociologists have been the most active in opening this area of social behavior to scrutiny and have made practical as well as theoretical contributions to its development. Sharp (1973), Hare (1968), and Galtung (1969) have made important contributions. Sharp's encyclopedic review of the history, mechanisms, and cases of nonviolent direct action is a benchmark work. Hare's analysis of nonviolent action in social-psychological terms, using the exchange and interaction theory of Homans and Bales, has moved the field ahead considerably. Galtung has suggested ways in which nonviolent action may be used in restructuring both national and global societies.

The social scientific study of nonviolent action is in large part the study of social innovation. Bondurant's (1965) analysis of the Gandhian satyagraha movement and Erikson's (1969) psychohistorical study of Gandhi are exemplary. Gandhi was an innovative personality and satyagraha was an innovative technique of waging conflict. Lakey and Oppenheimer (1965) place nonviolent action within the perspective of sociological analysis. Both the minority equal rights and the antiwar movements of the 1960s have encouraged research on these change phenomena, including examination of the socialization processes (Keniston, 1968; Elise Boulding, 1974) that produced the youth who participated in them.

Nonviolent action as social innovation has also been analyzed in the study of nonviolent resistance to invasion and the potential use of such resistance for the development of new national defense policies. Sharp (1973) and Roberts (1972) have researched the role of nonviolent direct action in past and future national defense.

Social science, then, has moved ahead in studying conflict regulation theory and technique. Accurate analysis of conflict situations and tested techniques for intervening effectively are essential for the development of the knowledge and skills of peacemaking. These areas are not yet within the mainstream of social science but, in the decades ahead, the press of violent and destructive conflict processes within the global system will place them there.

Even though conflict regulation theory and research have moved ahead in recent years, the record of their use to create new practical techniques of regulation and to train specialists for conflict regulation roles is rather dismal. However, there is a small but growing group of scholar-practitioners who are experimenting with the application of theory to conflict regulation problems. These people include international law specialists, psychologists, political activists, political scientists, and others, in addition to the sociologists cited thus far. Most of them work with theories and strategies, developed around actual problem solving, that reflect cross-level commonality and can be applied at levels of conflict other than those for which they were designed. Osgood's (1962) GRIT model, for example, may be equally applicable for conflict regulation at the international, intergroup, and interpersonal levels. In fact, Osgood characterizes his model as the application of theories of learning and of interpersonal communication and transaction to problems of international conflict.

Applied conflict research has a reasonably good foundation on which to build. Societies have accumulated a good deal of knowledge and numerous institutionalized methods for keeping conflict within bounds. Conflict does not occur unbridled and uncontrolled in social systems. Unregulated conflict tends to be more violent and therefore more noticeable, but regulated conflict is by far the more common. Let us examine several conventional models of conflict regulation.

Legal Regulation

This model is perhaps best known to political science and law. It assumes the existence of a set of explicit norms that parties in conflict agree to accept as standards for settlement. These standard guides for behavior and conflict management can operate to settle disputes. Law is a common device for regulating conflict within societies and operates through the interaction of legal representatives of conflicting parties who, within the system of jurisprudence or without, reach compromise settlements. It also works through such processes as *arbitration* and *adjudication*—by which courts rule in favor of one party or another. Law also functions to regulate conflict in the international system, though to a lesser degree, and less effectively than in domestic dispute settlement.

The legal model is perhaps the best-tested and most refined conflict regulation technique, but it has some serious weaknesses—especially in regard to interstate conflict:

1. It is generally biased in favor of the status quo and is by nature a conservative institution. This renders it inadequate for regulating asymmetrical conflict involving weak challengers and strong conservators. Distributive justice disputes, for example, are not easily settled by legal means since the law seems permanently stacked against those seeking change.

2. Legal conflict regulation is effective to the degree that enforcement of the law is possible. Within nation-states, where the government theoretically has a monopoly of force, conflicting parties can be forced to settle a dispute and to abide by legal decision. With an international system hampered by national sovereignty and the absence of a reliable enforcement agent for international legal bodies, legal regulation eschews violent conflict only where all conflict parties see nonviolent, lasting settlement as in their own best interests. Sometimes this is the case, and sometimes it is not.

Chai (1974) describes a South Korean–Japanese fishing rights dispute settlement that involved no adjudication and was achieved largely through the restraint of international norms and the empowerment process. A relatively weak Korea and a strong Japan, through face-to-face bargaining, pursued enlightened self-interest to achieve a more equitable power relationship. For every Korean/Japanese fishing rights settlement, however, there are numerous failures at international legal conflict regulation. With a national locus of power still prevailing, Falk (1968:41) asks the essential question: "Under what conditions can law contribute to the regulation of human conflict in a social system that is decentralized in the manner of the present international system?"

The Deterrence Model

Threat is a pervasive process in social relationships and deterrence is rooted in threat. This process, especially familiar to students of international arms races, operates where one has a balanced threat-counterthreat system. Superpower nuclear standoff is the most awesome example of this. Both Schelling (1963) and Kissinger (1969) analyze the dynamics of the deterrence mechanism. One must admit that in a bizarre and terrifying way deterrence seems to have operated in the past two decades to prohibit the use of the ultimate weapon. The weaknesses of deterrence, however, are glaring.

1. As Kenneth Boulding makes clear, stable nuclear deterrence is an illusion in a rapidly changing world.

> The attempts to build equilibrium systems of defence on stable deterrence seem to me to be doomed to failure. The world changes too rapidly and, as we have seen, it is the adaptive system, not the equilibrium system that will survive under these circumstances. The adaptive system which is required here is a world system of conflict control. By this I mean social institutions which will be able to throw in counter weights, or countervailing forces, which will prevent these systems from reaching the crisis point of system-breakdown into overt violence involving the use of national armed forces. (1968:126)

Deterrence tends to be upwardly unstable, as we can see in the present renewed spiraling of multiple nuclear warhead production and placement by the United States and the USSR. This instability is supported by the principle of technological development that says if something can be done, it should and will be done. Since deterrence is primarily built on threat, which in turn is built to a large extent on mistrust, the higher the potential level of violence, the less trust, and so on.

The deescalatory spiral is, of course, a possibility, as suggested by Osgood's GRIT concept, and in fact seems to have operated that way in rare instances like the Berlin crisis of 1961 and the nuclear testing agreement of 1963 (Etzioni, 1967). Although deterrence appears to have some conflict regulation potential, its inherently unstable vertical dynamics, pushing a conflict to higher and higher levels of threatened destruction and implying increased alienation of opponents at each new level, makes it an unlikely basis for stable peace. In addition, its propensity for horizontal instability in the form of nuclear proliferation (Willrich, 1975) increases the potential of violence.

2. A second weakness of deterrence is its tendency to encourage the refinement and promotion of violence at other levels. As a direct or indirect result of nuclear deterrence, nations have been pushed to advance the development of techniques of conventional warfare. Southeast Asia and the Middle East have both been testing grounds for the superpowers' conventional weapons systems. The policy initiated by the Kennedy administration of increasing conventional military capacity as an alternative to massive nuclear retaliation may well have set us up with the ill-fated capability and, therefore, the will to intervene in Vietnam.

3. Finally, while an element of threat can and probably does function creatively in all conflict regulation processes, deterrence seems to approximate a pure threat system, with regulation based almost entirely on the injury each opponent can do the other. If stable peace requires moving steadily away from threat and toward integration systems, deterrence is of low value as a long-range conflict regulation mechanism. I do not mean to suggest here that threat processes are necessarily dysfunctional. Mediators, for example, may use threat to good advantage in achieving a settlement. They are just less satisfactory in general for maintaining a stable peace.

Bargaining and Negotiation

The bargaining process regulates conflict by providing a framework within which parties may achieve, partially or fully, certain goals that conflict with those of an opponent. Bargaining involves give-and-take, concessions and gains, the combination of which results in a tolerable situation for each party. We ordinarily associate bargaining with a formal procedure involving face-to-face negotiation, such as industrial bargaining, where the compromise is explicit. Some conflict regulation, however, as Schelling (1963) notes, is achieved through tacit bargaining. Much of the agreement reached in the SALT I talks was a formalization of the tacit agreements between the United States and the USSR that had existed for years.

Bargaining commonly brings opponents together around clear-cut issues. It is a way of ritualizing conflict, of establishing some rules of the game. Through trade-offs, face-saving devices, and ranking of goals, opponents transform what was a win-all/lose-all or zero-sum game, purely competitive in nature, to a positive-sum contest with a partial-win/partial-win outcome. The latter contest is partially cooperative in character, and all parties are somewhat better off as a consequence of the bargaining.

Bargaining is a common mode of conflict regulation and dispute settlement at all levels of human experience. Examples are marital counseling, community dispute settlement (Nicolau, 1973), and interstate conflict resolution (Randle, 1973). The continuing disengagement of Israeli, Egyptian, and Syrian armies in the Middle East following the 1973 war was illustrative of bargaining among nation-state adversaries.

Two major weaknesses constrain bargaining as a conflict regulation device:

1. Bargaining seems to work well only in conflict formations that are primarily consensual (Kriesberg, 1973)—where opponents agree on at least some goals and objectives but disagree on the conditions for achieving them and on allocation of commonly desired resources or values. The Egyptians, Syrians, and Israelis now value a no-war situation in the Middle East and some sense of security for themselves, and are cooperating through bargaining to achieve it. Several years ago such bargaining would have been politically impossible. The two sides seemed then to have totally incompatible goals, and the Arab states had not yet accepted Israel's right to exist as a national state within its established borders. Dissensual conflict, then, is not very susceptible to control through bargaining.

2. Bargaining also assumes that parties to a conflict are ready to negotiate. In intense conflict this is often not the case, and until this will to bargain for a settlement develops, the bargaining mode is quite irrelevant. Considerable research has been done on the bargaining process and on means for rendering it more effective in settling disputes. Evan and McDougall (1967), for example, have tested with positive results the theory that internal dissensus within conflict parties substantially enhances the chances for settlement. With regard to the Middle East, the theory would seem to be empirically supported. This

proposition may not hold under all conditions however, since negotiators must be able to commit constituencies to agreements and enforce them, which might be difficult where sharp cleavages exist in constituencies.

In the bargaining process, there is generally a facilitator whose personal stature, credibility, and skill as mediator as perceived by all parties allow him to act as a catalytic agent. Names like Bunche, Nehru, Thant, and Kissinger come to mind as successful international intermediaries. The need for such persons is certainly a present limitation on the bargaining approach—such skilled intermediaries are rare—but it is not an inherent weakness. People can be trained for these roles, and Kissinger himself in his Pacem in Terris III speech called for the training of substantial numbers of professional intervenors.

Third-Party Intervention

The conflict regulation models suggested above may or may not involve intervention by a neutral or interested third party. In this next section I will turn to those that do and discuss attempts to develop techniques of intervention that are effective in moderating or totally eliminating conflicts.

We can place conflicts within quadrants according to how they are resolved, as in Figure 4. In this conceptualization, quadrant A denotes conflicts that are resolved through fighting

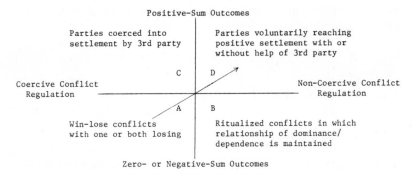

Figure 4. Conflict types and outcomes. (Derived from discussion with John Burton.)

or some other process by which one party is coerced into acceding to the other's demands. A war with a strong antagonist coercing a weaker one would be such a conflict. Quadrant B contains conflicts that are regulated through ritualized conflict, which involves a dominance-dependence relationship with a built-in zero- or negative-sum outcome. An autocratic marriage relationship with ritualized fighting that did nothing to change the oppressed status of one of the parties might be an example here.

Quadrant C contains those conflicts where a third party intervenes and forces the antagonists to resolve their dispute. Such resolution sometimes occurs in international conflict but is more common in labor/management disputes where binding arbitration is ordered by the judiciary. Quadrant D represents those conflicts where a third party intervenes and helps, rather than coerces, the parties to a settlement that advances the interests of both—in other words, the resolution processes insure that the conflict game is of the positive-sum variety in which all players win by settling their dispute.

What we have, then, are two sets of poles: a positive/negative sum continuum (i.e., at least one and often all parties lose in the latter case, while both improve their positions and maximize gains in the former) and a coercion/noncoercion continuum. In this section we are primarily concerned with approaches to intervention of third parties that have been developed to move conflicts from A into D. This process of creative intervention to facilitate voluntary settlement is the most promising and least-developed sector of the conflict regulation field.

Propositions

Let us consider some propositions identifying characteristics of the conflict regulation process that would concern an intervening third party.

1. *Conflict becomes more regulable as the threat factor is increasingly balanced with trust.* A conflict relationship becomes moderated as parties decrease the threat messages they send to their adversaries. Whatever third-party intervenors can

do to lower the threat level and raise the trust level will increase chances for resolution of the conflict. In any intense conflict, the mutual perception of threat is heightened. Communication of all but threat messages and distortions is interrupted. Negative *mirror images* form on both sides as each party sees the other as increasingly hostile and threatening.

One type of third-party intervention into such conflicts is what we might call *communication facilitation*. Intense conflict formations are difficult to regulate partly because opponents are normally not in direct communication with one another, are mutually hostile, and as Warren (1964) observes, often form a *conflict intersystem* in which each party is sustained by the conflict. The initial step toward settlement, then, must be some modification of the political atmosphere. Conciliation involves the intervention of a third party who establishes communication both with and between conflicting parties. These channels for dialogue between leaders make the setting more conducive to negotiation, mediation, and peace. United Nations conciliation is one illustration of this technique (Pechota, 1971). Quaker conciliation in international and intranational disputes is another. In the Middle East conflict (AFSC, 1970) and the East-West confrontation in Berlin (Warren, 1964), Quaker conciliators concentrated on penetrating the "belief-action" systems of each conflict party and shaking up their image systems sufficiently to permit some accomodation.

Yarrow (1978) identifies certain functions of the Quaker conciliator role: listening to each side's perceptions and rationale; identifying conditions that may permit partial solutions; proposing small steps away from dead-center confrontation; assessing realities on both sides of the "communications gap"; providing a medium for exchange between antagonists who may have no other direct contact; and personal visitation within and between the conflicting communities.

Jackson (1952) writes of Quaker efforts at communication facilitation within the United Nations itself. UNITAR (1970) has also concerned itself with this, as has Bailey (1970). This approach is designed to establish and improve accurate, non-threatening communication between antagonists so that eventually other forms of dispute settlement like mediation and arbitration can be initiated.

2. *Conflicts are generated and maintained by objective and subjective factors, and the latter must be dealt with first in the resolution process.* One interesting approach is Burton's (1969) *controlled communication.* His assumption is that accurate and controlled communication between conflict parties is a basis for eventual bargaining and settlement of a conflict. A conflict is viewed as a hard core of issues to be resolved, surrounded by a softer layer of subjective factors like miscommunication, misperception, stereotyping, and mirror images that must be dealt with and penetrated before bargaining can begin.

Experimenting with representatives of two warring states, Indonesia and Malaysia, Burton's team worked with the adversaries on reconceptualizing the conflict, establishing accurate communication, a joint-costing process in which each opponent assessed the potential gains and losses of continuing and terminating the conflict, and the identification of common superordinate goals. Doob and others (1970, 1973) have worked at moderating specific international conflicts through sensitivity training techniques. The risks of such experiments are illustrated in the Northern Ireland case, where several participants were subjected to extreme stress and even violence upon return to their communities.

One must have some reservations about the Burton approach. First of all, the willingness to resolve a conflict that controlled communication participants develop as a consequence of their experience will probably not be shared by their colleagues or superiors "back home." Conciliatory tendencies have been induced in an artificial environment, and the discontinuity of participant experience with that of their governments is a potential problem.[1] Secondly, as Druckman (1971) points out, we do not yet know the relative importance of cognitive and affective factors in the negotiating process. It may be unwise, therefore, to give too much weight to intervention techniques concentrating on communication facilitation—though my personal inclination is to stress its importance in order to balance its past neglect.

3. *Conflict is most readily resolved by eliminating its cognitive and perceptive aspects rather than its affective dimensions.* This approach to conflict resolution could hardly be further from the preceding ones because it holds that communication between the parties to a conflict may in fact exacerbate that conflict.

The cognitive conflict approach (Hammond and Adelman, 1976), used primarily to resolve conflicts in policymaking groups like industrial firms and governmental agencies, sees social conflict rooted primarily in the *differing cognitive systems* of decision makers. Two policymakers will employ different analysis models and arrive at quite different sets of conclusions about the same data. By examining those models it is possible to pinpoint the causes of disagreement and, by feeding back the information gained, resolve the conflict. Social judgment theorists use a computer technique known as interactive computer graphics to illuminate policymakers' differing judgment styles for them. Once disagreements are identified, conflicts are more easily resolved. This process is often carried out with little or no face-to-face interaction between antagonists.

Such an approach has been successful in resolving conflicts in situations where there is stability and controlled human interaction. It remains to be seen, however, how useful it would be in conflict situations where personal and group identities or entire political systems are at stake.

4. *Asymmetrical conflict is best resolved through intervention that empowers the weaker party.* The empowerment model of conflict regulation rests upon the principle that balance is desirable in a conflict situation, reminding one of the traditional balance of power theory. It operates primarily in conflict situations that are grossly asymmetrical, where there is domination of the weak by the strong. As the weak learn that there are certain weapons they can use (e.g., disruption, terrorism, nonviolent resistance) the conflict heats up. Interracial community disputes in the United States are a good example of this type of conflict; Arab terrorism in the Middle Eastern conflict is another. In the former case nonviolent resistance was used, in the latter terrorist attacks. As the

desperate and the oppressed gain some sort of power base in the conflict, some legitimate leverage of countervailing force, the conflict becomes more amenable to negotiated, nonviolent settlement. I am not implying here that the challenger of the status quo is necessarily the agent of violence. But his empowerment, by whatever means, increases both his own acceptability as a party in the conflict and his options for dealing with his opponent.

Curle (1971) builds his entire theory of peacemaking and conflict regulation on a sequence in which oppressed groups become aware of the conflict and reduce the imbalance of power through confrontation to the point where conciliation and bargaining can take place. This is the process of empowerment; in conflict formations where economic and political justice are central issues, it is an effective way of short- and long-range regulation. Himes (1966) likewise illustrates the empowerment principle operating in racial conflict in the United States.

Several organizations in the United States that train people in conflict resolution skills base their programs on the empowerment model. A crisis intervention team is used that includes a mediator, advocates, activists, and communications facilitators (Laue and Cormick, 1974). Activists and advocates work with the weak parties, helping them to build a power base and a viable position from which they can bargain.

An assumption central to the empowerment model is that gross asymmetry in conflict breeds either desperation on the part of the weak or absence of restraint on the part of the powerful or both. Either instance may increase the likelihood of violence. Palestinian terrorism and the conduct of the National Guard at Kent State are two cases in point. One drawback of the empowerment approach is the risk of uncontrolled escalation as the weak push for power. There must be built-in safeguards against "runaway crises."

5. *In crisis situations, violence can be minimized or eliminated through proper training and control of those directly involved.* Conflict is perhaps most difficult to regulate in a crisis situation for which the conflict parties are unprepared. Numerous tragic examples can be cited including the Attica prison revolt (NYSSCA, 1972), the Chicago police riot (Walker,

1969), and the Kent State shootings (Davies, 1973). In such unexpected situations of intense conflict several regulating factors are central: (1) accurate communication within and among conflict parties; (2) rumor control; (3) the availability of nonlethal weapons and the tight control of lethal ones; and (4) effective and responsible leadership directing a responsive command/control system. We have only to compare the 1968 Chicago and 1972 Miami Beach convention demonstrations to see the benign consequences of deliberate violence abatement procedures.

At the international level, the U.S. performance in Southeast Asia illustrates the command and control and lethal weapons problems. The military forces of the United States and the Saigon regime were a runaway violence machine. Command and control systems operated sporadically, communications were poor, and information was often falsified or inaccurate. I am not suggesting that violence was a totally unplanned consequence of U.S. involvement. It would be difficult to find a more deliberate plan of calculated violence than the Defense Department's Operation Phoenix. But one might argue that a major part of the violence was due to an inadequate preparation and control within the war machine itself and a poorly controlled influx of lethal weapons.

There are, of course, examples of successful *crisis management* at the international level. The Washington/Moscow hot line insures that crisis communication will be relatively accurate. Demilitarized zones created as buffer areas between hostile states are also a crisis management mechanism.

6. *Conflict is often regulated by modifying the environment giving rise to it.* One technique of environmental modification is *interposition*. At any level, if a neutral third party or other barrier is placed between combatants, regulation of the dispute is usually easier. United Nations peacekeeping forces best exemplify this approach. Interposition is a form of conflict regulation only to the degree that it buys time for other forms of intervention. In the Middle East, demilitarized buffer zones occupied by neutral forces currently control the conflict between Israel and Egypt, Lebanon, the Palestinians, and Syria (Schonborn, 1975).

In intranational conflict, similar approaches to territorial disputes have created buffer zones in urban areas, street patrols of citizens who replace the normal police presence, and neutral observers at mass meetings to monitor police and citizen behavior. Interposition of this sort has been used to moderate gang warfare in Philadelphia and communal riots in India, where the Shanti Sena peacekeeping corps intervenes (Desai, 1972).

In regulating interpersonal conflict, environment modification is sometimes useful. Gordon (1970) trains parents to regulate and resolve conflict with their children through active listening (providing a relationship-enforcing emotional outlet for the child), defining acceptable behavior, and reducing conflictful behavior by modifying the conflict environment. In Gordon's approach, the parties in the parent-child conflict first identify who "owns" the problem, in other words, they discover where the major locus of the conflict is (see Figure 5). Through expanding or contracting, enriching or impoverishing, or introducing an intervening force into a conflict environment, conflict intensity can be regulated.

A conflict dynamic that is especially common in interpersonal conflict is the offensive-defensive reaction. One or both parties feel directly attacked and the upward spiral begins. Where child and parent are the parties, the consequences of this dynamic can be particularly harmful for both the health of the relationship and the child's sense of self-worth. A decoding process and a nonthreatening mode of expressing emotions are ways of clarifying the problem and minimizing parent-child conflict and alienation (see Figure 6).

It is striking how much cross-level applicability there is with the models being discussed. Conciliators working in intense international conflict situations, for instance, report that a major function of theirs is to listen—to provide each party the opportunity to relate the history and present state of the conflict as they see it. This venting process is crucial in the transformation of a no-exchange relationship into one moving toward exchange. Gordon proposes active listening as an intergenerational conflict regulation technique that has been tested as such with excellent results. Active listening performs the same venting function at the interpersonal level as it does for representatives of nation-states or for leaders of conflicting

When the Child Owns the Problem	When the Parent Owns the Problem
Child initiates communication	Parent initiates communication
Parent is a listener	Parent is a sender
Parent is a counselor	Parent is an influencer
Parent wants to help child	Parent wants to help himself
Parent is a "sounding board"	Parent wants to "sound off"
Parent facilitates child finding his own solution	Parent has to find his own solution
Parent accepts child's solution	Parent must be satisfied with solution himself
Parent primarily interested in child's needs	Parent primarily interested in his own needs
Parent is more passive	Parent is more aggressive

A parent has several alternatives when he owns the problem:

1. He can try to modify the child directly.
2. He can try to modify the environment.
3. He can try to modify himself.

Mr. Adam's son, Jimmy, takes his father's tools out of the tool box and usually leaves them scattered over the lawn. This is unacceptable to Mr. Adams, so *he* owns this problem.

He can confront Jimmy, say something, hoping this might modify Jimmy's behavior.

He can modify Jimmy's environment by buying him his own set of junior tools, hoping this will modify Jimmy's behavior.

He can try to modify his own attitudes about Jimmy's behavior, saying to himself that "boys will be boys" or "he'll learn proper care of tools in time."

Figure 5. Problem ownership. (From *Parent Effectiveness Training* by Dr. Thomas Gordon. Copyright © 1970 by Thomas Gordon. Reprinted by permission of the David McKay Company, Inc.)

religious communities in India.

7. *Conflict regulation ultimately requires moving a dispute from the status of a fight to that of a debate.* This generally involves several stages: (1) encapsulating the conflict—estab-

"You are being a pest" is a very poor code for the parent's
tired feeling. A code that is clear and accurate would always
be an "I-message": "I am tired," "I don't feel up to playing,"
"I want to rest." This communicates the feeling the parent is
experiencing. A "You-message" code does not send the feeling. It refers much more to the child than to the parent. A
"You-message" is child-oriented, not parent-oriented.

Consider these messages from the point of view of what the
child hears:

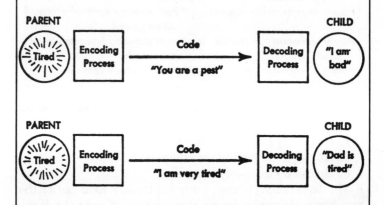

The first message is decoded by the child as an *evaluation*
of him. The second is decoded as a *statement of fact* about
the parent. "You-messages" are poor codes for communicating
what a *parent* is feeling, because they will most often be
decoded by the child in terms of either what *he* should do
(sending a solution) or how bad *he* is (sending blame or
evaluation).

Figure 6. Expressing and clarifying the problem. (From *Parent Effectiveness Training* by Dr. Thomas Gordon. Copyright © 1970 by Thomas Gordon.
Reprinted by permission of the David McKay Company, Inc.)

lishing some limits and some rules of the game; (2) the creation
or introduction of an agent to enforce the rules; and (3) an agent
to facilitate bargaining, arbitration, and other forms of dispute
settlement.

The current peacemaking process in the Middle East is again
a reference point. In recent years, some gaming rules have been

established. Open warfare has been temporarily renounced, mutual recognition of the rights to existence of all parties attained, and third-party mediation has achieved some success in conflict moderation. For some of the major antagonists in that conflict arena, the fight is just short of being transformed into a debate.

Conflict regulation in the Middle East demonstrates very effectively the dynamics and importance of efforts by a third party to assist directly in the settlement of a dispute. This may or may not involve face-to-face negotiations. However, it almost always involves bargaining, trade-offs, face-saving devices, and other forms of accommodation. It might be described as the process by which a relationship primarily characterized by threat becomes largely one of exchange. Essential components of the process include mutual trust in the integrity and impartiality of the mediator, the identification of trade-off points, clarification of the issues, and timing.

8. *The development of commitments to more inclusive communities among members of conflicting groups can reduce a conflict.* We have suggested how this happens in community disputes, where loyalty to the community as a whole dampens the fighting spirit of those in factions or subgroups. In global relations, international conflict may be moderated as subnational groups increase supranational allegiance through the development of transnational networks. These nongovernmental channels of communication, exchange, and influence bypass the official relationships between nation-states and can reduce conflict between them. Multinational business, educational, and religious networks, scientific associations, and hundreds of other networks linking individuals and groups, from philatelists to photographers, will play an increasing and generally moderating role in international relations. One should note, however, that the same transnational network (e.g., multinational corporations) might in one instance serve to moderate conflict and violence (as in the Middle East conflict) and exacerbate and promote it in another (as in Chile).

Common Threads

Though each of the intervention models described was developed at a particular level of the conflict taxonomy, it is interesting to note how many characteristics they have in common. More than half involve the *intervention of a third party* into the conflict as mediator, communication facilitator, or in some other role. Nearly all involve some *alteration of communication* patterns to promote settlement of a dispute. Every model's success depends heavily on the *credibility and trust* it is able to generate in the situation. The mediator must be credible and trusted, and the opponents must become credible and trusted as well. Even in the deterrence process, credibility is the key to success or failure. If one opponent's threat is not credible, the other may attack and deterrence fails.

Legitimacy is another crucial and common element in the models. Empowerment succeeds when each party achieves a sufficient stake in the sociopolitical system to accord it legitimacy. Bargaining only occurs when all parties have accorded the others the right to negotiate. Legal arbitration and judicial decisions in international disputes are rooted in the legitimacy of the system of law.

Many of the models seek some type of *perceptual shift* within the conflict parties. How opponents view each other and the conflict is a vital factor, and the shattering of mirror images is a central objective of many conflict regulation strategies. Most approaches rely heavily upon compromise and trade-offs, in other words, some *modification of original goals*. This tendency toward compromise is closely related to a *move from threat toward exchange* as the basis of the relationship.

Finally, *each model's applicability is transferable* to at least one conflict level other than the one for which it was created. The empowerment model, for instance, works equally well in marital conflict, community racial disputes, and international conflict. Where gross inequality and awareness of same exists, there will likely be intense conflict, whether it be between spouses, racial groups, or Southern and Northern hemispheres.

Intervenor Roles and Training

The success of intervention techniques depends upon persons trained to use them. The roles that conflict intervenors

may take must be more accurately defined, e.g., *mediator, arbitrator, conciliator*. A division of labor in dispute settlement
must evolve, with specialists trained in each of the roles. As we
broaden our concept of conflict regulation to include intervention in highly asymmetrical relationships (Laue and Cormick,
1974), we must invent new intervenor roles like the *activist*
(who helps a latent conflict to become manifest), the *advocate*
(who helps to clarify issues and to formulate bargaining
positions), and the *communication facilitator* (who is responsible for maximizing the accuracy and utility of communication in a conflict situation).

There now exist organizations that train people for conflict
intervention roles. The most imaginative training is done with
professionals who will be able to directly apply it in their
working lives. These include police (Bard, 1969, 1971), who are
often called upon to intervene in crises and intense conflicts
(e.g., hostage-taking, and intrafamilial or gang fighting);
community leaders, whose skills in negotiation are increasingly essential (Nicolau, 1973); and international civil servants
and military officers who must learn new skills for international dispute settlement and peacekeeping (IPA, 1971;
UNITAR, 1973).

Bard has developed an imaginative program for training
police as neutral third-party intervenors that (1) emphasizes
their role as peacemakers over their role as enforcers of law
and order; (2) sensitizes them to the nature of the conflict
process and to how it can be creatively handled without
violence; and (3) permits them to identify more closely with
the community and its members—to serve rather than to
oppress them.

Educational institutions have been a central arena of conflict
for more than a decade now, and there have been some efforts at
training intervention teams (ISR, 1970; Morgan, 1972; Chesler,
1969) to create shared-power systems in universities and public
schools. Such systems are the key to the restructuring of
these institutions and to the control of conflict and the abatement of violence within them.

In recent years, there has been considerable refinement in
the techniques for conflict resolution used by trainers in or-

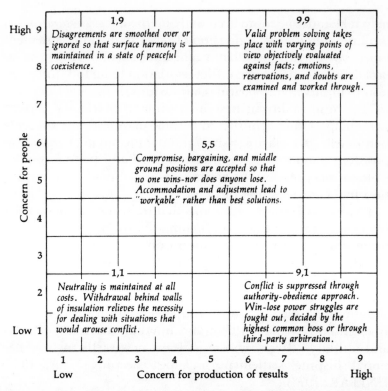

Figure 7. The conflict grid. (Reproduced by special permission from The Conflict Grid figure from "The Fifth Achievement," by Robert R. Blake and Jane Srygley Mouton, *Journal of Applied Behavioral Science*, 1970, 6(4), pp. 413-426, NTL Institute for Applied Behavioral Science.)

ganizational development. Primary attention has been paid to the resolution of interpersonal conflict in pursuit of greater organizational efficiency. Walton (1969) has researched intraorganizational conflict in industrial relations and suggests specific techniques for facilitating communication and creative confrontation. Blake and Mouton (1973) present the concept of the *conflict grid* (Figure 7) to assist in locating the proper mix of concern for people's growth and welfare, and concern for production of results in an organization's handling of its conflict problems.

Ethical questions may be raised in connection with this type of conflict resolution. Intraorganizational conflict resolution will tend to increase the effectiveness of that organization. Many of the complex organizations (e.g., the U.S. Air Force) now interested in internal conflict management are tools of official policies that we may question on ethical grounds. Do those of us engaged in conflict regulation really want to resolve conflict within organizations designed to make war or generate other forms of organized violence? Conflict regulation within health-related organizations may be socially beneficial; within war-related organizations it may not.

Over two decades India's Peace Brigade (Shanti Sena) has developed an effective training program for its crisis intervention/development teams (Desai, 1972). Such teams train for nonviolent third-party intervention by living and working with the inhabitants of communities. Shanti Seniks are not outsiders who intervene in communal riots; they are community members whose peacemaking capabilities depend upon the close relationships they develop and on their commitment to social and economic development. The teaching of attitudes necessary for intervention, self-discipline, the development of a national and world citizen self-concept, and economic and social development theory and field work are all important parts of the Shanti Senik's training.

In the United States, a number of organizations (Appendixes A and B) train persons for conflict regulation in community disputes, prison conflict, and environmental disputes. In such training programs, a dispute settlement strategy that assumes a need for basic social change and tough bargaining shapes the techniques. Also stressed are empathy skills development, trust establishment, timing, settlement psychology, and the assessment of costs and payoffs among conflict parties.

Edited video replay of selected individual and group actions in role plays provide positive and negative feedback of the effect of individual and group behavior on the resolution of conflict, and the video-playback enables the trainees to see themselves in the group process as others see them. Perception of oneself in the group process promotes self-awareness and enables the trainee to substitute new behaviors for those which do not function to individual and group advantage.

The course is structured so that each role play actively builds from the previous one and toward the next. Communication problems and frustrations in the first negotiation role play set the stage for the introduction of a mediator in the next simulation. Observing a mediator as he (or she) assembles an agreement provides a role model for students whose next assignment is to mediate a conflict. The student mediation role play tests ability to transfer training to practice and performance. In observing each other as mediators and in their critiques of peer performance, students also practice and reinforce learning in the seminar.

In the three simulated conflicts, each student assumes an activist role, an establishment role and a mediator's role. For most, one or the other of these roles is a reversal of their actual life and/or work role. . . . Role players are constantly put in the position of having to look at a problem from another person's perspective . . . to view disputes from all sides, a key element in both the mediation and negotiation process. (Nicolau, 1973)

Conflict regulation training at the international level is considerably less developed. The Burton and Doob experiments have already been cited. Another approach, which focuses on the training and retraining of international mediators, third-party intervenors, and peacekeeping specialists, is that developed by the International Peace Academy (IPA). The IPA's training session on techniques of mediation and negotiation covers the following areas: sensitivity to and analysis of incipient and actual conflict situations; selection of bargaining and other negotiating postures; group bargaining and negotiation; timing of third-party intervention in conflict; and change in third-party efforts from stage to stage of the mediation process (IPA, 1971).

Training should also be available for representatives of nation-states who might come into conflict. "Joint-costing," the Burton exercise in which diplomats of conflicting states "cost-out" the conflict and seek alternatives, would be extremely useful. Fisher (1969) suggests training for national policymakers in both tacit and explicit negotiation by way of

MAP

	DEMAND The decision desired by us	OFFER The consequences of making the decision	THREAT The consequences of not making the decision
WHO?	Who is to make the decision?	Who benefits if the decision is made?	Who gets hurt if the decision is not made?
WHAT?	Exactly what decision is desired?	If the decision is made, what benefits can be expected? —what costs?	If the decision is not made, —what risks? —what potential benefits?
WHEN?	By what time does the decision have to be made?	When, if ever, will the benefits of making the decision occur?	How soon will the consequences of not making the decision be felt?
WHY?	What makes this a right, proper, and lawful decision?	What makes these consequences fair and legitimate?	What makes these consequences fair and legitimate?

Every feature of an influence problem can be located somewhere on this schematic map. The nature of a given problem can be discovered through estimating how the presumed adversary would answer the above questions.

Figure 8. The influence map. (From Roger Fisher, *International Conflict for Beginners,* copyright © 1969 by Roger Fisher. Reprinted by permission of the author.)

the *influence map* (Figure 8). Here, antagonists decide what they wish opponents to do and formulate the "yesable proposition," which maximizes the possibility of their opponent's doing it. Concepts such as these should be built into formal training programs.

Conflict Intervention Training

We must first train persons to select conflicts appropriate for intervention. Then we must teach them how to enter a conflict situation, what to do while in it, and how to leave it with some assurance that a settlement will not come undone. As part of our modest program at the University of Colorado, I suggest a series of steps and cautions which intervenors might follow.

CONFLICT INTERVENTION GUIDE

I. *Mapping the Conflict*

II. *Decision to Intervene.* Many conflicts are not ripe for intervention at a particular time. Some will never be. Judging whether or not intervention in a conflict is wise is difficult and should depend on several criteria:

1) *Accessibility:* does one have sufficient credibility to gain entry to the conflict?

2) *Tractability:* does the conflict offer some hope of success given the intervenor's time, energy, skill, and funds?

3) *Divisibility:* can one intervene in only one issue or segment that might be more manageable?

4) *Timing:* is it too early . . . are the parties hurting enough to welcome intervention? Or too late . . . has it gone too far?

5) *Alternatives:* is nonintervention riskier than intervention in terms of the well-being of the conflict parties and others?

III. *Entering the Conflict Situation.* Each conflict situation has entry points where intervention can best begin. The optimum entry point is likely to be through a sharing of the conflict map with the conflict parties and influentials in the conflict situation.

A. *Credibility:* intervenors must already have or be able to establish credentials as someone with past success in settling disputes. In addition to professional credentials, the good offices of respected persons and backing from authoritative organizations outside the conflict situation are helpful.

B. *Neutrality:* intervenors must have no commitment toward any party in the conflict except that to a mutually satisfactory resolution of it. Naturally, the intervenor will have a personal investment in helping to resolve or regulate the conflict since its resolution will increase his/her personal credibility and professional standing.

IV. *Withdrawing from the Conflict Situation.* This can be the most important stage of intervention. The durability of the settlement and the reputation of the intervenor rest on the effective implementation of it. One part of this is creating a monitoring agency to hold all parties to their agreement. Another is to leave behind, if possible, established conflict regulation procedures for dealing with similar conflicts in the future.

V. *Essential Peacemaking Skills.* No third-party intervenor will be effective in conflict management in every type of conflict situation nor will they be equally proficient in the diverse skills that successful intervention draws upon. The following are skills or propensities that seem important for third-party intervention—a sort of guide for skills development. No rank order is implied in the listing.

1) *Conflict situation analysis/fact-finding:* parties, issues, goal clarification.

2) *Empathy:* ability to understand positions of antagonists without subscribing to them.

3) *Listening:* "active listening" helps parties to vent hostility and frustration, gains trust for intervenor.

4) *Sense of timing:* judging when conflict is receptive to intervention, when negotiations are appropriate.

5) *Trust and credibility development:* establishing "credentials," trust relationships with conflict parties and between them, intervenor objectivity.

6) *Mediation:* a set of skills that includes scheduling negotiations; helping negotiators formulate "yesable propositions"; clarifying and getting parties to agree to trade-offs; insuring full implementation of an agreement.

7) *Communication:* facilitating and validating communication among conflict parties; accurate verbal and non-verbal messages.

8) *Imagination:* the capacity for eliminating impasses through imaging creative alternatives, recombining alternative solutions or parts thereof, priority goals reranking.

9) *Joint-costing:* helping conflict parties to accurately assess the costs of the conflict to each, and the potential benefits of resolving it.

10) *Crisis management:* minimization of hostility and violence in extremely tense conflict situations through such measures and rationalizing the command-and-control system of forces of order, controlling access to weapons of violence on all sides, rumor control.

Conflict Regulation Exercises and Field Work Possibilities

1. *Future Imaging / Role Invention Exercise* (Appendix H). Have trainees read some of the futures literature, then write a conflict scenario for some future period when conflicts over environmental issues, resource scarcity, control of marine wealth, and the like are predominant. Have them design a conflict-regulation role for themselves. The exercise is designed to (1) sharpen their future-imaging capacity and the types of conflict situations and conflict management techniques the future will require, and (2) help them conceive of professional and lay roles in working creatively with conflict.

2. *International Conflict Resolution Exercise* (Appendix I). Gain knowledge of current conflicts in one of several regions of the globe for which maps with continental boundaries and "center capitals" are provided. The

assignment is to create strategies for intervention to resolve the conflict selected.

3. *Bomb Shelter Exercise* (Appendix J). An exercise to sharpen value clarification, future imaging, problem solving, and the resolution of value-based conflict. The exercise also sensitizes the student to the dangers and realities of nuclear war.

4. *Attica Negotiation Exercise* (Appendix K). In-depth examination of negotiation situations having negative or positive outcomes. An illustrative case of the former type is the Attica prison rebellion and massacre. There are some excellent media resources available: (1) the report of the New York State Commission on Attica (1972), particularly the section on negotiations; (2) a 16mm free film produced by the American Bar Association (from an ETV documentary videotape) of both the rebellion and the investigatory hearings; and, if there are media funds available, (3) a second film, "Attica," Tri-Continental Film Center, P.O. Box 4430, Berkeley, California. The exercise consists of (1) reading the entire book; (2) viewing the film and discussing it; (3) rereading carefully the section on negotiations; (4) analyzing where negotiations went wrong; and (5) discussion of restructuring or abolishing current prison systems.

5. *Analysis of Crisis Management Exercise.* Failures and successes in crisis management can be extremely useful for conflict regulation training. Attica, Kent State, Jackson State, and the 1968 Chicago police riots are all excellent cases for study. The Miami Beach convention case and the Cuban missile crisis are examples of successful management. In such cases, the problems of conflict regulation, contingency preparedness, and violence abatement intersect. Students in small working groups might select crises such as those cited that ended in disaster and create strategies for managing the crises that might have worked.

6. *Simulations* like the InterNation simulation (Guetzkow et al., 1963) or the Parker High School simulation (Appendix F).

7. *Community Peacemaking Exercise.* Select current conflicts close enough at hand for you to become involved directly. Strategize resolution techniques and even test them if possible. Intervention need not take the form of directly resolving a particular conflict. The intervenor may present ideas he or she feels will be useful to the actors in a conflict to resolve it. Testimony before investigatory or policymaking bodies becomes one effective means of intervention as citizen participation increases as a value in good government (Appendix L).

8. *Internships.* Locate internships—paid or nonpaid positions with organizations likely to be involved in conflict and conflict regulation. These might include urban school districts, community action organizations, peace action groups, police departments, university administrations, and national and international conflict regulation training groups.

9. *Global Futures Game.* Conflict at the global level within and between nations will be increasingly generated by scarce resources such as food and energy. This game illustrates the interplay of the components of national and global survival (food, population, technology, education) and the relationship of the have and have-not nations as concerns conflict and cooperation over those components. Game available from Earthrise, Providence, Rhode Island.

3. Self-limiting Conflict: The Gandhian Style

I have mentioned two basic categories of conflict regulation scholarship. In the preceding section we concerned ourselves with the first, specialists engaged in third-party intervention research and experimentation—intermediaries, negotiation, conciliation, communication control and modification. The second involves the study of ways of waging conflict that tend both to keep it within bounds and to limit its intensity or at least the possibility of violence—nonviolent social movements, nonviolent resistance on the part of individuals and groups, nonviolent alternative national defense strategies. Let us look at conflict processes that are self-regulating in nature, i.e., that have built-in devices to keep the conflict within acceptable bounds and to inhibit violent extremism and unbridled escalation.

Socialization is an important determinant of the style and effectiveness of conflict regulation in any society. If Tolley (1973) is correct in placing the formative period for attitudinal and behavioral patterns concerning peace/war issues and conflict regulation styles at ages 4-12, then learning creative approaches to conflict regulation through family, school, mass media, and other primary learning environments is essential. There are a few sources dealing with this problem (Nesbitt, 1973; Abrams and Schmidt, 1972).

There are societies and groups within societies that socialize their members in effective conflict regulation. Bourdieu (1962) describes Berber Kabyles of North Africa as a society held together by a process of balanced and strictly controlled conflict in which members are socialized to avoid violence. Elise Boulding (1974) observes that there are certain types of family environments and child-rearing practices that tend to produce persons with nonviolent proclivities and creative response patterns to conflict. Ultimately the socialization process, political socialization in particular, is probably the most important conflict regulation device. We should soon learn some interesting things about the impact of a decade of involvement in an unpopular war on the attitudinal and behavioral patterns of America's youth.

Etzioni's *self-encapsulation* concept is very useful here. It is a process in which certain conflicts are increasingly limited by their own nature and by the nature of the host system, so that the "range of expression of the conflict is curbed." Certain modes of conflict and weapons are excluded by mutual, sometimes tacit, consent, and the conflict becomes ritualized—the game is played by the rules, so to speak. Dahrendorf's analysis of the institutionalization of labor/management conflict over the past half century is an excellent illustration of self-encapsulation. In the United States, encapsulation occurred as a consequence of third-party intervention, when the federal government decided to protect labor's right to strike. It was also self-propelled encapsulation to some degree, as both labor and management decided that it was rational to place strict limits on their conflict—in other words, to maximize gains and minimize losses all around.

The Gandhian Model of Self-Limiting Conflict

Self-encapsulation can also occur through both ideological restraints and tactical approach. If at least one of the parties to the conflict develops an ideology that by its very nature limits the weaponry and violence used in the conflict, it is in an important sense self-encapsulating. Mahatma Gandhi's satyagraha (a word taken from Sanskrit, meaning "insistence on truth") movement in the first half of this century used such techniques, and other movements for social justice and self-determination have developed variations on this theme of nonviolent direct action. The Martin Luther King, Jr., and Cesar

Chavez movements are the best examples in recent North American history, though there are interesting Latin American nonviolent movements as well.

The satyagraha movement was a series of direct action campaigns aimed at calling into question the validity and moral legitimacy of the dominance-dependence relationships existing in India and South Africa. The movement challenged white rule in South Africa, British rule in the Asian subcontinent, and the caste structure of Indian society itself. As do all major social movements, Gandhi's had a discrete ideology, well defined roles, a strong leadership, and clear goals. It challenged a set of social structures with highly inequitable distribution of privilege, access to authority, and life chances. The movement's primary objective was to refine a technique for making latent conflict manifest and waging it without violent means or consequences.

Specific political goals included the winning of political independence of the subcontinent from Britain, the liberation of oppressed minorities such as the outcastes, and the creation of a new and appropriate model for Indian economic, political, and social development. There were philosophical objectives as well. The search for social and spiritual truth gave form and direction to Gandhi's strategic and tactical approaches. The concepts of ethnic, religious, and social community were also central to the movement's ideology.

The Gandhian Conflict Style

We will focus on the Gandhian techniques of waging conflict that served to limit the hostility—to inhibit the "runaway processes" within conflict dynamics, as Coleman (1957) terms them. How was Gandhi able to successfully propel yet control a movement that had such great potential for massive violence and reactive repression? In large measure the answer lies in both the strategy and tactics of confrontation that Gandhi developed and in the movement's ideological bases.

Step-wise Strategy. Perhaps the most obvious self-limiting aspect of Gandhi's confrontation style was its step-wise rather than spiralling escalation. Each satyagraha campaign involved a series of steps, each more challenging to the opponent than the preceding one. It would begin with *negotiation and arbitration*. This would be an extremely elaborate and lengthy stage including (1) on-site accumulation and analysis of facts, with opponent participation; (2) identification of interests in common with opponents; (3) formulation of a limited action goal acceptable to all parties and mutual discussion of same; and (4) a search for compromise without ceding on essentials (Naess, 1958). Gandhi did much to avoid further escalation; at this preliminary stage he established the close, cooperative, personal relationships with opponents that would later limit the antagonism normally generated by the escalation process.

If the conflict was not resolved at that initial level, the satyagrahis would prepare for direct action, then move on to agitation, ultimatum, economic boycott and strikes, noncooperation, civil disobedience, usurpation of governmental functions, and the creation of parallel government (Bondurant, 1965:40). If in any of these stages, the conflict was resolved, those subsequent would be unnecessary. After each new step, however, there was a built-in period of withdrawal, reflection, and analysis of one's own and one's opponents' positions and tactics. Missing was the escalation of normal conflict, in which a hostile response evokes an even more hostile response in an unbroken upward spiral. This strategy maximized the role of rational and conciliatory action on the part of all concerned, while providing for an intensification of the confrontation as needed to achieve the goals of the movement. The step-wise approach and the interaction of reflection and action allowed the movement leadership and rank-and-file participants to control, channel, and direct the dynamics of the conflict situations they had created. One might say that the movement's peculiar "self-consciousness" served to gauge the impact of each step in a campaign, to continually reassess its effectiveness and nonhostile intent, and thereby to maximize its self-limiting capacity.

The step-wise approach suggests that Gandhi's model of the conflict process is phasic rather than cyclical, with a confrontation proceeding through a series of escalatory steps. In the

Gandhian perspective, the conflict should lead the parties to a new level of truth, not back to the point where they began.

Ideological Self-Limitation. An essential concept in the Gandhian model of self-limiting conflict was *ahimsa* or non-violence. Each satyagrahi had to give unqualified commitment to nonviolent action and was resocialized for this by movement leadership. Although the nonviolent ethic in Hinduism, Jainism, and Buddhism did reinforce satyagraha's nonviolent belief system, satyagrahis from these and other religioethnic sects who were accustomed to battling each other violently had to be resocialized into new forms of confrontation.

The internalization of this ideological commitment gave satyagraha a unique form of self-control. No tight command-and-control system existed within the satyagraha movement. The leader and participant roles, individual and collective behavior, the influence of norms and peer expectation were all rooted in individual and group self-control. It was primarily because of this personalized self-control that such a massive movement developed with surprisingly little violence. Resocialization was essential to this self-control—where it was incomplete, violence would often erupt and Gandhi would halt a campaign.

Nonviolence is by its very nature an ideology that moderates the intensity of a conflict. An inherent theoretical assumption is that a nonviolent act will elicit a similar response from an opponent and will thereby increase the chances for conciliation. In practice, however, the dynamic is much more complex. In his analysis of nonviolent action as a form of interpersonal behavior, Hare (1968), using Homans' exchange theory and Bales' interactional analysis, shows how nonviolent protestors may evoke violent responses from police and bystanders.

The nonviolent actors usually intend to take downward (submissive), backward (advocating social change), and positive roles in their confrontation with others, especially those in authority. When they can maintain this role they seem to be able to "pull" a dominant-positive response which may lead to social change. However, if they become negative, or appear to be negative, then they pull a hostile response. (Hare, 1968:12)

Small group experiments (Shure et al., 1965; Bartos, 1974) have also suggested the potential risk that pacifist or conciliatory responses may increase the aggressiveness of an opponent. The point to be made here is that the training and discipline of nonviolent actors and their understanding of the interpersonal dynamics of nonviolence are important. Socialization into and internalization of the role of nonviolent actor is critical for the self-limiting capacity of nonviolent action.

Controlling the Dynamics of Escalation. Social scientists are now aware of certain growth dynamics of conflict—dynamics that in most conflict situations are unobserved and uncontrolled. Perhaps the most thorough analysis of the dynamics of intensification is that of J. S. Coleman (1957). I will describe a number of these dynamics and suggest how Gandhian conflict techniques tended to control them—particularly the "runaway responses" to which Coleman refers.

In community conflict situations certain changes normally occur as the conflict develops:

1. *Movement from specific to more general issues and from original to new issues.* This shift sets the stage for a wider and more intensive conflict as it alerts more potential parties to the controversy, uncovers fundamental cleavages and differences in the community, and clouds the basic issues. All of this, for obvious reasons, makes conflict resolution more difficult. Where a social movement like satyagraha is involved, such an issues diversification dynamic increases its opponents and inhibits its focus and sense of achievement. The Gandhian tactic for controlling this dynamic was to tie each campaign to a single issue and a sharply limited arena. The limited issue in each campaign, however, was subtly and cleverly tied into larger questions like the end of colonial rule. The effect was to limit the potential allies of the opponent, to retain as much issue clarity and simplicity as possible, and to insure moderate and continuous success feedback in limited increments. With each limited success, the nonviolent action device gained

credibility both with its adherents and its opponents. This tended to encourage both increased commitment to non-violence and more conciliatory attitudes on the part of opponents.

2. *Movement from disagreement to antagonism as the conflict develops.* Issue-based conflict is transformed into *ad persona* hostility—the conflict is personalized. Attacks are no longer on opposing positions but on those who hold them. This naturally heightens the conflict parties' sense of perceived threat and intensifies the conflict; it increases the "life-stakes" involved, so to speak.

The Gandhian model of conflict-waging inhibits the conflict personalization process. It reduces threat by stressing the maintenance of good personal relations with opponents while pressing the issues. An exemplary case was the Ahmedabad Satyagraha during which Gandhi maintained close friendly relations with several millowners while persuading them (and finally coercing them through fasting) to make concessions. Gandhi, by personalizing his relationships with his opponents, often accomplished individual "conversions" to his position. By this process of separating the person from the issue, he was able to shake the loyalty of opponents to their respective groups (e.g. millowners, members of the Brahmin caste), to sufficiently break down group identification and increase opponents' propensities toward conciliation. This technique was often employed to limit antagonism in satyagraha campaigns.[2]

The Gandhian model recognizes both the necessity and danger of polarization. Without it the issues cannot be clarified. The challenging movement needs it to survive and grow. Yet, in Gandhian conflict theory, confrontation is not a zero-sum or even a positive-sum game as much as it is a joint process of truth seeking, with the settlement emerging from that process. Gandhian conflict simultaneously provides for confrontation and maximizes the potential for conciliation. Gandhi developed a delicate mix of polarizing and conciliatory tactics that both produced and moderated confrontation. His view of conflict as the joint pursuit of truth rejected absolute ideological and tactical positions, thereby restraining the polarization process.

3. *Distortion of information.* As the conflict grows, according to Coleman, informal communication modes supplement
and may even replace formal media as a result of an increased
demand for information by more people who are alerted and
involved. Rumor, slander, innuendo, and inaccurate data tend
to aggravate the conflict. The sense of threat is heightened
between the parties as they become more secretive. What is the
other side planning? The worst is imagined. Information
that contradicts threatening images of opponents is filtered
out. Gandhi's conflict style, countering this dynamic, maximized the flow of information between the movement and its
opponents. His techniques and tactics were openly discussed.
Steps in the campaign were made known to opponents beforehand. He used the mass media to acquaint everyone with movement plans. Misinformation and secrecy were eliminated, reducing perceived threat among opponents and lessening
public fear and ignorance.

4. *Mutual reinforcement of response.* Coleman emphasizes
the process of reciprocal causation, the stuff of which conflict
escalation is made. Cycles of hostile response develop and feed
the polarization process. Negative images of the other party
are continually confirmed. Hostile acts call forth hostile
responses that in turn evoke more hostility and so on. Conflict
resolution is largely the discovery of a means to break into
escalatory reciprocal causation and reverse its direction. Oberschall (1973:266) notes that reciprocity is also the basis for
dispute settlement. The "ethic of symmetry" requires that each
give as well as take, and refrain from taking unreasonable and
extreme positions.

The Gandhian conflict style uses positive reciprocal causation. Nonviolent action theoretically calls forth a nonhostile
response from one's opponent. As I noted earlier, this principle
may not always operate—where nonviolent actors are poorly
trained, for example. Even when the nonviolent actors are
disciplined, the initial trauma of an unexpected nonviolent act
contravening established custom and threatening privileged
status may anger and frustrate opponents and encourage them
to respond violently, as was often the case in the early months

of the sit-in movement in the South (Wehr, 1968). The theory of nonviolent action asserts that while an opponent's initial response may be hostile, nonviolent response to that hostility will increasingly modify and ultimately transform it. The experience of the Gandhian and similar movements tends to lend supportive evidence to this proposition, although, as Bondurant observes, police excesses were common in official response to satyagraha.

> An American journalist, Webb Miller, reported that after one raid on a salt depot he counted, in a hospital, 320 injured, many still insensible with fractured skulls, others writhing in agony from kicks in the testicles and stomach. (Bondurant, 1965:97)

5. *Emergence of extremist leadership.* To curb the operation of Gresham's Law of Conflict (Coleman, 1957:14), by which extremist leaders increasingly replace moderate ones as the conflict heats up, Gandhi selected his first- and second-level leadership carefully, and, as Sharp (1973:470) notes, they were disciplined and trained thoroughly in preparatory periods before each campaign. Wherever possible, Gandhi would lead a campaign personally, with his stature as a leader permitting him to control access to leadership positions. His pledge of nonviolence acted as a brake on extremist elements. The Gandhian principle of self-reliance also helped the movement to stay clear of alliances with other political forces that did not share its commitment to nonviolence. The emphasis on cooperative, constructive programs in each satyagraha campaign reinforced the positive, creative aspects of the conflict technique. One was not challenging established norms and structures without exemplifying alternatives. The habits of cooperation in improving sanitation, nutrition, and education were essential dimensions of the satyagrahi's role.

Other Limiting Aspects. The principle of self-realization in satyagraha was a conflict-limiting device in two respects. (1) Any conflict was viewed as a self-realization process for all parties involved. Such a view sees the opponent as one to be persuaded or one to be persuaded by, not as one to be eliminated, humiliated, or bested. (2) For the satyagrahi, the conflict was an empowerment process. Satyagraha as a technique gave the hitherto powerless a strength, a unique identity and status vis-à-vis their opponents. This identity-producing dynamic encouraged a symmetry in the conflict that reinforced its self-limiting qualities. Violence is often a product of desperation and asymmetry in a power relationship. Satyagraha provided both a power balance that facilitated eventual conciliation with minimal violence and a concern for the opponent as someone with an identity deserving of respect.

Coleman identifies a number of factors working for moderation of conflict in communities—cooptation of the opposition, resort to normal techniques of handling problems, the existence of preconflict relationships that cross-pressure participants, identification with and investment in community institutions. Though Gandhi exploited these factors wherever possible, he was primarily concerned with institutionalizing new conflict processes, creating new rules by which conflict might be waged—encapsulating the conflict, to refer again to Etzioni's concept.

We find, then, in Gandhi's model of conflict built-in inhibitors of violence, rancorous escalation, and extreme polarization—three processes that facilitate destructive consequences in normal conflict waging. The specific self-limiting aspects discussed above are rooted in a conception of conflict as a truth-seeking process in which the objective is not to win, but to achieve a fresh level of social truth and a healthier relationship between antagonists. This is what Bondurant called the Gandhian dialectic.

> In every case of satyagraha the conflict is to be understood in dialectical terms. The immediate objective is a restructuring of the opposing elements to achieve a situation which is satisfactory to both the original opposing antagonists but in such a way as to present an *entirely new total circumstance* [emphasis mine]. (Bondurant, 1965:195)

This rather innovative view of struggle, then, insured that the techniques of waging it would be self-limiting. The conception of struggle as truth seeking produces in Gandhian conflict an escalating dynamic somewhat different from the normal one, which Kriesberg has described:

> Having expressed hostility and coercive action against another party, the alleged reason for it assumes importance commensurate with the action taken. The cause is endowed with additional significance and there is increasing commitment to it. In addition, as the other side reciprocates with coercion the threats and injuries suffered also induce feelings of loyalty and commitment . . . [that justify] increased effort toward their attainment and the willingness to absorb, without yielding, the coercive efforts of adversaries. (Kriesberg, 1973:155)

In the dynamics of Gandhian escalation, to the contrary, persuasion in theory replaces coercion, though, as Klitgaard (1971) notes, this did not always occur. The escalating commitment is not to "winning" but to the discovery of the truth of social justice, a commitment that admitted the possibility of the opponent's truth.

> Gandhian philosophy does not exclude compromise as a device for the accommodation of differing positions at a point where conflict has not become explicit and basic principles have not been challenged. But once conflict materializes the Gandhian technique proceeds in a manner qualitatively different from compromise. What results from the dialectical process of conflict of opposite positions as acted upon by satyagraha, is a synthesis, not a compromise. The satyagrahi is never prepared to yield any position which he holds to be the truth. He is, however, prepared—and this is essential—to be persuaded by his opponent that the opponent's is the true, or the more nearly true, position. In the working out of the Gandhian dialectical approach, each side may, of course, yield through dissuasion any part of its position. But this is not compromise. When persuasion has been effected, what was once the opponent's position is now the position of both antagonist and protagonist. There is no sacrificing of position, no concession to the opponent with the idea of buying him over. Non-violent resistance must continue until persuasion has carried the conflict into mutually agreeable adjustment. Such adjustment will be a

synthesis of the two positions and will be an adjustment satisfactory to both parties in the conflict. There is no victory in the
sense of triumph of one side over the other. Yet, there is no
compromise, in the sense in which each side would concede
parts of its previous position solely to effect a settlement.
There is no "lowering" of demands, but an aiming at a
"higher" level of adjustment which creates a new, mutually
satisfactory, resolution. (Bondurant, 1965:197)

What unfolded in the Gandhian dialectic was a process similar
in many ways to the consensus formation traditionally used by
Quaker bodies and in certain traditional political systems
(Bourdieu, 1962). No one wins or loses. Antagonists arrive at
a "meeting of the minds," so to speak.

Gandhi was ostensibly one of the opponents in the satyagraha campaigns, but his style and commitment to the process
made him, in a sense, a third party to the conflict. Kakasaheb
Kalelkar, one of Gandhi's satyagraha leaders, has called him a
"master in the art of synthesis."[2] This skill at facilitating a
convergence of positions among antagonists is, unfortunately,
impossible to analyze in any but a superficial way here.

Applicability of the Model

Is the Gandhian model as a conflict regulation device transferable, in part or whole, to other conflict arenas? In fact, it
has been adopted and adapted for use in other social movements—e.g., the Martin Luther King, Jr. (1961) and Cesar
Chavez (Matthieson, 1970) movements for equal rights in the
United States and the Danilo Dolci movement in Sicily (Mangione, 1972). Its tactics were borrowed by wartime resistance
movements in Norway and Denmark and by the movement in
Czechoslovakia in 1968, to cite the most prominent cases. It
has been used effectively by groups and individuals not ideologically committed to nonviolence but who have recognized
its practical value. Gandhian self-limiting conflict may provide future tactical possibilities for both liberation movements
and civilian defense programs.

Of equal interest is the potential applicability of parts of the model for conflict regulation in marital conflict, community disputes, and international peacemaking. Its transferability will be greatest where conflict involves the total identity of the opponents, where a restructuring rather than a mere reallocation of values is called for. Yet in most conflict situations the information maximization tactic would tend to reduce threat and encourage conciliation. Training people who are likely to be involved in intergroup conflict how to break into an escalating spiral with a nonhostile response would help to regulate conflict. Training people to distinguish between antagonist and issue in their conflict waging is a third Gandhian tactic that would help limit conflict.

One final conflict-limiting mechanism in the satyagraha approach that might be used effectively in conflict regulation training is that of timing. Conflict is rarely, if ever, waged "on schedule." Gandhian confrontation was self-limiting partly because it was well timed. Runaway processes were precluded by careful, self-conscious weighing of each action and the opponent's likely response to it. Even in conflicts where maximization of gains is the primary objective for each party, training both parties and third-party intermediaries in timing and scheduling could increase the potential for conciliation.

Satyagraha has several prominent weaknesses, however. For one thing, it is quite culture-rooted, with concepts like self-suffering and nonviolence difficult to transplant. Yet the Gandhian method of creative confrontation is not as culture-bound as is popularly believed. The research of Sharp (1970) and others suggests that many of the techniques of satyagraha were borrowed from Chinese, Russian, and Irish nonviolent resistance movements. While a major part of its genius lay in the way it was skillfully shaped out of Indian tradition, as a means of struggle it has had substantial cross-cultural transferability.

The Gandhian movement was fueled by the charismatic leadership of one man, though it produced other men of somewhat lesser stature like Ghaffir Khan and Vinoba Bhave. When that leadership was withdrawn, the movement declined rapidly. Whether nonviolent movements are any more susceptible to such a dynamic than other movements is a debatable point, but with Gandhi and King, movement dependence on their leadership was both strength and weakness.

A third possible weakness concerns the vulnerability of satyagraha to cooptation by opponents. The confrontation/conciliation mix is an extremely delicate one and the movement may take much less than it could get from opponents in order to maintain the balance. Most revolutionaries would argue that compromise has no place in a struggle movement—that it is only diversion.

Finally, Gandhi's methods did not always work for even Gandhi himself. A number of satyagraha campaigns were abortive or produced violent confrontations. It will be interesting to see how successful the current resurgence of the satyagraha movement in India will be. It has had some major successes in confronting corrupt governments in Gujarat and Bihar and the Desai government is committed to Gandhian principles, but it is too early to measure lasting impact.

4. Self-limiting Conflict: The Norwegian Resistance

Nonviolent resistance in the Gandhian tradition is one example of self-limiting conflict. Social scientists are also researching and creating other uses for nonviolent action. Scholars have begun research on nonmilitary forms of resisting both external invaders and oppressive regimes. Sharp (1973), Roberts (1969), Boserup and Mack (1975), and Ebert (1969) have all published research in this area.

As armaments become more destructive and more limited in their applicability, the pressure to explore alternative techniques for protecting national territory and sociopolitical institutions from external attack will increase.[1] Embryonic theory on civilian defense draws heavily at this point on analysis of historical cases like the one that follows, in which nonviolent civilian resistance proved to be effective to some significant degree.

The Norwegian Resistance

Norway during the German occupation of World War II represents a classic case of nonviolent resistance. We will deal with one dimension of that resistance—the communication media and structures developed to provide the backbone of widespread opposition to nazification. The analysis is in large part based on primary sources—both documents in the Norwegian national archives at Oslo and the author's interviews with persons instrumental in building the resistance communication system. Special emphasis is placed on the means by which peacetime political and social structures, voluntary associations, and channels of communication were modified for clandestine resistance to an attack on deeply rooted institutions.

The Setting

The Wehrmacht invaded Norway on April 9, 1940. Initial and sometimes spirited resistance by Norwegian armed forces lasted for weeks but ended with their demobilization and the flight of the Norwegian government to England, where it functioned in exile until the end of the war. As the invasion began, Vidkun Quisling, the leader of Norway's small and ineffective Nazi party, the Nasjonal Samling, prematurely proclaimed himself the new chief of state and presented a hurriedly appointed cabinet, several of whom had not been consulted beforehand and who subsequently refused to serve. The German Reichskommissar Terboven, who mistrusted and despised Quisling, quickly removed him (Quisling was not to appear again in public office until February 1942, when he had succeeded in persuading Berlin to allow him to form a puppet state as minister-president). After an unsuccessful attempt to fashion a subservient indigenous government with some semblance of popular support, Terboven created a Council of Commissioner Ministers—manned with Quisling supporters for the most part, but controlled by German administrators.

By the end of 1940, several hundred thousand German combat and support troops had occupied Norway. Many were building massive fortifications along the coast in anticipation of an Allied invasion, which never materialized. "Fortress Norway," as certain Third Reich strategists referred to it, was an important segment of Germany's northwestern defense perimeter, and the Germans were dead serious about both its internal and external security.

Yet, the occupation was a comparatively benign one. As Hitler had made clear in his personal order initiating the invasion:

Above all, the aim must be to give the operation the character of a peaceful occupation which has as its goal the armed protection of the neutrality of the Nordic states.[2]

German soldiers were generally correct in their behavior toward Norwegians, who were regarded as Nordic cousins to be integrated into the greater Reich. The economic situation was initially favorable for individual Norwegians, particularly if one agreed to contribute to the German war effort. In short, life under occupation began with relative ease and little hope for outside assistance, and the situation was not conducive to the development of resistance to the occupying power. From April to September, Norwegians passed through a period of shock and confusion, and then adjustment. The psychological polarization of occupied and occupier necessary for the emergence of a resistance movement, and the perception of threat that triggers this polarization, were yet to come.

Holdningskamp

The first phase of the *holdningskamp*, or "battle of the wills," involved the clear drawing of battle lines, creating a dichotomous image in the public mind—"them and us" and "right and wrong"—without which resistance would have been impossible. This psychological polarization was centered around and achieved through the unique social and political characteristics of Norwegian society, two of which were especially important. Norway has a parliamentary system with a number of parties representing various economic and religious communities in the Storting, or parliament. At that time there was much provincialism, with different regions politically and geographically isolated from one another having strong traditions of local self-government—reflected in the jealousy with which communities guarded their autonomy. Resentment of restrictions on this regional and personal autonomy and on valued democratic traditions were inevitable in such a political environment.

The second major structural characteristic of Norwegian society relevant for an understanding of *holdningskamp* was the central role of voluntary associations in Norwegian life. The most important of these represented specific occupational groupings (e.g., doctors, lawyers, teachers, labor). Others were centered around largely avocational activities such as sports and the arts. Each association had a national office—usually in Oslo—a secretariat, branches in various cities, and a communications system. These associations were "the communications media for all essential group interests" (Wyller, 1958:315).

In addition to their communication and training functions, these organizations had political influence as well

> through the activities of the pressure groups at different state levels, through contacts with the parties, as administrative bodies working for the State, as sources of recruitment to public bodies, as groups supplying experts, and as elements in the general political situation. In conjunction with the organs of the State and the political parties, the organizations had come to play so important a part in the underpinning of the demo-cratic structure of the State that one can without exaggera-tion describe the Norwegian system of government as an "organization-democracy." (Wyller, 1958:315-316)

One might say that *holdningskamp* formally began on September 25, 1940, when Terboven decreed that all political parties and organizations excepting Nasjonal Samling (NS) were illegal. Since most Norwegians held NS in high con-tempt, the formerly quasi-political voluntary associations became their sole means of exerting political influence. From the NS perspective, the associations could be used to enlist popular commitment to the "New Order" and to integrate Norwegians into a visionary corporate state, which would immediately make peace with Germany and become her sover-eign fighting partner.

> Basing themselves in part on the fascist doctrine of the corporate state, which regarded the parliamentary system of representa-tion as outmoded and wanted instead a congress composed of spokesmen of professional, trade and other economic interest associations, the Norwegian Nazi authorities began planning a system whereby the NS party could control these associations

and in that way exert pressure on the members. (Riste and Nokleby, 1970:26)

As the *Reichskommissariat,* assisted by NS, sought to bend this firmly established organizational infrastructure to a new political purpose and ideology, a growing awareness of the threat to an entire way of life developed within these organizations.

Legal Resistance. For a limited period the effort to coopt the associations for the purposes of a Nazi state, and the resistance offered by the legitimate leaders of the organizations, was carried out on a legal plane. The organizations existed as before, while Terboven, through the fall of 1940, attempted to persuade leaders to publicly join the Nazi cause and to influence their members to do likewise. Approached first were groups that appeared to be more politically conservative or potentially tractable, like the medical professions, civil servants, and agricultural and sports organizations. As the Nazis pushed, leaders resisted and took initiative by mobilizing their constituencies to protest specific government policies that contradicted national traditions and values. Protest was sometimes voiced by an association's leaders, as in the open letter to Terboven of May 15, 1941, signed by national representatives of forty-three professional groups. In other instances, leaders would urge individual members to protest directly. The letter-writing campaign of communal administrators in January 1941 was in response to the interior minister's demand that all civil servants take a loyalty oath to the Nazi state. Most—up to 98 percent in certain communes—sent letters of protest and refusal (Malm, 1945:4).

Through the fall, winter, and spring, the sparring continued with the Nazis alternately cajoling and threatening in an effort to bring organization leaders to heel. Each issue broached and each organization approached raised the conflict to a higher level of intensity. The critical issue in this early period seems to have been the absence of justice and good sense in the appointment of persons to direct public affairs. The Justice Department's decree of November 14, 1940, claiming the right

to dismiss jurors from courts and replace them with "politically reliable" persons, brought a sharp reaction from the
legal professions and ultimately the supreme court's resignation. The creation of NSPOT in February 1941—an NS office
with total authority over appointments of persons to public
office—brought a more general protest. Unqualified persons
with questionable motives would replace existing uncoopera-
tive leaders—the threat to both the society and the individual
was becoming clear.

The Norwegian bishops' letter of January 15, 1941, and the
protest of doctors at Oslo hospitals condemning the brutal
activity of the *Hird* (the Norwegian equivalent of the German
SA) were other prominent examples of legal, open resistance.
All such actions were mobilized through the communications
networks of the individual professional groups. The protest
letter from the forty-three organizations on May 15 produced
a watershed. On June 18, 1941, an infuriated Terboven sum-
moned the leaders of these groups to Akershus. He had six of
the forty-three arrested there and either disbanded or placed
under NS tutelage all of the signatory organizations. From that
point on, it was clear that resistance required solidarity, cooperation, and effective communication—all of a clandestine
nature. In early September, a period of martial law, arrests, and
executions underscored both the growing threat to the Norwegian way of life and the risks of participating in resistance
activity. The battle lines were now clearly drawn for the
leaders, and illegal clandestine activity accelerated sharply—
their major task became one of clarifying the lines for the larger
population.

From Open to Clandestine Communication. From July
through December 1941, two developments essential to the
resistance took place. Second-level leadership in the disbanded
or NS-controlled associations began to organize for action. In
some, this occurred with the blessing or at the instigation of
top-level leaders. Where NS-appointed or faint-hearted leaders
were in command, such organizing was initiated by younger
officials—often in the secretariats—who cemented contacts
with reliable people at all levels in their organizations and

established relationships with counterparts in other associations. Most of these leaders were already key persons in their organizations, with middle-level positions that afforded them effective access to communication and control.[3]

The emergence of these middle-level leaders sometimes produced awkward situations. During the transition from legal to illegal protest, associations often had a double leadership. NS-controlled leaders existed simultaneously with unofficial leaders who usually formed "action committees."

> These committees sounded opinion among the membership, they gave directives to members and led cooperative action within the extreme factions (of their respective organizations), they kept contact with each other and with other Home Front organizations. . . . In order to continue contact (with members) down the line, each built its own communications apparatus. (Wyller, 1958:277)

By the end of 1941, most of these quasi-clandestine networks were in place.

This period also saw the development of double memberships in these associations. There had been mass withdrawals from many of the organizations affected by Terboven's decree, particularly after the creation of an Associations Bureau to monitor members' loyalty. The result was often the shell of an organization, deprived of a vast majority of its members and directed by Nazi officials, and a reconstituted illegal, clandestine organization serving a growing constituency. The essential fact of this transitional period is that the interlevel and interregional communications networks of these organizations not only remained largely intact, but were extended and refined to transmit illegal messages, provide feedback from members, and coordinate resistance.

Developing the Integrated Network

The integrated communications net had its origins in the "Protest Action of the 43." The planning for that action had

brought representatives of those organizations together for the
first time in a resistance framework. Resulting contacts later
provided the nucleus for the *Koordinasjonskomiteen* (KK),
which was to develop both the centralized network and a
number of ancillary services.

In October 1941 a secret meeting was called in Oslo by Dr.
H. J. Ustvedt, the vice-chairman of the junior medical association.[4] Present at the meeting were an engineer, the chief of
communal administrators, a lawyer, a pastor, a school principal, a university lecturer, and a teacher—all of them important
men in their fields (Malm, 1945:7). It seems that personal
acquaintance was as influential as considerations of strategic
representation in the selection of these particular men, and personal relationships continued to be a vital factor in resistance
communication.

The group decided that a nationwide network of reliable
contacts was needed to distribute directives and organize local
resistance to nazification. Such a net would use, wherever
feasible, existing contacts of different national organizations.
The coverage represented at the meetings, however, was limited
to eastern Norway. Ustvedt called to the meeting Dr. Ole Jacob
Malm, a colleague, fellow amateur musician, and fellow
activist in the association's illegal faction. Malm was charged
with the responsibility of developing a nationwide organization of local committees in the "natural communications
centers."

> In the course of the last months of 1941, then, the foundations
> were laid for a communications network, partly through (my)
> visiting in individual towns, partly as people who had been
> designated contact-points . . . were called to Oslo and instructed
> there as to their future activity. (Malm, 1945:8)

Malm found the challenge stimulating. He resigned from his
hospital, quietly withdrew from all other normal activities,
and began "writing" a nonexistent thesis on bone diseases. For
two months he carefully developed plans for the system. He
traveled to each of twenty-one centers to contact and instruct
persons designated for the net. Travel within Norway was

tightly controlled, but Malm had a perfect alibi for the trip. His "research" afforded him a legitimate reason for traveling to hospitals all over Norway, and with his set of X-rays and proper permits, he constructed the basic net without interruption.

In December 1941, a trial directive was sent out to test the system. It was successful and by early 1942 the network was operative.[5] The system was to maximize both security and effectiveness and was so carefully thought out that it survived over three years despite ingenious attempts by the Gestapo to crack it and was still operating at the time of liberation. The network was a multiplex system for information gathering and distribution and was used primarily for the *parole*—a directive to a certain population instructing it to adopt a certain position or take a specific action in response to a government policy. This directive was the primary technique for controlling and shaping the attitudes and actions of large numbers of people. A *parole's* effectiveness would be determined by the extent of its coverage (i.e., how many people reached and how rapidly) and the authority and authenticity accorded it by the receivers. Both coverage and credibility would be enhanced through a multimedia, multichannel system for getting the word to local action committees and beyond. A general *parole*, then, would normally be sent out by the KK via four separate means of transmission.

1. *The Underground Press.* By the time the KK and its net had been formed, the underground press had already appeared in many cities. KK saw it as a potentially significant part of the network and quickly formed a press committee to coordinate illegal press activity and harness it for *parole* distribution. Members of this committee traveled throughout Norway locating underground papers and integrating them into the net. Clandestine papers provided one of four means of *parole* dissemination. The most important paper was the publication *Bulletinen*, which first appeared in mid-November 1940, and became a major vehicle for "spreading the word." By late 1941 it had developed a distribution system in various cities that was later used by KK (Hansen, 1946:1). The underground press, then, carried the word directly from KK to the individual.

2. *The Postal Service.* A second medium of transmission—this one to the contact person or local committee who passed the word to the inhabitants of the region—was the directive sent by mail. The *parole* was written between the lines of a quite ordinary personal letter, but in invisible ink. Nazi censors developed detection fluids but KK had informants in the appropriate offices and whenever an effective fluid was developed, the ink formula was immediately changed. Besides transmitting the message itself, the letter had to insure the authenticity of its source, for there were false *paroles* emanating from both Nazi sources and nonofficial resistance groups. Authenticity was established through a code, like the length of certain sentences and the distinctive handwriting of Malm's secretary, Sigrid Steinnes, who wrote every single message during the occupation and provided continuity as Malm and successive coordinators were forced to flee.

> Neither her conduct nor her manner suggested that she had the remotest thing to do with illegal activity. Officially she was a secretary in a little doctor's office on Storting Street in Oslo. The other floors (of the building) had been taken over for *Hird* (Nazi SA) offices. Who would suspect that the medicine bottles contained chemicals for clandestine writing, and the prescriptions were *paroles* for the entire nation? (Steen, 1950, vol. 3:299)

Letters were carried by an official/unofficial postal service. Malm and Ingvald Lid, chairman of the Norwegian Postman's Union, created an interesting parallel postal service, using essentially the same personnel and apparatus that handled the regular mails. With the contacts of Lid, Malm, and others in and around KK, a nationwide clandestine postal service was established.

> When Malm sent out KK paroles, it was usually in sealed envelopes bearing return addresses of fictitious companies. Malm most frequently brought these letters home to Lid in packages which were picked up there by postal truck . . . which delivered the mail to Solli post office . . . where reliable persons took the letters and sent them through the stamping machine at

a time of the day when there was no German controller present. (Lid, 1962:188)

Through a system of assumed names, false addresses, office "fronts," and trustworthy personal relationships, this second channel of communication carried directives from the KK to local contacts with striking reliability.

3. *Couriers.* A third dissemination technique used personal envoys. These were always legitimate travelers, not special messengers. Travel about Norway was difficult and the Nazi police were effective. Only people who were reliable and unlikely to be suspected by the authorities were selected to carry *paroles* and other important messages. With contacts in the travel permits office and travel agencies, KK was regularly supplied with a list of persons with legitimate travel plans and permits. Of these, the most reliable were enlisted to carry messages—always in verbal form. There was to be no written evidence if someone were taken. With contacts at Fornebu Airfield near Oslo, KK was even able to enlist north-bound German aircraft as unsuspecting couriers for the long haul to North Norway. With minute containers of microfilm inconspicuously attached to their fuselages, they dispatched messages with the usual Teutonic efficiency. Messages were also sent with railway personnel who traveled throughout Norway on the job. Often the courier never met the person for whom his message was destined. It would be left at a shop or passed to an intermediary or "cut-out." Because courier transmission was risky both for the individual and the organization he temporarily served, this technique was relied upon less than the others.

One of the reasons that the (network of) contact points held up as well as they did was that communication with the center was based to such a slight extent on couriers. . . . A courier could be arrested and pulled in with important information. A little film could at worst be found. . . . However, it happened that throughout the war, not one report or message from the KK was intercepted on route. (Steen, 1950, vol. 3:298)

4. *BBC Broadcasts*. Finally, each major *parole* would be broadcast over the BBC Norwegian Service. The message would be smuggled to Sweden and sent by radio or courier to London. Now and then, *paroles* would make their way to England via the North Sea fishing fleet. Receiving the word in this way was not simple, as all radios had been confiscated in September 1941. Each local community, however, generally had access to a clandestine set, and the *parole* would make its way to the same destination as those arriving by other means.

Each of these four media—letter to the local contact, underground press, courier, and the BBC—supported the others and provided cross-checks on authenticity. If a directive arrived by three of the four channels, it was fairly certain to be authentic. If it was also heard on BBC, all doubt was removed.

Regional and Local Nets. At the regional and particularly the local levels the system had a very personal dimension since the web of relationships in Norway's rural and small-town society was used to spread and gather information. The directive came initially to the regional contact. By 1945, these *kontaktpunkt* had increased in number from twenty-one to perhaps thirty-five throughout the nation. All of these people had false addresses—shops where mail was delivered to a pseudonym and from there delivered elsewhere for pickup.

Contacts were selected for reliability, personal relationships with those at the center, and their strategic position. Often they were what Rose has termed ecological influentials— persons whose role or location in a society makes them natural facilitators of communication through "mediating ideas" among several groups (Rose, 1968). Professional people like teachers, doctors, and lawyers who were tied into the national system through their professional associations, who were respected and trusted by local people, and who had regular contact (or legitimate reason to have it) with many people were often optimum contacts. On the other hand, persons with responsible positions were sometimes too cautious for this dangerous and exacting work. The "comers" with minimal vested interest were often the best local communicators because they were willing to take the risks.

Once contacts were identified and asked to organize their region—an entire valley, for example—they would receive the *parole* by letter and courier and would distribute it as rapidly as possible. Each would contact all persons he trusted, who would in turn function as information "buds" by contacting trusted friends, thus creating a multiplier effect. Whole valleys could be alerted in ten hours with this method.

The local nets, like the national network, were operated with a curious mix of stable personal relationships and anonymity. Personal acquaintanceship and interdependence facilitated communication, and anonymity secured it. The word traveled but it was impossible to locate its source—a condition that frustrated potential informers. Even so, precautions were taken to protect local contacts. Okkenhaug tells of his writing *paroles* in invisible ink between the lines of Nazi literature that he then sent to local communicators.

Communication was the initial basis for and function of the local contacts. There was, throughout the war, an overwhelming popular hunger for news from inside and outside the country. Contact people responded naturally to this need. In early 1942, Olav Drivnes, a teacher at Hardanger, began to receive material from the KK's contact in Bergen. Drivnes knew no one above his level in the system, but began to pass information further down within the teachers association in the villages. Illegal newspapers, banned books, Allied propaganda, and information sheets from his own BBC-based news service made their way through him.

Through a unique "sixth sense" one knew where to place trust and to whom one should pass information. This non-verbal communication of certainty that others would follow one's lead was essential for building local networks. It gave the leaders, and ultimately the people at large, the courage to act.

Communication was at the same time the most essential and **the least threatening resistance activity and was therefore the** perfect vehicle for mobilizing local populations. Passing information to friends was in the beginning a relatively low-risk activity and many were willing to do it. As resistance developed, the communication system both expanded and differentiated to respond to other local problems, like distribution of money to families of strikers and prisoners. People in the system became willing to participate in increasingly risky actions. Individual commitment, then, was captured initially through communications activity and grew from that point.

Generating feedback was another major function of local contacts. Intelligence-gathering and its transmission to the center was continuous. The success of the *parole* depended heavily on the KK's skill in judging popular response before sending it out. This capability rested in turn upon continuous soundings of opinion from hundreds of people at the periphery. Pre-*parole* estimation and post-*parole* evaluation were thereby assured.

Tapping the Network. The network was so meticulously constructed that, as noted earlier, it outlived the occupation. The attrition rate among top-level communicators such as Malm and Okkanhaug was high but such people were not discovered in their KK roles. Malm, for example, was forced to flee after he became involved in the Jewish rescue operation, not because of activity with the communications network. Nazi police tried to tap the net for information that would lead them to key people. One imaginative and effective technique was "play in the negative sector." Nazi agents planted in resistance groups were allowed to feed them information that might, and indeed did in rare instances, result in the loss of German troops. Their credibility thus established, these plants could then subtly turn their groups away from resistance goals and toward Nazi objectives, while providing the authorities with incriminating data.[6] Despite their natural reserve and mild xenophobia, the Norwegians were sometimes easy prey for such "negative play." For example, isolation and hope led people to accord unwarranted authenticity to things English. Persons using English idiomatic phrases, recent English newspapers, or English cigarettes were often too readily trusted. The illegal press was another vulnerable dimension of the network. Police would merely observe the distribution pattern, starting at the limits of regional circulation and following the lines to the source.

On the whole, however, the network was secure for several reasons. It was planned, not spontaneous, in its origin; and its design minimized points of vulnerability. First of all, the cardinal principle of legitimacy in the transmission process was carefully observed. When couriers were used, everything possible about them was legitimate. Nothing written was ever carried, and as little as possible was written by any one at any level. Wherever possible, established and legitimate communications and authority structures were used, like the voluntary associations. By using them, the network identified special interests more closely with national interest and legitimized clandestine leadership for the average Norwegian, decreasing the chance of detection.

Second, a modified cell system existed in the network's structure. A cell system protects itself by severely limiting the knowledge a person at any level has about the rest of the organization. With no horizontal communication between cells and only one member of a cell communicating vertically, it is difficult to expose the organization from any one point. The Norwegian system minimized horizontal communication at the upper levels, where it could be most damaging and where individuals were most vulnerable, while maximizing it at the bottom where it mattered primarily that the word reach as many as possible and from where the original source was especially difficult to trace.

Responses to the Parole

The *parole*, like much of the basic structure of the communications net, had its roots in prewar Norway's political and social systems. Political parties and professional organizations had used *paroles* widely to communicate policy decisions to members and to urge them to act in a particular way. This continued during the legal phase of resistance. Leaders were known and legal, and communication was unhindered. A national organization could inform and shape the attitudes and actions of its membership as demonstrated by the massive protest of communal officials in January 1941, when a flood of letters forced the cancellation of a proposed loyalty oath.

As the *holdningskamp* intensified, however, and associations went underground, led by unknown men, the *parole* had to be reshaped to meet new and difficult criteria. When directed at specific occupational groupings it was necessary to pull not only the correct reaction from the group but a supportive response from the rest of the population as well. The general *parole*, directed at the total population, was a new concept that posed serious problems of coverage and technique. The most difficult task, though, was to devise means of giving authority to these directives, which came from a group of unknowns with initially no legitimate status in the eyes of most Norwegians, even though their messages travelled the same organizational channels as before.

Paroles used during the occupation varied greatly in content, purpose, and form. They ranged from emotionally charged slogans like "No Norwegian For Sale!"—which found their haphazard way around the country—to the KK's complicated directives. A *parole* normally contained three elements: information, commentary, and conclusion. The receivers would be told of a certain policy being prepared by the Nazi government. The commentary would explain how the new action would affect the population and would generally include propaganda to render the individual more receptive to the conclusion, as well as some threats to those who might fail to follow the directive. The conclusion would combine an appeal to resist with a formula for the actions, such as a carefully worded paragraph of refusal or protest that all members would send to the government office concerned. Initially these formulae for action were presented as recommendations, but, as the *holdningskamp* heated up and the KK gained full control of the *parole* system, the directives became orders to be followed.

An effective *parole* achieved two objectives. It brought about the desired and near unanimous response from the target group, and it invested the KK with increased authority and legitimacy by the fact that it was followed. Credibility increased with each *parole*, thereby strengthening the resistance and its leadership. The success of a *parole*, then, depended on (1) obtaining precise information about planned government moves with enough lead time to get a directive out through the network, and (2) shaping the *parole* so that it would have every possible chance of being followed.

From informants in government offices, word would reach the KK's Operating Group (OG) of some new tactic to draw an organization into the proposed corporate state. The OG would meet, often with only five or six hours to formulate and disseminate a *parole*. It would discuss the government's action, what response was needed from the people, and what the actual *parole* should be. In cases of extreme urgency three or four OG members were forced to make such decisions.

The *parole* drew its authority largely from an innate logic or sensibleness that the KK built into the *paroles*. If an individual held certain values, could he retain his self-respect and reason other than by following the directive? The individual's answer to this question, if the *parole* was properly constructed, had to be in the negative. This rationality rested on a moral undergirding carefully fashioned from a deeply rooted sociopolitical ethos. Playing on such values as patriotism, self-determination, nonviolence, and professional responsibility was a powerful technique. The fact that the initial *paroles* were successful with those occupational groupings considered to be the guardians of national morals (i.e., teachers, clergy, judges) greatly influenced the *parole's* later success as an appeal to national conscience and professional integrity.

The emphasis on moral responsibility was matched by a call for group solidarity. One was called upon to act—to commit oneself—but one's colleagues, receiving precisely the same *parole*, would do likewise. The individual was not isolated. He could identify with his fellows and with a national moral leadership. This identification was extremely important during the early occupation years when the traditional value system had been shaken, when "normal" behavior was vaguely defined, and when the need, in a highly ambiguous situation, to belong to a well-defined community of ideas and mores was strong indeed.

Observers who recall that period say that there were no sharp distinctions of class, personality type, or sense of national loyalty differentiating Norwegians who fell victim to nazification from those who did not. Often it seems to have been largely chance. Had the KK, with its communications network and *paroles*, not existed to sharply define the right/wrong and good Norwegian/traitor dichotomies, providing means for the rank and file to identify with the proper groups and value sets, nazification might well have succeeded.

The *parole* greatly increased interpersonal communication at all levels of Norwegian society. It helped to dispel the insularity, suspicion, and fear generated by the occupation. It had a binding effect and lent a sense of common purpose and solidarity to people's lives. The *parole* made clear the coincidence of individual, group, and national interests and thus inspired the willingness of the average Norwegian to resist. The *paroles* had a certain internal momentum. Each built on the effectiveness and authority of the preceding one. A poorly conceived or distributed *parole* could therefore be disastrous. One could plot a "credibility curve" for *paroles* beginning in early 1942. Initial KK *paroles* drew a positive response from perhaps 75-80 percent of the target group, with the curve moving upward toward stability at around 90 percent or better throughout the remainder of the occupation.

The Teachers' Front

How well the communications system actually functioned can be illustrated in a brief analysis of the "teachers' front." On February 5, 1942, a directive from the Ministry of Church and Education required teachers to become members of the national teachers' union. Membership implied willingness to teach Nazi ideological principles of the "New Order." In the first major test of its system the KK, acting in the name of the nation's teachers, dispatched a *parole* to the 14,000 teachers urging them to protest the requirement by mailing in a standard letter of resignation on a certain day. Twelve thousand letters arrived at the ministry, most of them on the same day. In response, the minister threatened to dismiss all teachers.

There came, today, a new decree: All teachers who send in resignations from the Teachers' Union will be expelled [from their

posts] without leave, pension (there we have our "Free Norway!") . . . or other [possibilities for] positions in "Society's"
productive work. [The authorities] are impossible desperados!
. . . *that they could be Norwegians!*[7]

Only a handful of teachers gave in. To extricate itself from an
embarrassing position, the ministry declared a month's school
holiday because of a "fuel shortage."

> Fuel holiday . . . for lessons, then, we will use my house. Can the
> reason . . . be that so many teachers have sent in resignations and
> refused to be in the union? . . . Mrs. E. said today that 98 percent
> had declared themselves out of the union. Ninety-eight percent!
> Those are *real* teachers in the high school, eh? But there is no
> reason to doubt that teachers in the folk- and youth schools will
> do less. . . . Today I sent my letter to the Norwegian Teachers'
> Union in Oslo. I signed [the statement] that I could not defend
> Norway's youth through this clause . . . which is at variance
> with my conscience. . . . That the decision was dangerous, that
> is completely clear to me. This can perhaps endanger both my
> job and my life—all that is clear; but this thing must never-
> theless take its course now . . . and then shall no one say about
> me that I cried when the darkness descended. No! . . . Forward
> Norwegian lads! Forward, we will without shame defend the
> good old native land! Certainly we are without weapons; but
> we possess another [type of] sword![8]

The sense of solidarity and outrage reflected above was
characteristic of teachers all over Norway. They saw in the
membership requirement a direct threat to their professional
integrity founded on guarding the truth and the nation's
youth. Despite the subsequent arrest and internment of 1,100
teachers—500 of whom were sent to a concentration camp at
Kirkenes and greatly abused—the "teachers' front" held and
few gave in. Regular information about government plans,
explicit directives, and funds to support deprived families all
passed through the KK network to insure continued resistance.

On April 25, the ministry declared that its directives had been
"misunderstood." The teachers' union was to be apolitical and
membership implied no obligation to work with the Nazi

youth federation (which, of course, it had). The ministry's plan
to draw the teachers into the proposed *riksting* had failed
miserably. Other groups were subsequently attacked but the
example of moral resolve set by the teachers was replicated
many times.

The death blow to the *riksting* concept—the cornerstone of
nazification—came when KK learned in July 1942 of a secret
memorandum from NS Ombudsman Whist that had suggested
a new divide-and-conquer tactic to be used.

> Such large actions, which could imply a certain risk of new con-
> flicts, are not wanted at present. In order that we—in spite of
> difficulties—will continue to move forward, and in the shortest
> possible time, to achieve the organizational framework for
> commerce that both it and the society now need, it will be
> necessary . . . to organize a group of organizations *singly*, when
> the necessary preparations are made and the operation can be
> done without risk of major disturbances. (The Ombudsman
> proposes . . . that they begin with business and the banks,
> "where the risks of difficulties are minimal.") (Malm, 1945:10)

The KK devised its strategy accordingly; and when it was
learned that the NS planned to establish the *riksting* with a
national meeting in September, it torpedoed the scheme by organizing protest among the commercial associations. A *parole*
went out urging members to withdraw from their organizations. A law was passed making membership compulsory; a
second *parole* followed that resulted in near-total withdrawal
from commercial organizations and trades unions.

The failure of the Quisling government marked the end of
the effort to nazify through the associations, although the
propaganda war continued. By the autumn of 1942, the *holdningskamp* had brought the communications network to a
point where it ceased to focus on specific segments of the population and became a more general leadership/communication
structure for total resistance, used in later campaigns like the
"labor service" action.

The Coordination Committee

As both the source of the *parole* and the hub of the distribution system, the KK was the nerve center of the operation (see Figure 9). The committee averaged thirty members with representation reflecting the significant groupings of voluntary associations in Norway, thus providing the KK with a broad capacity for authoritative communication with the population. Each representative had knowledge of and contacts in a limited sector of the population. To keep the formal structure simple and secure while casting the contacts net as wide as possible, organizations not represented in KK were kept in touch through KK members rather than integrated into the committee itself.

The KK was strengthened, too, through its overlapping membership and communication with other leadership groups (Kretsen, Milorg, Landsorganisasjon), which together with KK comprised the Home Front. Kretsen included several men of great stature such as Paal Berg, chief justice of the supreme court, who gave credibility and legitimacy to the Operating Group and other middle-level personnel in KK.

A striking characteristic of KK's internal structure was its utter simplicity. There was no hierarchy of positions, in fact no leadership except the coordinator's direction. The absence of political structure undoubtedly was related to the non-political backgrounds of most members. Each represented a professional grouping or constituency that had theoretically equal importance for the resistance movement. Decisions were made through a consensual process similar to the one used in Quaker business meetings.

> Divisions were never permitted to stand—a matter was discussed until there was agreement. One person, naturally enough, would have greater influence than another, both because of personal qualities, wealth of information, and breadth of contacts. (Wyller, 1958:281)

The Operating Group. The advisory and executive functions of KK were separated, for a group of thirty-odd men was much too large for safe or effective execution of policy. A smaller Operating Group was responsible for the operation of *paroles* and other KK activities. Members of OG interacted with the entire committee on a one-to-one basis thereby informing and obtaining from it direction, support, and contacts in the rest

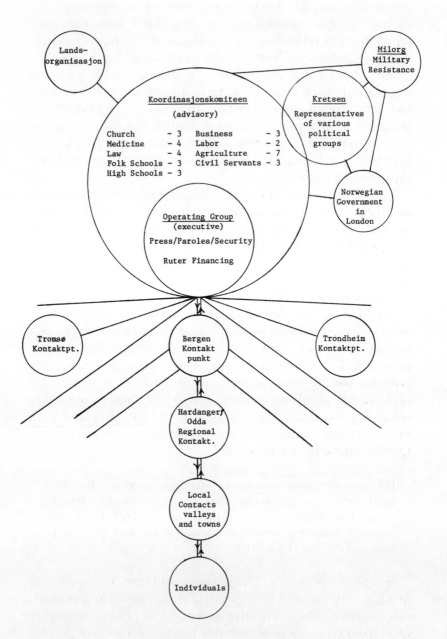

Figure 9. The KK network.

of Norway. OG members—usually not more than twelve in number—had regular contact with one another. One meeting locale was in the back room of an Oslo tobacco shop. Messages could be left there in person or by telephone. Matches placed in the front window signalled that it was dangerous to enter.

When vital new information reached the OG, as many members as could be reached would gather to construct a *parole* to counter the planned government move. For three years, the OG was the most powerful group of individuals in Norway, their anonymity notwithstanding. It is noteworthy that none of them moved into the government after the war—all returned to professional life. Almost none of them were politicians, and it was perhaps because there were no individual political ambitions to hinder the OG's operation and the consensus it depended on that the KK system ran so smoothly.

KK Functions. As noted earlier, the primary function of KK was to integrate numerous communication and authority systems for the goals of the resistance movement. This integration occurred at two levels. First, the networks of individual associations were integrated within KK. Second, as the KK developed, it assimilated networks that cut across professional lines and had developed in response to particular contingencies. A case in point was the cross-professional system developed for support of persons arrested or dismissed from their posts. Fifty million crowns were borrowed in the name of the government-in-exile for this purpose. Collection and distribution called for a system of contacts and channels that were quite naturally assimilated by the KK.

What occurred, then, was a differentiation of the initial communication function and the structure of KK over time, similar in some respects to Parsons' (1961:235) differentiation process. This happened both through internal development and through assimilation of other groups' functions and nets. This process of growth through differentiation continued throughout 1943-44. By late 1944, KK was responsible not only for *paroles*, but also for support of families in need because of their resistance activity, for intelligence and security for the civil resistance, for financing, editing, and distributing illegal papers, and for maintaining *ruter* (routes by which people escaped arrest and imprisonment—both internal routes and those leading to Sweden and Britain).[9] When all of these services were operative, the KK had a permanent staff of sixty people in Oslo alone.

The KK performed three additional functions for the resistance movement. It was by far the most active and effective of the four Home Front Leadership (HFL) groups. It was the KK that gave HFL its effectiveness as a parallel government. The sense of being led by competent and authoritative men activated resistance. Paralleling KK's activating function was its controlling function. Resistance violence had to be controlled. The Norwegians, it was assumed—and probably correctly—were not prepared to withstand violent reprisals for sabotage and assassination. To sustain the will to resist, resistance had to be limited and, wherever possible, executed within existing structures, norms, and values.

As the war drew to a close, the KK was confronted with a final problem, the task of winding down the resistance and developing transitional institutions. Resistance sentiment, hatred of the occupation forces, and desire for revenge on Norwegian Nazis all ran high. Legitimate political institutions had not operated for nearly five years. The HFL wanted order not chaos, justice not revenge, and a smooth transition to political normalcy—the KK functioned effectively to ensure these goals. (An added motivation was a fear among the HFL that Britain would occupy Norway unless indigenous institutions were in place immediately upon German capitulation.) A viable transitional civil administration was created: police officers, civil servants at all levels, city and county councils, and top officials for all government departments were appointed and notified through the KK network. For months there was a "shadow administration" ready to assume direct responsibility at the moment of liberation.[10]

A related effort was made in the political sphere. A committee was formed representing four principal points on the prewar political spectrum (Right, Left, Farmers Party, Workers Party). Its role was to create a common political program for postwar Norway. Through ingenious communication, the committee consulted with the Norwegian government in London and with Norwegian political leaders in Sweden, in the Grinni concentration camp, and in camps like Sachshausen in Germany itself (Aanerud, 1963:4). A draft document was accepted by the government-in-exile that provided Norway with a reasonable degree of postwar political consensus.

Another dimension of preparing for peace concerned the depolarization of public sentiment. The illegal press was especially important here for it had a major role in shaping the polarized attitudes that had created immunity to nazification. This process now had to be reversed. Black/white perceptions once again had to be modified to include shades of grey. People had to be resensitized—reprogrammed so to speak—for reconciliation with the enemy among them. This resensitization involved a conscious effort in resistance literature to reorient readers away from the oversimplifications upon which *holdningskamp* had necessarily been based.[11] That effort may have been partially responsible for the remarkable pace at which reconciliation of the Norwegian population took place after the war.

The Example of the Norwegian Resistance

It would be invalid to generalize from the Norwegian case since this particular response to military occupation grew from unique conditions especially conducive to massive nonviolent resistance. Several conclusions can be drawn, however, that contribute to an understanding of the general nature of civilian resistance.

The Role of Communication

Viewed within a communications frame of reference, what were the most salient factors in the Norwegian experience and how did communication influence them?

1. *Psychological polarization* was essential for the development of resistance. It occurred as Norwegians were forced to think of themselves as a distinct community threatened by the occupiers and their collaborators. Polarization of attitudes and

group solidarity first developed as a consequence of being attacked—a natural response of a community that feels its existence threatened.[12] As nazification was pressed, it drew resistance, but, as Coser points out, this particular conflict dynamic occurs only under certain conditions.

> If the basic social structure is stable, if basic values are not questioned, cohesion is usually strengthened by war through challenge to, and revitalization of values and goals which have been taken for granted. (Coser, 1956:90)

Communication within the population, as developed by the KK, clarified those values, used that structure, and defined the moral boundaries of the national community sufficiently for the threat to be visible to all. The necessary in-group/out-group dichotomy might otherwise have been too blurred to support active resistance. Clandestine communication acted as a binding, community-defining force that set the boundaries of the national community, with its exclusive set of symbols, values, and communications media.

2. The *role of the subnational group* was vital in mobilizing resistance. The development of a sense of threat and the identification of the individual with community occurred at two levels, national and group. The voluntary associations were especially influential. They provided an identification link between individual and nation, and they personalized the issues for people, helping to integrate occupational and national roles for them, and thereby facilitating collective action. A precondition for collective action in a potential conflict situation is the emergence of self-defined subgroups around which conflict is generated, as was the case in the 1964 Berkeley Free Speech Movement (Heirich, 1971). In Norway, the voluntary associations, by providing subgroup identity for individuals, were essential for generating resistance. A fatal error of the NS was its attempt to use these organizations for alien purposes, for in the process it helped activate them as resistance communities.

The use of existing structures for resistance purposes was especially valuable in the Norwegian setting where political institutions had been suspended and the government-in-exile was resented by many for having ill-prepared the nation for war. Whatever national image citizens normally identify with and fight for was initially weak indeed. It was strengthened immeasurably through citizen participation in institutions like the associations that continued to exist. The communication function of the subgroups was most important. A symbiotic relationship grew up between resistance communication and the voluntary associations. The associations offered resistance leaders a structure for communicating with the population and facilitated collective action; their use as a communications infrastructure revitalized them as national institutions.

3. The concept of *legitimacy of leadership* looms large in the Norwegian case. To whom individuals should accord obeisance and the right to lead when normal political life was suspended was a difficult question. There was not merely a leadership vacuum. To activate and control resistance, new and unknown "pretenders" had to establish their legitimacy with the people. This they did largely through a remarkable system of clandestine face-to-face communication. NS leaders were not accorded this legitimacy, partly because they were not chosen democratically, but mainly because they lacked control of the nation's basic social communication systems. As Deutsch observes:

> Without effective control of the bulk of the actual face-to-face communication networks . . . the nominal holders of the legitimacy symbols may become relatively helpless vis-à-vis those groups that do have this control. . . . Perhaps we may suspect, accordingly, that it is rather in the more or less far-reaching *coincidence* between legitimacy beliefs and social communication channels that political power can be found. (Deutsch, 1963:153)

Resistance leadership also established its legitimacy by clearly distinguishing legality from legitimacy and identifying NS leaders with the former and themselves with the latter. Resistance came to be rooted in what people considered just and legitimate according to a set of "higher laws." The KK defined these laws for the larger population, then gained a following by giving people the opportunity to make them operative.

4. The *reinforcement of indigenous values and norms* in a situation where anomie threatened was striking. Defining the legitimacy of behavior types under new and stressful conditions was as important for the resistance as establishing leadership legitimacy. Values reinforcement through *paroles* was extremely successful in Norway because the values in question were strongly held and operative.

> The *paroles* were a most original weapon in a political power struggle. They could . . . only have been used successfully in a society marked by the most basic agreement on certain fundamental values and in a conflict where precisely these values were under attack. (Wyller, 1958:291)

Norway was the most democratic of societies. Democracy, justice, self-determination, and other antitotalitarian values were not merely ideals for Norwegians, they were universally held operating guides to sociopolitical behavior. Once the KK network permitted individuals to act collectively in response to a threat to these, values and the norms rooted in them were revitalized. Resistance communication, by galvanizing the values and the sense of threat, made certain that nazism, representing an opposing normative set, had no chance. The importance of norm and value reinforcement under foreign occupation cannot be overstated. Heroes in a resistance movement are much more rare than popular literature would lead us to believe. Norway was no exception. Most people will follow a normative tone set within the occupation context. Whether that tone is resistance-oriented and strongly nationalistic or the opposite determines with whom the masses cast their lot.

The primacy of communication in the building of a civilian resistance movement is attested to by the Norwegian experience. One could say communication in Norway was the genesis of resistance, with other aspects of the movement developing from it in a modified process of structural/functional differentiation. Leadership was created and legitimized through communication. KK personnel at all levels were drawn into positions primarily because of their personal contacts—in other words, their capacity to communicate. Their legitimacy and control of the situation were likewise assured by this capacity. That communication was the key to legitimacy is evidenced by the fact that leaders remained anonymous, having access thereby to none of the other devices for obtaining and retaining power. Resistance occurred through and because of communication. Organized resistance can develop only where a population is informed, instructed, and views itself as a community. The KK network and supporting services, by performing these functions, made possible the various collective acts of resistance. Without it resistance would have been sporadic and disorganized.

The very personal and incidental way in which much of the KK's communications system developed suggests that it would be impossible for an invader state to anticipate and counter such activity. Three of the organizers of the KK, for example, came together quite incidentally when one was vaccinating the school class of another who was an acquaintance of the third. The importance of such situational factors in communications development would increase the deterrence value of a civilian defense policy. An occupier might rather quickly gain control of the more technical aspects of intranational communication, like the mass media, but would be quite powerless to prevent a clandestine face-to-face network from forming. The adoption of civilian defense as a viable national policy depends heavily on how refined and invulnerable a clandestine communication system strategists can devise. Creators of such a system could draw profitably from the success of the Norwegian resistance but would do well to grant sufficient allowance in their planning for the operation of the situational, innovative, and personal factors that figured prominently in that success.

Nonmilitary Defense

The Norwegian resistance to Nazi occupation suggests both the difficulties and the possibilities of alternatives to military defense of national territory and sociopolitical institutions. My emphasis here is, once again, on the self-limiting and goal-attaining characteristics of the methods used:

1. *Minimal use of violence by the civilian population.* When violence was used upon occasion by civilian saboteurs, it was publicly condemned by Norwegians. This avoided inevitable reprisals by the German military and the subsequent spiral of violence that occurred in Denmark and other occupied areas.

2. *Focus on protecting their institutions, not liberating already occupied territory.* This located the conflict around values rather than material possessions and *within* the Norwegians themselves. It was a struggle of wills rather than arms and could, therefore, be waged without violence. It also served to reinforce those core values that nazism threatened: nonviolence, reason, justice, and autonomy.

3. *Providing control through creating unity by way of existing structures and networks.* This had two major payoffs: (1) it was the most effective way of mobilizing Norwegians for resistance, and (2) it permitted movement leadership to control extremist elements. This was undoubtedly a major reason for the absence in Norway of the excesses, internecine warfare, and anomie that characterized so many European resistance movements of that period.

Alternative Means of Conflict

The study of such historical cases is useful for what it contributes to the development of future alternatives to violent means of conflicting. Considerable research has been done recently on the subject of *transarmament*—shifting nations from armed defense, to mixed armed/unarmed strategies, and finally to nonmilitary defense. Roberts (1969, 1972) and Boserup and Mack (1975) provide transarmament feasibility studies commissioned by the Swedish and Danish governments. Although a debate continues on the practicality of and most effective approach to civilian or nonmilitary defense, it is at least a potential supplement to existing defense strategies, especially for militarily weak states, whose negligible armaments may do nothing more than provide an excuse for subversion or invasion, drain off valuable resources from economic and social development, and increase technological and economic dependence on major powers.

Case studies of nonviolent action may suggest some faulty conclusions. It is not true that nonviolent approaches to bringing about basic social change within a society are rational, conscious, and moral while violent approaches are not. Theorists and practitioners alike, including persons as dissimilar as Mao Tse-tung, Herman Kahn, and Frantz Fanon develop hyperrational, calculated strategies in which violence, for exceedingly moral motivations, is included as a necessary strategic and tactical element. Most revolutionary movements combine nonviolent and violent techniques, with the former playing the dominant role and the latter carefully controlled. Likewise, nonviolent revolutionary movements generally contain both coercive and persuasive elements in their strategies and tactics.

One cannot conclude that nonviolent movements are functional and successful and that those using violence deliberately are dysfunctional. If, however, an objective of conflict regulation research is to minimize violence and contribute to the development of peaceful change techniques and dynamics, we need to be working at helping social change movements to increase the effectiveness and predominance of nonviolent methods.

5. Self-limiting Conflict:
The Rocky Flats National Action

From time to time one comes upon an event that illustrates several of the types of conflict regulation discussed in this book. The antinuclear demonstration at the Rocky Flats nuclear weapons plant near Denver is an example. This event took place in April 1978 and was successful largely because different conflict regulation processes worked well. Empowerment, self-limiting conflict through nonviolent direct action, crisis management, and mediation all played significant parts in the successful planning, implementation, and public response to the event. The Rocky Flats National Action took place within the context of a global antinuclear movement and mounting concern about the risks of nuclear war, radiation contamination, and nuclear terrorism. Our analysis of the event must first be set within this larger context.

The Rocky Flats plant is a target of both the USSR's strategic priorities list and of environmental and peace activists in Colorado. It is the United States' only producer of plutonium trigger components for nuclear weapons. It was built in 1952, long before state and local involvement in such decisions was considered necessary. For twenty-three years the plant was managed by Dow Chemical Company under contract with, first, the Atomic Energy Commission, and then the Energy Research and Development Administration. In 1975, Rockwell International assumed management of the plant.

The plant's history has been punctuated with a series of errors in judgment, acts of negligence, and false information given to state and local officials and citizens. That series includes:

1. Original miscalculation of prevailing wind patterns at the plant site. Readings were taken at Stapleton airport where winds generally blow away from Denver rather than at the site, where winds blow toward the city.
2. Several major plutonium fires; one in 1969 was the most costly ($50 million) industrial fire in the nation's history.
3. Open-pit burial of radioactive wastes near the plant, without accurate maps recording locations of the burial sites.
4. Inadequate outdoor storage of plutonium-contaminated machine oil, which leaked from corroding containers and saturated the soil over a substantial area. Management's solution to the problem was to pave over the plutonium (with a half-life of about 24,000 years) with asphalt (with a useful life of perhaps 10 years).
5. Seepage of radioactive material from the plant into the municipal water supply of nearby Broomfield (Figure 10). Management claimed it was not even aware that such material had come into the plant.
6. Release of detectable amounts of plutonium into the air that was blown by prevailing winds toward Arvada, Westminster, and other sections of metropolitan Denver (Figure 10).

Rocky Flats illustrates well the global nature of nuclear risks. It is at the center of a global nuclear network. Raw plutonium comes to it by air and road from Washington State and South Carolina plutonium fabrication plants. It is also brought inside nuclear weapons being recycled from deployment and storage areas throughout the world. New plutonium triggers are made, old ones are reconditioned, and all are shipped out to find their way around the globe. Nuclear high- and low-level wastes leave the plant by rail for storage elsewhere.

Public Response

By 1974, local concern about plant safety and security was

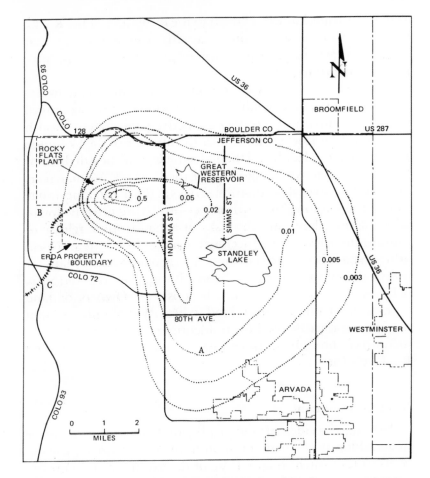

Figure 10. Rocky Flats plant, showing (A) the plutonium contamination contours, (B) the site of the Rocky Flats National Action, and (C) the sites of Rocky Flats Truth Force track occupations. (Adapted from USERDA, 1977:2-93)

mounting. Governor Lamm and Congressman Wirth, whose district includes Rocky Flats, formed the Lamm-Wirth Task Force on Rocky Flats. This panel of specialists and public officials worked for a year, held public hearings, and produced a report (LWTFRF, 1975) assessing the hazards of the plant for its environs. It issued a set of recommendations that included the suggestion that the federal government relocate plutonium operations out of the area. The report established that there were significant hazards and led to the formation of the Rocky Flats Monitoring Committee, a citizen/expert panel that meets regularly to press for implementation of the task force recommendations.

Other public and private responses due to increased awareness of plant risks are notable. The task force report encouraged state and county health officials to actively research the health risks posed by Rocky Flats. Both the director of the Colorado Department of Health and the Jefferson County health director have become active antagonists of the Rocky Flats managers around the issues of occupational risks at the plant, long-range cancer risks among the million persons living directly downwind of the plant, and the risks of a catastrophic release of plutonium from a critical accident or major fire. State and local officials have been forced to draft emergency response plans for use in the event of such a release, although no one seriously believes an evacuation would be possible. Owners of land beyond the plant perimeter, land so heavily contaminated that it can no longer be used for residential or industrial development, have brought suits against the federal government and Rockwell International for $7 million.

Nuclear Terrorism

Although accidental and negligent release of radioactive material has been fairly common in the past, there is growing concern that intentional release or diversion may be a greater threat in the future as nuclear terrorism becomes more likely.

Recent research into the phenomenon of terrorism (Hyams, 1975; Hamilton, 1978) notes an alarming global increase not only in the incidence of terrorism but in the sophistication with which it is carried out. Furthermore, research (Carlton and Schaerf, 1975) indicates the emergence of international links between political groups employing terrorism to the point where one can now speak of an international terrorist network. Through such channels pass both persons and material to be used in terrorist acts.

Some students of terrorism (Jenkins, 1977) are convinced that terrorists will increasingly direct their activity toward nuclear installations and materials as they increase in number, size, and volume. Because of their unusually destructive capacities, such facilities would also have greater threat and blackmail value, a primary consideration for terrorists. The risk of terrorism poses a special problem for an installation like Rocky Flats that uses and stores substantial quantities of plutonium. As a transportation hub for such high-grade nuclear material, Rocky Flats could well be a "terrorist act waiting to happen." This may be increasingly the case as international terrorism is exported to the United States in the near future—as some experts feel is inevitable.

The Nature of Terrorism

Simply defined, terrorism is the calculated use of terror and anxiety or threat of same to achieve an objective. It can be implemented by various means: kidnapping and hostage taking, infiltration, theft of explosive or toxic materials, blackmail, threatened or actual destruction of persons and property. Terrorism can be categorized according to the nature and motivation of the perpetrator. *Insurgent* terrorism is most common and normally involves a rebellious group acting against the state, often to gain attention for its cause. *Idiosyncratic* terrorism occurs when a psychologically disturbed individual commits an open act of violence against society at large out of derangement or hope for personal attention. *Criminal* terrorists are motivated by expected economic gain, and are generally in pursuit of a scarce and valuable commodity like plutonium, or are terrorists for hire.

State terrorism involves the application of terror by a state to a population or to another state. This may include the use or threat of using weapons of mass destruction. The primary purpose of the nuclear destruction of Hiroshima and Nagasaki was to terrorize the population of Japan and thus bring the war to a swift conclusion. That destruction proved both the feasibility of nuclear war and its threat potential. The current system of nuclear deterrence rests squarely on the terror the nuclear threat generates and the credibility of that threat. The level of terror increases with each advance in nuclear weapons technology. The enhanced radiation weapon, for example, appears more terrible to populations because of its unique killing properties.

Rocky Flats is vulnerable, as are all nuclear weapons and energy facilities around the world, to all four types of terrorism—insurgent, idiosyncratic, criminal, and state terrorism. The plant is to some degree open to the first three types in spite of its elaborate security systems. It is vulnerable to state terrorism as well because it is high on the target priorities list of the USSR (and for this reason the metropolitan population surrounding it is a hostage) and because it is a key to the United States' capability to retaliate.

The Risks

What are the possibilities for terrorism at Rocky Flats? It should be noted that threats and attacks against nuclear installations are becoming ever more common. Between May 1969 and August 1975, ten known attacks in the United States and Europe on nonmilitary nuclear facilities alone were recorded (Flood, 1976:31). Incidence of such attacks has increased since that time. In the United States in 1972, airline hijackers used an Oak Ridge reactor as a bargaining chip, circling the facility and threatening to crash the plane into it if their demands were not met. Conscious of this embryonic nuclear terrorism, we must make judgments about the risks of terrorism at Rocky Flats against the backdrop of an appalling lack of security at sensitive U.S. military installations around the world. Two examples of this security lack will suffice:

1. The discovery that nerve gas weapons inventories at Colorado and Utah depots had been deliberately falsified to conceal discrepancies. The author was personally responsible for the initiation of an investigation that uncovered this practice and has resulted in a worldwide inventory check of all such weapons (*RMN*, 1978; *BDC*, 1978).

2. The disclosure that nuclear weapons in Hawaii were being routinely transported through densely populated urban areas, accompanied by skeleton crews, and that information concerning the routes and schedules of

these shipments could be obtained from local police (Lind, 1976).

Security at Rocky Flats is undoubtedly better than at other weapons facilities, but how much better? If security against terrorism is adequate now, will it continue to be so as terrorism and the illicit plutonium market expand? Several problems are of particular importance.

1. *Diversion of fissile material by plant personnel.* Although there is apparently no known case of such theft at Rocky Flats, diversion by either criminal or political terrorists is not unthinkable. In 1977, the head of security at the Rocky Mountain Arsenal nerve gas storage depot was arrested and later convicted as the organizer of a theft ring marketing $300,000 worth of goods stolen from federal facilities (*DP*, 1977). Among the items he sold or offered to sell undercover agents were plastic explosives and nerve gas. Were a similar diversion to occur at Rocky Flats, only two kilograms of plutonium would be needed to construct an implosion-type nuclear weapon (Hayes, 1977). A theft of that magnitude could conceivably go undetected if it occurred over time, and if an insider knew how to effectively "manage" the plant's units accountability system. Ironically, each step in the accountability process—transfer and weighing, records computerization, inventory adjustment, chemical recovery—presents simultaneously an opportunity for greater system control and for system failure.

2. *Interception of plutonium transport.* In 1974 alone, there were 372 shipments within the United States involving 1,600 pounds of plutonium (Hayes, 1977). A significant part of that total was raw plutonium oxide travelling to Rocky Flats from the Hanford and Savannah River plants, and from Rocky Flats, as weapons components, to Pantex, Texas, and elsewhere for final weapons assembly. Plutonium travels, often in strategic quantities, either by road in Safe Secure Trailers or by air transport through the Stapleton, Jefferson County, and Buckley airports. Observant terrorists with carefully gathered information about the shipping procedures could intercept shipments at any point along the routes, though with the

trailer immobilization and penetration deterrence systems now being developed, many of the security weaknesses noted in the past (CGUS, 1977) may be eliminated. Despite the elaborate precautions taken with plutonium shipments, a determined and sophisticated terrorist group could intercept a substantial if not strategic quantity of it. For each safeguard system—Safe Secure Trailer, irregular routing and scheduling, armed couriers, air surveillance, postdiversion location techniques—countertechniques can be developed. True, the fabrication of a nuclear device would require more plutonium than is normally carried in one shipment, but lesser amounts could be used for nuclear blackmail.

3. *Intentional catastrophic release.* A third type of risk would involve an act of sabotage within the plant or an attack on it from the outside. Such an act could be either politically motivated or a consequence of personal psychological disturbance. At least one major fire at Rocky Flats has already succeeded in breaching its multiple filtration systems, and a determined saboteur could cause such a fire. A catastrophic release could be most easily brought about by aircraft penetration. While it may be that air space over the plant is now restricted, there is no way that a guided crash into a "hot" area of the plant could be prevented. Metropolitan Denver has one of the nation's highest aircraft-per-capita ratios and a profusion of airports and landing strips. Surface-to-surface missiles could also be fired at the plant from a distance. Knowledge of the plant layout and location of its strategic buildings is not difficult to obtain. In fact, a resourceful terrorist could, without too much difficulty, learn the locations of disguised Buildings 1 and 2 (USERDA, 1977:I-3-28), which would yield the largest penetration and fire releases of plutonium. Releases might range from 0.1 percent of the total in the case of metallic plutonium to 40 percent of the total where plutonium is contained in combustible contaminated waste such as machine oil. The crash of a large plane could release as much as 1,000 grams of plutonium into the atmosphere (USERDA, 1977:I-3-19).

The risk of terrorism and other possibilities for radioactive contamination have combined with a concern about the plant's nuclear weapons production to make Rocky Flats anathema for both environmental and peace activists.

Collective Behavior in Response to Nuclear Threat

The melding of religious, environmental, political, and peace organizations in the antinuclear movement makes it an unusually interesting case for students of collective behavior. What are the origins of this rapidly growing movement, and how does the current debate among collective behavior theorists further our understanding of it?

The antinuclear movement, represented in Colorado by the Rocky Flats campaign, emerges from earlier phases of what might loosely be called the peace and disarmament movement. The Campaign for Nuclear Disarmament of the early 1960s, most visible in Great Britain, Japan, and the United States, gave way in the mid-sixties to the campaign against U.S. involvement in Indochina. Once that threat terminated, the peace movement returned to a focus on weapons proliferation and its contribution to the persistence of war and poverty, and more recently the linkage between nuclear weapons and nuclear energy. There are exceptions to the rule (as, for example, in Japan, where groups with a socialist orientation condemn both nuclear weapons and nuclear energy while groups with communist affiliation condemn the former but support the latter), but generally the antinuclear movement treats the two issues as one.

The vitality of the movement is reflected in the growing incidence of public demonstrations and civil disobedience against nuclear facilities. The 1977 occupation of the site of a proposed nuclear generating station in Seabrook, New Hampshire, produced 1,400 arrests. Subsequent detainment and legal costs placed that state in a serious fiscal bind. In the Federal Republic of Germany in 1975, 28,000 persons occupied a nuclear reactor site at Whyl continuously for eight months. The protesters won a court order delaying construction of the plant, which has yet to be built. Equally significant actions have occurred in France, Holland, Denmark, England, and Spain. The 1977 Malville march to protest construction of

France's commercial-scale fast breeder reactor involved an estimated 60,000 participants. Antinuclear sentiment combined with a desire for Basque autonomy to produce a rally of 150,000 in Bilbao, Spain.

Antinuclear campaigns vary in the degree to which leaders and participants are committed to nonviolence. In some European countries, where radical political parties direct campaigns and security forces have greater license to use force, strictly nonviolent demonstrations are more rare. In the United States, where movement leadership is more likely to be religiously than politically motivated, nonviolence is a cardinal principle. Here, leaders and participants are often veterans of the nonviolent antiwar campaigns of the 1960s who have merely shifted their focus. The experience with nonviolent direct action is there and the issues remain largely unchanged: weapons production, sales, and proliferation; corporate exploitation of the third world; overconcentrated economic and political power; unmet human needs; and economic conversion to peaceful production.

One can analyze the antinuclear movement within the framework of the lively debate of recent years among theorists of collective behavior. This debate was sparked by Smelser's (1962) book on collective action that found challenge movements to be nonrational, discontinuous with established institutions and norms, and manipulated by cynical leaders who used "generalized beliefs" (i.e., myth) to mobilize followers. This characterization hardly seems to fit the antinuclear movement as I have observed it, and Smelser's critics offer analysis to support my observation.

Oberschall (1973) notes that Robert Merton, in his theories of social organization and change, makes a clear distinction between the deviant and the nonconformist in society. The former does not challenge the rightness of norms and laws but contravenes them for personal gain. The latter, by contrast, challenges the very legitimacy of a norm, often calling upon a "higher law" to justify the infraction. The deviant breaks the law anonymously and in secrecy, if possible, to avoid punishment. The nonconformist, quite to the contrary, breaks the law or norm openly and is prepared to accept the punishment to the end of changing the law, as in the case of civil disobedience. Smelser would treat deviance and nonconformity as variants of the same process, while Oberschall sees them as opposing phenomena.

Smelser emphasizes the nonrational elements of collective behavior, in particular emotion and generalized beliefs, which he sees as the primary motivation for mass participation. It is true that such beliefs (e.g., nuclear weapons cannot defend) are motivating forces in the antinuclear movement. Leaders of the movement, challenging the legitimacy and wisdom of certain laws and policies, can draw upon moral indignation and emotion to mobilize people to action. Generalized beliefs, however, need not be entirely or even primarily nonrational. They may contain important elements of rationality, self-interest, and facts-based perception. The major antinuclear organization, Mobilization for Survival, roots its program in the belief that unless governments' policies on nuclear weapons and energy are revised, and soon, humankind will have an abbreviated future. There is considerable empirical evidence and intuitive knowledge to support that belief.

Gamson (1975) maintains that each social movement has a strategy of conflict—a calculated, reflective, potentially self-correcting course charted by movement leaders. The emotional, the nonrational, and the manipulative no doubt play a part in this strategy, but no more so than they do in other social processes. Our analysis of the Rocky Flats campaign will illustrate how the rational and nonrational elements of collective behavior are integrated to achieve movement objectives.

The Rocky Flats National Action

Social movements depend for their energy on dramatic public events. These events illustrate the collective nature of the action, clarify movement goals and principles, and encourage potential adherents to commit themselves. For the antinuclear movement in the United States, the Rocky Flats National Action was such an event.

The Action originated in 1973 within the American Friends Service Committee (AFSC) Colorado Area executive commit-

tee. A professor of preventive medicine concerned with radiation hazards, an AFSC peace educator, and a sociologist
engaged in peace research discussed the possibility of a citizen
inquiry into Rocky Flats. The committee endorsed the idea and
the AFSC set about forming a coalition of concerned environmental, religious, and academic organizations—the Rocky
Flats Action Group (RFAG). For three years the coalition
met regularly, educated its members about Rocky Flats, organized different task groups, and held public demonstrations.
The latter were generally limited in size, with fewer than 100
persons participating.

RFAG organized a statewide conference on nuclear issues
(Wehr and Carpenter, 1976), and engaged in and published
(RFAG, 1977) the results of research on the risks posed by
Rocky Flats. RFAG members gave verbal and written testimony in public hearings on Rocky Flats, contributed a member
to the Rocky Flats Monitoring Committee, and continued a
public education program. It became a constant irritant to
the federal and corporate managers of the plant. RFAG activists were not sure precisely when Rocky Flats would command
national attention, but they were encouraged by a visible and
growing concern in metropolitan Denver.

By early 1977, nuclear weapons and power issues had gained
substantial national notice. The citizens' lobby Common Cause
adopted the Rocky Flats problem as a primary focus for that
year. By mid-year, three national organizations—the AFSC, the
Fellowship of Reconciliation (FOR), and the Mobilization for
Survival (MOBE)—had agreed to cosponsor and help organize
the Action with RFAG. Additional impetus came from three
sources: the United Nations Special Session on Disarmament
planned for May-June 1978, the national debate over development and deployment of enhanced radiation or "neutron"
weapons, and an alarming three-year increase of 25 percent in
world military expenditures to an estimated $400 billion in
1977 (Sivard, 1977). The time for the Action was right.

The Action as Drama

In addition to the collective behavioral framework, drama-
tism is a useful frame of analysis for viewing such an event.

The dramaturgical perspective has been used effectively by Goffman (1959) to analyze diverse social situations and by MacCannell (1973) to study nonviolent demonstrations. According to this frame of analysis, a nonviolent demonstration, like any other social situation, is an exercise in impression management, a crafted dramatic presentation in which all characters have expected behaviors and consent to agreed upon forms of interaction.

The presentation is rehearsed beforehand, takes place on a stage before an audience, and reaches a wider audience through the mass media. Its success depends on good advance publicity, adequate rehearsal, and all persons—organizers, speakers, musicians, marshals, civil disobedients, ordinary participants, police—playing the roles for which they were trained. Spontaneity does occur, of course, but is only a part of the event. Following the demonstration, press and broadcast accounts are watched and read as eagerly by organizers and participants as are opening night reviews. The Action, then, was nonviolence as an art form.

As Gamson (1975) observes, challenge movements have limited economic and political resources. Popular sympathy and support are potential resources that must be mobilized. The staging of dramatic events is one means to that end. Such events serve also to activate third parties (e.g., the Colorado Department of Health, congressional representatives) to intervene on behalf of the cause.

Preparing the Presentation. Six months of planning, negotiating, communicating, travelling, and rehearsing preceded the National Action. The organizing committee had to secure national and local commitments to participate. Local authorities, from police and Denver city officials to the Rocky Flats managers, had to be negotiated with for permits, space, transportation routes, and traffic control plans.

The committee negotiated with a four-person team from Rockwell International and the Department of Energy over space near the plant that could be used for the rally and parking, and how organizers and security would communicate during the event. A willingness of those in power to negotiate with challenge groups is normally an indication that the group has gained acceptance. Such negotiation, however, must be done in good faith and with mutual respect. Although the Rocky Flats team agreed verbally to space allocation, they refused a written agreement, claiming to be men of their word. As the rally was to begin, they betrayed the organizers and refused to open the area agreed upon. The State Patrol finally ordered it opened for parking to relieve a massive three-mile traffic jam. A note of irony: Rockwell, one of the nation's major radioactive polluters, constantly sent its "ecology people" around the demonstration and occupation sites to check on the condition of its "fragile pastureland." Organizers were asked to fill out "environmental impact" forms.

During the final months of preparation, movement personalities were lined up for on-stage participation, and relationships with mass media representatives were developed to insure the fullest coverage. A specialist in training for nonviolent direct action came to Colorado to rehearse the production. In Denver and Boulder, hundreds of marshals and civil disobedients had to be trained for their roles. This was vital because of the sensitive security problems that characterize any event in the vicinity of a nuclear weapons facility.

This planning, strategizing, reflecting, and reviewing by the organizing committee illustrates Gamson's point about the predominance of the rational over the nonrational in social movements. Leaders had well-defined objectives they went about achieving systematically. In addition to its rational attributes, collective behavior is, in large part, learned. Organizers had participated in similar campaigns before and had learned, for example, the importance of contingency plans and back-up systems, like generators for loudspeakers.

The Presentation. There were three public events in the Action. On the morning of April 29, over 1,000 people gathered at the Federal Building in Denver to hear Congresswoman Schroeder, Daniel Ellsberg, Stokely Carmichael, and others speak about the risk and waste of military spending and the need to transfer these resources to meet domestic human needs. The second event was the demonstration at Rocky Flats later that day. The third was a "Celebration of Life" on the following day, which included an interdenominational religious service and workshops to prepare participants to continue the campaign.

As drama, the demonstration at Rocky Flats did in one respect suggest theater of the absurd. A confrontation between 5,000 peaceful unarmed citizens ranging from babes in arms to octogenarians with the kingpin of the most awesome military machine the world has yet known does have a ring of the absurd about it. Yet there was much more high than absurd drama in the confrontation, which brought face-to-face two powerful forces: the overwhelming potential for nuclear destruction and the nonviolent truth-seeking process. It was, one might say, a modern equivalent of a medieval morality play, complete with audience participation.

The physical setting for the play enhanced the sense of drama (Figure 10). The backdrop in-the-round included the papier mâché–like Rockies looming behind the demonstrators, the nuclear weapons plant with its 100-odd buildings spread out a mile to the east, and metropolitan Denver sprawling to the north, south, and east beyond that. The juxtaposition of the villain, the heroes and heroines, and the humanity to be saved reinforced the sense of theater. Brisk winds, intermittent rain, and a turbulent sky heightened the drama as did the observation helicopters and planes that circled continuously. No doubt the feeling of being tested under fire increased the protesters' determination.

Protesters converged on Rocky Flats from every direction and by almost every conceivable means. Delegations from mountain settlements to the west protested uranium prospecting near their towns. Three hundred people marched the nine miles south from Boulder, while others jogged, biked, bused, car-pooled, and even roller-skated the distance. From the east and south, car caravans several miles long brought people from the Denver rally, while others from elsewhere in the nation and world arrived by plane, bus, and automobile. A large truck carrying mock radioactive waste barrels had followed the "plutonium path" from a South Carolina nuclear reprocessing plant to Rocky Flats.

Participants were of surprising diversity. The majority were in their twenties and thirties, but there were babies, children, oldsters, and pets. Representatives of religious organizations and political parties mingled with those from towns and cities ranging from Gold Hill, Colorado, to Tokyo. Banners, signs, and clothing reflected diverse motives: from religious pacifism ("Quaker Testimony for Peace") to political radicalism ("Only Governments Need the Bomb—Anarchy"); from opposition to nuclear weapons and energy ("AtomKraft, Nej Tak") to meeting human needs ("Stop Making Bombs: Buy Life Instead of Death"); and from the deadly serious ("We Have 30,000 Already") to the half humorous ("Hell No! We Won't Glow"). Even pets communicated with signs ("Close Rocky Flats, I Don't Want to Be a Hot Dog"). One or two counterdemonstrators reminded the crowd that the whole world was not of one mind.

As a dramatic presentation, the Action had its costumes and props: someone dressed as Death, radiation protection suits and respirators, mock radioactive waste drums, helium-filled balloons with finder-return tags climbing into a turbulent sky. From the stage within a stage came music and the spoken word. For four hours speakers and musicians presented reports from similar events around the world and the Action themes: the clear and present danger of the plant, the need to convert such facilities to alternative energy research and production, and the elimination of nuclear weapons.

Although the tone and demeanor of the Action was that of a nonthreatening, sober celebration, it was viewed quite differently by the Rocky Flats managers. For plant security officers and local police responsible for securing business as usual, the Action had created a crisis situation. Days were devoted to fashioning a security strategy. The sense of crisis had been dissipated somewhat by the candor and friendliness of the organizing committee, which had fully disclosed its plans. Security forces may also have been reassured by the Action's training program, which provided for a good measure of self-policing.

Despite the inevitable tension, Action/police cooperation facilitated effective crisis management. Both organizers and police had learned from a decade of antiwar protests: good police command-and-control; spatial separation of police and demonstrators; police out of sight where possible; noninflammatory speakers; and crowd self-policing.

The Occupation. The climax of the demonstration was the occupation of the railroad track over which nonradioactive materials enter the plant and radioactive wastes leave it. (Figure 10) Plutonium, except for trace amounts in the wastes, is transported by road. The occupation, of which security forces had advance notice, was to be symbolic since no trains were expected for days and there were no plans to support a group on the tracks beyond one night. Nevertheless, the occupation was an illegal act since the track was off limits to unauthorized personnel.

With methods refined in recent years (Coover et al., 1977), 150 persons had been trained in civil disobedience and organized into ten or more affinity groups much as in the Seabrook occupation of a year earlier. As the groups entered the restricted area, morale and sense of purpose were high. People spread along the track, singing, praying, and silently facing the crowd beyond the fence.

The Truth Force

With cold wind and rain, and with the temperature dropping steadily, by nightfall a number of the occupiers had left. More did so after an uncomfortable night of huddling together in a few tents. The planned occupation was over, the unplanned was beginning. During that first night on the tracks, searching discussion produced a group of forty committed to remaining for a longer period. Representing a number of affinity groups, they reformed themselves into a new one, the Rocky Flats Truth Force.

The decision of the Truth Force to "continue on the right track," as they put it, was not well received by the Action organizers, who were exhausted. They held that a symbolic occupation had been agreed to by all beforehand and that continued occupation would disrupt a planned meeting with visiting President Carter and antagonize local authorities. In dramaturgical terms, further occupation could torpedo the successful impression the management of the Action had achieved. Prolonged occupation had not been rehearsed; spontaneity of that sort, the organizers felt, would make it difficult for local activists when the occupation ended. Truth Force members, on the other hand, felt continued occupation to be a natural outgrowth of the Action—an act of conscience that could not be denied.

A good part of Day 2 on the tracks was spent settling this dispute. Mediators, including the author, intervened and as tempers cooled, agreement was carefully crafted around a clarification of positions, restatement of a common purpose, and organizing for press liaison, support services (e.g., food and shelter), contacts with security forces, and other important tasks. By common agreement the Truth Force became a separate entity with moral and some logistical support from the organizing committee, but very much on its own.

A tent city was quickly erected around a communal shelter of loose railroad ties and sheet plastic installed atop the rails. This was to house frequent group meetings, a library, press conferences, and other common activities. There were, in addition, a cooking tent and sleeping tents. Each day new symbols of the community would appear: an American flag, chemical toilets, a tree planted, a play area formed, a carefully lettered mailbox tacked to a fencepost. The Truth Force was well supplied from the outside with hot and cold food, warm clothing, sleeping bags, press coverage, legal counsel, medical care, letters and telegrams of support, and visits from friends. Along with solid links with the outside world, the group had an identity and reality of its own. It was very much a community.

The weather was uniformly miserable. Rainy and cold, it nonetheless kept down the plutonium-contaminated dust and sustained the sense of sacrifice and solidarity within the group, which was spared the privation of two feet of spring snow only by arrest on Day 7.

Use of drugs and alcohol was prohibited by the group, and tension release through play and humor was important. Play could create as well as relieve tension, however, in the shadow of a nuclear weapons plant. During one celebration, a group of fifty formed a human train and innocently started down the track in the wrong direction, toward the plant. Instantly, busloads of armed security police appeared in the distance and security vehicles were everywhere. This sobering experience reinforced a pervasive sense of the danger and gravity of the situation.

Truth Force members were mostly young students representing thirteen states. Two middle-aged exceptions were a local Mennonite minister and Daniel Ellsberg, the systems analyst who released the Pentagon Papers and has become a militant "radioactivist." The Truth Force chose a group of remarkably stable people—short on the personality aberrations one might expect to find in such an "antisocial" activity as a nuclear blockade. This stability helps to explain the group's effective decision making, reaching consensus and closure under both stressful conditions and the ubiquitous eye and ear of the media. Ellsberg, as a folk hero and elder statesman in the group, could have tried to manipulate and control decisions. He chose instead to assume a rather low profile in decision making and seemed to purposely reinforce the democratic and consensual potential of the group.

Truth Force communication with the outside world flowed through numerous channels: press conferences, open letters to President Carter and other officials, letters and telegrams to and from other parts of the antinuclear network, an unwelcome prayer for nuclear disarmament offered at a Presidential prayer breakfast, talks to university classes, messages to Sunday church services, telephone calls to relatives. The group's overriding concern was that its message—stop the nuclear arms race—be heard.

There was considerable continuity of life on the tracks with more institutionalized behavior. As Gamson and Oberschall maintain, there seems to be more continuity than discontinuity between collective and institutionalized behavior. The civil disobedients engaged in commonplace activities like writing letters to the editors of local newspapers, calling political representatives, and other routine processes. Track-sitting was a point on a spectrum of challenge activities that hundreds of thousands engage in each day.

The Arrests. On Day 7, a train came and the Truth Force was arrested for the first of many times. In a blinding snowstorm, the group locked arms and stood in silent meditation as police approached. Jefferson County sheriff's deputies, after a thirty-minute warning, walked the protesters and their belongings to a waiting bus. Some embraced deputies as they were led away. In the bus, an assistant district attorney apologetically informed them that their right to protest was recognized and that Rocky Flats managers, not the county, had requested their arrest. They were thanked for their peaceful demeanor and were taken, singing, to the county fairgrounds. They were photographed, fingerprinted, given citations for criminal trespassing and blocking a passageway, told to report for arraignment, and released on personal recognizance.

The arrest of a group dedicated to nonviolence and truth seeking to prevent it from "impeding normal plant operations" that produce weapons of mass destruction clarified the moral issues involved. Such civil disobedience clearly illustrates the distinction between deviance and nonconformity discussed earlier. The civil disobedients disclosed their plans to authorities well in advance, accepted arrest willingly, clarifying at each step precisely why they were disobeying the law: to change policy and the law protecting it.

Following the release, the Truth Force used a Boulder church center to relax, hold a press conference, and strategize. Reoccupation of the tracks occurred, but in smaller groups. New persons would join some current members, while those not returning to the tracks would form a truth squad and work on public education about Rocky Flats hazards. Still others would return to final exams at their universities. There followed a series of reoccupations that had involved over 250 individual arrests at this writing.

The Truth Force and its supporters also conceived numerous alternative events on the tracks at Rocky Flats: a graduation ceremony at which a score of University of Colorado graduating seniors and faculty in academic gowns participated and alternative diplomas were awarded; weekly ecumenical religious services; and various seminars and solidarity rallies.

A social movement must end each public event before it

loses its dramatic potential and the force of its message dissipates. The occupation and arrests at Rocky Flats could not continue indefinitely, but how to end them meaningfully and gracefully?

Conclusion

Terrorism and other risks posed by nuclear installations are likely to increase in the future, and the antinuclear movement will continue to develop in response to those risks. The Rocky Flats National Action, as part of that movement, succeeded in achieving its more realistic objectives. The environmental contamination and war risk issues were well dramatized. Antinuclear sentiment along the Front Range of Colorado was given a new visibility and the coalition was strengthened. The Action is no doubt a benchmark on the path of the developing antinuclear movement.

The impact of the Truth Force occupation is more difficult to assess, in part because it has not yet ended. Once it was clear that the Truth Force was taking civil disobedience seriously, it generated the support of many people. It may also have alienated many, but on the whole, the Truth Force punctuated the National Action and probably strengthened the larger movement.

As examples of collective behavior, the Rocky Flats National Action and the civil disobedience it spawned support the theory that collective action is primarily rational and purposeful social behavior in pursuit of well-defined values and interests. It was carefully planned and well executed. Nonrational elements were important but no more so than in routinized behavior.

As nonviolent direct action, the Action was exemplary. It demonstrated that a large public expression of concern and dissent could occur without violence, with good planning and participant training and with security forces who are disciplined and informed of demonstration plans. The success of the Action was in sharp contrast to many recent European antinuclear demonstrations where large crowds of untrained protesters, edgy officials, and brutal police responses have combined to produce chaos.

Action organizers learned anew that the movement must and can make peace within itself. Internal peacemaking skills were continually being discovered and sharpened. Conflict avoidance is one of these skills; the emergence of the Truth Force illustrated the importance of precluding conflict by providing for the spontaneous and unexpected. A nonviolent dramatic presentation may well move some participants to initiate new forms of protest. Here is where dramatic nonviolence departs from theater: the curtain in the former may not drop on cue.

Finally, the Action suggests the increasing refinement and cumulative learning of the methodology of nonviolent protest as a means of purposive social change. With ever-increasing concentrations of political, economic, and military power in governments around the globe, that methodology will continue to grow in sophistication and significance as a tool for the less powerful.

6. Regulating Environmental Conflict

Environmental Conflict

We can view environmental conflict as one consequence of the interaction of several populations that survive and often prosper by using resources of one kind or another and in turn provide resources for each other's survival. As used here, the term *population* refers to a category of living things: humans, lower animals, plants, microorganisms, and the like. When the allocation of resources for those populations is mal-distributed, conflict within and between them results.

Environmental conflict has increased measurably in recent years with a more acute awareness of resource finiteness and scarcity and of the polluting of the natural system by what we might call the sociotechnological system. Environmental conflict is not dissimilar to other types of conflict. It involves multiple parties with multiple needs and objectives, conflicting usually over multiple issues. Diverse approaches for resolving conflicts are necessary. Currently, litigation is the common method of resolving it, but legal or judicial settlement is increasingly ineffective and costly for resolving value-based conflict. Normally, litigation takes the decision out of the hands of the communities who must live with its consequences. Other methods of conflict management are now evolving that may be more effective—methods that involve communities in environmental decision making rather than excluding them.

Who will get what of the scarce resources? How much ought we to permit deterioration of the natural environment in the allocation process? These two questions are the foci of most environmental disputes. The first question concerns *interest conflicts* between parties motivated by economic and other interests. Whether the oil shale industry or agriculture will get the larger share of Colorado River water in Colorado is primarily an interest conflict. Rarely, however, are environmental disputes purely interest-generated. To rephrase the second question, how much ought we to pollute or permanently alter our natural environment? This issue concerns ideological or *value conflict*, which mingles with interest conflict to greatly complicate environmental peacemaking.

A third influence on environmental decision making involves *differences in intellectual assessment or judgment* about what is the best policy to follow with any particular problem. Here the question is: What is the wisest and most efficient policy choice? Judgment-based conflict normally involves political and administrative decision makers, but increasingly citizens' organizations are drawn into the policy selection process. Finally, because humans are self-conscious beings, emotion and verbal communication enter the scene; and so we must deal with *tension* arising over environmental issues among individuals and organizations. To better manage conflict we must understand and reduce these diverse forms of strain in environmental policymaking.

The Sociotechnical Imperative

Humankind has greatly altered its natural environment. The deforestation and cultivation of the European and North American continents and the elimination of the Great Plains bison have had immeasurable environmental impacts. The coal-fired industrial revolution must have had an air-quality impact similar to that of automobile emissions now. The magnitude of current world population growth and the increasing sophistication and widespread use of machine technology moves us to an ever higher level of impact.

The interaction of social and natural systems in the past seemed more in balance than that of today, particularly in the vast rural areas. As a boy on a Vermont mountain farm in the 1940s, I was made constantly aware that nature was the dominant actor. Labor, learning, leisure, and physical survival seemed subordinate to weather, the seasons, disease, wildlife, and the unyielding quality of the land. My family did constant battle with the local fauna over the fruits of our labor in the garden. We often lost. My father—the gentlest of men—finally declared war when the abundant porcupine population succeeded in devouring parts of first the porch and then the woodshed of our farmhouse. The severe winter temperatures, upon occasion reaching -40⁰ F, nearly killed my brother one afternoon on the two-mile hike from school.

Nor was the region's past reassuring. Colonial Roxbury had been a way station on the northward migration route of early settlers from Massachusetts. A mile from the farm were to be found the remains of a once flourishing community nearly wiped out in the last years of the eighteenth century by a smallpox epidemic. The old cemetery, its headstones bearing dates as early as 1780, and the overgrown foundation holes of a tavern and several dozen farms gave testimony to the predominance of natural over social forces. The few survivors of the original Roxbury had retreated to the valley below. In succeeding generations the town they established was part of a continuing if modest sociotechnical impact on the area's natural environment. A railroad came through the valley, a quarry produced fine marble, and local pulpwood cutters harvested area forests. As my family left Vermont for Connecticut, a rope tow and ski jump in nearby Northfield hardly anticipated the winter sports explosion to hit the area little more than a decade later.

When I revisited the Vermont homestead several years ago, I was struck by the changes that had occurred. Seven miles away, on the western side of Warren Mountain, was Sugarbush, one of Vermont's largest ski resorts. Interstate highways 89 and 91 now give rapid access to the area from Boston, New York, and Philadelphia. By no means has all of the change been detrimental to the natural and social environments. A formerly depressed economy is now much less so. Vermont legislators have produced some of the nation's most progressive environmental protection legislation. The natural-over-social imbalance of my childhood seems, nevertheless, to have been reversed.

The reversing process began while we still lived in Roxbury.

A series of technological jumps made it possible. Vehicular mobility was one. My father bought the first jeep in the state in all seasons overnight. Technological diffusion at that time I felt as its four-wheel drive quadrupled the family's mobility overnight in all seasons. Technological diffusion at that time occurred no more rapidly in rural Vermont than did other cultural innovations, but when I returned two decades later, four-wheelers were everywhere and so were people. The inaccessible had become accessible.

I recall my experiences here not out of nostalgic indulgence, for the dominance of natural forces in that time hardly reflected a healthy balance. Nor, I might add, is the present imbalance of the sociotechnical over the natural a healthy one. I reflect on that past because the impact of sociotechnical developments on the largely rural locus of our subject here—Colorado's Western Slope—is similar in so many ways to that in Vermont. The impacting events—the inflow of investment capital from beyond the region, the revolution in winter sports technology, the interstate highway system, vacation home affluence and leisure, the off-road vehicle, the flight of nearby urban populations—all are common to both regions. Technological jumps continue to quicken the rate of impact. In 1978, the introduction of a new DeHavilland STOL aircraft has more than doubled the carrying capacity of one of the two airlines feeding Colorado's ski resorts.

What should be sought is a dynamic equilibrium of the social and ecosystems. The term *equilibrium* implies a functional balance. The concept *dynamic* implies change, not necessarily physical growth, but continuous movement in balance. Where growth occurs, it should be balanced and controlled rather than what Mesarovic and Pestel (1974) refer to as "undifferentiated" growth. Change implies conflict; we must learn to manage this conflict in striking a balance between resource consumption and conservation, between human and nonhuman populations, between economic growth and protection of natural and social environments.

An Arena for Environmental Conflict

No state offers greater potential for environmental and

resource-related conflict than does Colorado. In the macro view, it is experiencing a monumental interpenetration of the social and natural systems, with water, wild and scenic areas, and fossil fuels and other natural resources at the center. The micromanifestations of this interpenetration—the specific disputes involving identifiable parties—are the subject of our research. Colorado's environmental conflict is prototypic. If it can be regulated successfully there, the rest of the nation will benefit from its experience. The state's natural wealth has made it a focal point for environmental tension in a time of expanding national demands and contracting resources.

Water. Along the peaks of Colorado's Continental Divide, fifty-three of which exceed 14,000 feet, accumulates an annual snowpack that melts in the spring and flows eastward and westward in the headwaters of many of the continent's great rivers: the Colorado, the Rio Grande, the Arkansas, the Platte, and the San Juan. The water flowing in these rivers is both an interstate and an international resource. What policies Coloradans follow in this immense watershed to impound that water, to use more of it than they previously have, and to pollute it will directly affect millions of people in the upper and lower basins of these rivers. Elaborate plans now being implemented in Colorado may over the next decades sharply increase the salinity and decrease the usefulness of the Colorado River water that reaches Mexico. Conflict over water in Colorado thus has both regional and international implications.

Within Colorado, water conflict reflects regionalism as well. Western Slope communities (those to the west of the Continental Divide) resent and resist the transmountain diversion of Western Slope water to feed the rapidly growing urban strip along the Front Range or Eastern Slope. Normally the split has West confronting East, but occasionally Western Slope parties will cooperate with one Front Range municipal water board against another if it furthers their interest in minimizing the eastern flow of "their" water.

It is difficult for non-Westerners to comprehend the economic, judicial, social, and political centrality of water in Colorado and neighboring states. In more humid regions, "water rights" are unknown. In Colorado, water may well be thicker than blood: it is a key resource that interconnects with every other environmental issue in the state. Its allocation, treatment, and use is governed by the state's most complex body of law. It is more valuable than land or precious metals and for over a century has fueled interfamilial feuds and inter-organizational struggles. Colorado sits at the source of much of the West's lifeblood, which supplies the nation's and increasingly the world's grain- and meat-producing area. It supplies a new energy-producing region as well.

Finally, Colorado water sustains the urban growth in the central Rocky Mountain region. Real estate may well be Colorado's largest industry, though it is difficult to measure because land and water speculation are highly secretive. The key principle of real estate marketing is to buy big and sell small, in other words, to subdivide. Permission to do so in Colorado requires proof by the developer of sufficient water supply for all units projected. Water for domestic use, then, including lawns, swimming pools, and other inappropriate habits that immigrants bring here from more humid regions, is once again the key to real estate speculation and commercialization.

Land Resources. Leisure and sport are social activities that require a set of resources: open space that is topographically stimulating and aesthetically pleasing, that has wildlife, an attractive climate, and some suggestion of adventure. Colorado's Western Slope provides all of these. Winter sports growth has been exponential there in the past decade. Summer recreation use increases, too, as winter sports complexes are modified to become less seasonal. The Western Slope now has over thirty ski areas, and the U.S. Forest Service has identified ninety more sites developable for skiing in Colorado.

It is for living space that human and other warm-blooded populations compete most sharply. Colorado is a major stock-raising state; it also has a most diverse wildlife population that includes elk, bighorn sheep, mountain goats, pronghorn antelope, cougar, deer, eagles, and a variety of game fish. Nearly 50 percent of the land area in the state is federally owned and managed. This further opens the state for leisure use and for energy development.

Energy Resources. The OPEC oil embargo, and subsequent petroleum price jumps, and dwindling national reserves have made Colorado much more attractive to energy industries. Coal previously uneconomic for power generation can be profitably mined and oil shale production costs come within reason, though the latter are not yet commercially competitive. With world petroleum reserves now estimated at thirty-five years at present consumption rates, coal and synthetic fuel technologies like coal gasification and oil shale refining look even more attractive. Exxon (1975) estimates that the current Western states coal production of 80 million tons will rise to 580 million tons by 1990.

Not the least of Colorado's energy resources is its potential for energy conversion—for example, at sites for mine-mouth generating stations like those at Hayden and Craig in the Yampa Valley. Coal liquefaction and gasification sites are being considered and further hydroelectric stations are planned. The requisites for such plants are: (1) sufficient fossil fuel nearby, (2) adequate water for the generating or conversion process, (3) a reasonably sparse population in the area to minimize public environmental concern, and (4) transportation for the fuel or power. The current and proposed energy development in the Yampa Valley exemplifies the convergence of all these requisites. The coal is there, 751 million tons of it (BLM, 1976: Table RIV-2). So is the water: the Yampa River contains the largest portion of unappropriated water in Colorado. Moffat County has 1.4 people per square mile and Routt County 2.8 (BLM, 1976: Table RIV-35): this meets the sparse population requirement. As for transportation, a railroad reaches Craig from the east and transmission line sites are numerous.

Availability of water will be the most serious constraint on energy generation and conversion in Colorado. Reliable estimates put the water requirement of a single 1,000 megawatt (MW) coal-fired plant at 12,000-15,000 acre-feet/year (AF/Y) (NGPRP, 1975:71). Including water for coal washing, water loss through evaporation from reservoirs supplying the plant, and irrigation water for revegetation of mined lands, each 1,000 MWs produced might require 20,000 AF/Y. For coal development alone, the Northern Great Plains Resource Program estimates a water consumption of 849,700 AF/Y by the year 2000.

In energy, water, and recreation development, federal control of large areas in Colorado complicates environmental policy-making. Mining rights for coal, oil shale, and oil and gas can be leased, timber can be sold and forest land leased for ski development, all with little participation from state and local authorities. An additional set of environmental disputes created by a sizable federal presence in the state centers around government installations producing toxic military materials. Two of these are situated in the Denver metropolitan area. The Rocky Flats nuclear weapons plant (LWTFRF, 1975; Wehr and Carpenter, 1976) is at the center of a nuclear contamination controversy, and the Rocky Mountain Arsenal is a source of nerve gas contamination.

Policy decisions on how much water, leisure space, and energy resources will be used for what purposes (if they shall be used at all) call for a clarification of the tradeoffs involved. One starts with water, the key resource, upon which the development of the others depends. Water is a finite resource in any given year. By mid-August the well is dry, so to speak. Schneider and Meserow (1976) feel that Colorado River headwaters may be more scarce in the future than recent experience suggests since regional precipitation varies cyclically and we are heading for a downswing. Water allocated for industrial use and bought for oil shale refining will not be available for other energy technologies, for wildlife preservation, or for recreational development. The more water used for meat-producing rangeland in Western Colorado, the less there will be for crop irrigation in Utah and swimming pools in southern California. Clean air in the Yampa Valley may be traded for more ski days in the Eagle Valley or for clean air in the valley of the Roaring Fork. Both valleys will draw power from Yampa Valley power stations, and Aspen's proposed electrified light rail transit system will decrease auto use there but increase plant emissions along the Yampa.

The risk is that multiple use or overuse may destroy the resources in question—Hardin's (1972) "tragedy of the commons" played out on the Colorado stage. The questions for state and local policymakers come into focus: What is the wise balance between resource exploitation and resource conservation? How does one measure noneconomic values like wildlife and quality of life? Which sets of tradeoffs make the best sense for the health and future of our communities and their ecosystems?

The Magnitude of Impacting Change

That conflict-producing change is occurring in Western Slope communities is suggested by some rather startling data. Eagle County's 1960 population totaled 4,677. The Vail ski complex opened in 1964 and during its first season, the county's only ski resort served 146,000 skiers. A decade later, Vail was serving 815,000 skiers annually, and Eagle County's permanent population had increased to 7,498 (Donald and Patterson, 1975). When the Beaver Creek complex is finished in five years, the annual recreational influx will increase by another million skiers (USFS, 1976), and the total county population projected is 21,050. Although the impacting population is largely seasonal, the physical and social infrastructures developed for it are not. Pitkin, Summit, Routt, and other ski counties are experiencing development impacts of similar magnitude. We might note that the doubling of a largely rural population of 4,000 may well have proportionately greater consequences than would the doubling of an urban population of 100,000.

In the energy production sector, development has been equally spectacular. In nineteen Colorado energy towns (Fitch et al., 1975b: Table 2) the aggregate population had increased 28 percent during 1970-74 and was expected to continue to grow by 85 percent by 1977. Yampa Valley communities were among those showing most rapid growth. Hayden's 1970-77 projected increase was 4.0 and Craig's was 2.3. A fourfold demographic explosion like Hayden's is not uncommon in this energy boom region. The number and range of proposed

TABLE 1
Proposed Energy Projects in Colorado

1) Coal Mines (underground and strip)	35 (total production ca. 51 million tons/year by 1980)
2) Oil Shale (mine/retort complexes)	7 (total production ca. 355,000 bls/day)
3) Coal Gasification	1
4) Coal Liquefaction (slurry pipe lines)	2 (water requirements from 8-15,000 AF/Y)
5) Electricity Generating Plants	
a. Coal-fired	16 (6280 megawatts)
b. Nuclear-powered	1 (1100 megawatts)
c. Hydro-electric	4 (297 megawatts)
	(7677 megawatts) Total

Source: Fitch et al, August 1975.

energy projects in Colorado is impressive. The current and proposed projects are listed in Table 1 (data from Fitch et al., 1975a). Oil, gas, and uranium prospecting and production are also substantial in Colorado.

Impacting Populations. We may categorize people moving into the energy, water, and recreation resource areas as *transient, quasi-transient,* and *permanent.* The transient population includes the recreation seekers and their pets[1] from eastern Colorado and from other states. In 1974-75, the four major ski counties registered 3,706,000 skier visits (Donald & Patterson, 1975:94); that figure was up considerably in 1975-76. Summer visitors to federal parks, lands, and monuments in Colorado are numerous as well.

Quasi-transients include (1) the *construction labor* that must be imported to build projects like water diversion systems, ski resorts, or generating plants, and (2) the *service labor* needed for maintenance of energy and water projects and operation of recreational complexes. Though some of these people are drawn from the local labor pools, the communities cannot supply either the skills or the sheer numbers needed for these massive projects. Members of this population may remain for the duration of the project, move between service and construction jobs, or, in a few cases, settle permanently in the community. Rapid turnover affects both the construction and service labor groups, but though individuals may come and go, the impact of the quasi-transient population is a continuing one.

The permanent impacting population includes part-time residents like vacation-home owners or persons coming into the area to fill permanent positions with development industries or governmental organizations like the Bureau of Land Management whose expansion is generated by development. An increasing number of retirees also swells this population.

Impacted Populations. The impacted areas have native human and nonhuman populations whose existence is substantially altered by development. *Long-time residents* of Western Slope communities have been visibly affected. The commercial people, the elderly, the youth, and the agricultural people are all affected economically in different ways, both positive and negative.

Domestic livestock and food/forage crops are populations that often bear the brunt of development, generally decreasing in importance in both economic and ecological terms. In Eagle County, for example, in the 1970-73 period, while annual private nonfarm earnings were rising from $16,431,000 to $26,706,000, annual farm earnings dropped from $2,201,000 to $452,000 (Donald and Patterson, 1975:14). This drop in farm income reflects both a movement of farm labor into the recreation/construction sectors and the sale of agricultural land and water rights to developers. The human and nonhuman agricultural populations were, in either case, severely depleted.

Wild fauna and flora are affected as well. Winter and summer feeding grounds and migration routes of elk, deer, and antelope are invaded, and water habitats for fish and animals are altered by diversion, sewage, and salinity. A diversion project can, by state law, dry up a watercourse if unallocated water is needed for development. The "beneficial use" concept in Colorado water law nowhere considers minimum stream flow as a priority. Storage dams inundate areas inhabited by wildlife and timber. Air, water, land surface, and social and economic structures are all measurably altered by the entrance of sizable transient, quasi-transient, and permanent populations.

A regional analysis of air and water impacts like that done by Lord et al. (1975) for the upper Missouri basin, would show how development now taking place in the valleys of the upper Colorado basin will also affect and bring into conflict populations far from the development site. The increase in downstream salinity and the decrease in quantity of Colorado River water resulting from impoundment and appropriation within Colorado illustrates the region-wide impact of localized development.

Interestingly, impacting populations sometimes become the impacted. Many attracted to the Eagle Valley by the Vail development retreated down the valley as Vail grew and now resist further developments like the Beaver Creek and Adam's Rib projects. Some of these people have become environmental activists, exemplifying the "last pioneer" syndrome so common among migrants to the West.

There are concentrations of *ethnic minorities* in some of Colorado's high-development areas. In the Four Corners region, Indian reservations contain large fossil fuel and uranium reserves now being tapped. In the San Luis and Upper Eagle valleys, Mexican-American communities experience severe cultural stress as a consequence of development projects (FUND, 1975). The way-of-life changes are much greater for most ethnics, whose more traditional family structures and work and leisure patterns are more vulnerable to the impact of development than those of nonethnic peoples.

Response to Impact

The ability of Western Slope communities to cope with the impact of development and the conflict it generates varies from community to community and is determined by several factors. The size and makeup of the resident population seem to be important. More densely populated valleys tend to have more public participation in growth decisions. A larger proportion of nonnatives seems to produce more controversy and discussion of growth and environmental issues. The longer development has been going on, the more experienced local leaders become in controlling development for the benefit of the community. As Wolpert (1976) notes, the experience of these communities with initial development is their bargaining power with future developers. As they learn the ropes, so to speak, their controlling capacity increases.

In general, the Western Slope is not well prepared to manage growth. Its population is sparse and concentrated in a few towns. The major part of its lands are controlled by the federal government. It is media-poor, with an underdeveloped press. Mountain topography makes telecommunication difficult and isolates communities from one another and from the Eastern Slope-oriented state government. The Councils of Governments, created in 1972 to integrate local and state-level decision making, work well in only one of the six Western Slope regions (Figure 11). This institutional underdevelopment inhibits effective response to the massive changes thrust upon Western Slope communities. The officials of these communities resent unilateral state policymaking as much as the state resents unilateral federal action. Both press for cross-level consensual decision making, but they have far to go.

Local environmental policy formation is further hampered by an instability of the political culture on the Western Slope. Political participation by transients tends to be erratic and governed by short-term perspectives and objectives. Recent legislation grants local suffrage to any resident with a registered automobile. Local politics have consequently become more volatile. Many voters will not stay long enough to live with the consequences of their votes. The degree of political permanence necessary for sustained and well-reasoned public participation in environmental policymaking is hard to come by on the Western Slope; trends suggest even less stability in the coming years.

The Environmental Conciliation Project

Colorado institutions of higher learning must respond in some useful manner to the environmental stresses outlined above. There is increasing pressure in the state for public universities to justify their claim on public funds by providing useful services to Colorado communities. Although such pressure, if taken to an extreme, can be destructive of the

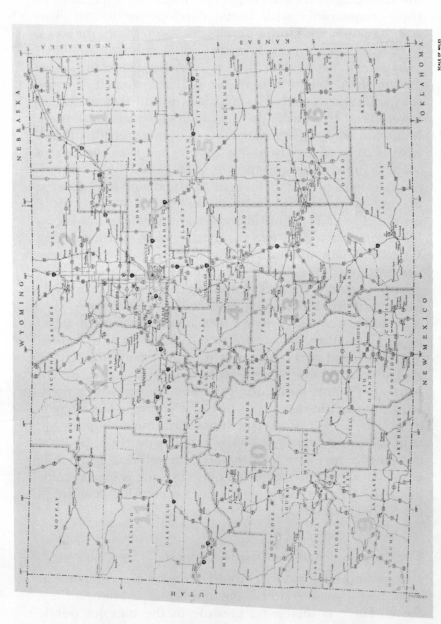

Figure 11. State planning and management regions. (From the Colorado Planning Division)

purpose of higher education, in moderation it stimulates applied research. Several of us at the University of Colorado became interested in working with communities to resolve specific environmental disputes. As our thinking developed, we defined three objectives:

1. *Helping Western Slope communities to manage environmental and resource-related conflicts.* We would locate three communities willing to work with us.

2. *Testing and refining conflict management methods* not previously used in environmental dispute settlement. Three quite different approaches to conflict management would be used. (1) *Tension reduction in the impacted community.* A controversial environmental decision, either before or after it is made, may generate tension and hostility and produce a psychological environment unconducive to sound policy formation and implementation. Joyce Frost, a specialist in interpersonal conflict reduction, would work with community leaders where such a condition existed toward producing a better decisional climate. Frost would go beyond temporary change to help develop patterns and networks of interpersonal communication among leaders that would continue after she left. (2) *Resolution of dissensus in policy judgments.* A second type of environmental conflict is an often sharp divergence in the subjective judgments of policymakers like planners, county commissioners, and environmental activists over the "best" policy. Kenneth Hammond, a social judgment psychologist would use a computer-assisted technique for reducing that divergence among participants in an environmental decision. Unlike Frost, who focuses on the emotional and verbal communication aspects of conflict, Hammond works on cognitive conflict in a limited decisional context. His objective is to produce judgment convergence among those responsible for a social policy decision (Hammond et al., 1975). Like Frost, Hammond seeks not only to resolve a particular dispute but also to illustrate a social policy conflict resolution method that could be used where appropriate in future decision making. (3) *Conflict clarification and mediation.* Environmental disputes are commonly made less tractable by (a) confusion and (b) the absence of a bargaining or mediating

structure. Paul Wehr would work with community leaders
engaged in an environmental dispute to better understand and
structure that dispute for settlement. This involves, first,
clarification: identifying *parties* (who are not always readily
identifiable); *issues* (some of which may not be obvious); and
costs and benefits of the proposed action for different segments of the community. Secondly, it may involve the mediation of various interests and values active in the dispute toward
a comprehensive and satisfactory settlement. Wehr's approach,
like those of Frost and Hammond, illustrates certain techniques of conflict reduction that parties to the dispute can use
in future policymaking. One method is to find ways of increasing the supply of a scarce resource or of decreasing the
demand for it. Lord et al. (1975:25) cite ways for a community
or region to increase its water quality and quantity through
technological innovation and to decrease demand through
waste elimination.

3. *Training for new roles.* To make a continuing contribution to communities under environmental stress, the university
must train advanced students in the policy sciences, law, business, and public affairs in the theory and technique of conflict
resolution. Conflict management specialists, social policy con-
sultants, environmental monitors—these are certain to be
future professional roles. Experience gained in this project
would shape new areas in the university's graduate curriculum.
Such specialized training would be a direct service to Colorado
communities.

Selection of Communities

Environmental conflict involves different levels of government. We prefer to work at the local level where the immediate
impact of environmental decisions occurs and disputes seem
somehow more manageable. On the Western Slope, river
valleys form natural communities and mountain topography
shapes them. Communication, commerce, and governmental
activity flow with ease along the rivers, highways, and rail
lines within valleys, but with some difficulty between valleys.
Towns within the same county and only a few miles apart by

crow-flight are quite isolated from one another. As Deutsch (1974) observes, even such topographical constraints can be overcome and mountain ecology substantially altered by technology, as Swiss transmountain highways and tunnels have opened links between formerly unconnected valleys. In the Colorado Rockies, mountain barriers continue to shape political and social behavior. The most prominent of these barriers, the Continental Divide, establishes a psychological estrangement of populations on either side that greatly influences environmental policymaking.

Western Slope valleys are natural ecological communities. A decision to build generating stations further down the valley from Craig will influence the air quality up the valley in the Steamboat Springs resort area. Valleys are also natural communication systems. Since information is often a scarce resource in environmental controversy, maximizing the flow of information in these valleys encourages a greater involvement of citizens in environmental decisions and ultimately wiser and more equitable decisions.

We set out to identify several valleys where there were water, energy, and recreational development impacts. We discussed the proposal first with federal and state officials. They helped us identify areas of the state where conflict over these issues was great. Three valleys in the state Division of Planning Region 12—the Yampa, the Eagle, and the Roaring Fork—were selected for further consideration.

The Communities

The Yampa, Eagle, and Roaring Fork valleys each present a broad range of environmental conflict potential. Each valley, as we shall see, has a different conflict development level. All of them host boom towns heavily affected by development projects, but they differ in how long development has impacted them. A "boom" implies unmanaged growth that in turn generates community tension and social disorganization as well as economic expansion. Gilmore (1976) describes a phasic response within a community to boom conditions that suddenly disturb its economic and social equilibrium: phase I, enthusiasm about growth; phase II, uncertainty about meeting demands for public services; phase III, near-panic over an anticipated revenues/expenditures gap; phase IV, problem solving. Gilmore sees adequate information about the changes occurring and likely to occur as the key to an effective response to booming. Controlling the boom involves coping with its effects and perhaps limiting the development generating it. The problem-solving phase may include questioning in the community of how much development is wanted and should be permitted.

Gilmore's phases parallel three community conflict stages that we might label (1) preconflict, (2) early conflict, and (3) advanced conflict. Conflict here is over development in the valley—how much is healthy, who benefits and loses by it, how it will affect the quality of life, how best to guide and control it. Each of our three valleys seems to be at different response and conflict phases. The Yampa Valley, confronted with a major coal-mining and power-generating program (BLM, 1976), is in the preconflict stage and somewhere between Gilmore's phases I and II. The Eagle Valley has experienced major growth in the Vail section of its upper region and will experience another growth spurt with the mid-valley construction of the Beaver Creek winter sports complex. The county must decide in the near future whether to permit a third complex, Adam's Rib, in the down-valley region near Eagle, the county seat. Interested parties are grappling with the Adam's Rib issue—the county is in the advanced conflict stage on that issue and somewhere between phases III and IV in response to the Beaver Creek development.

The upper Roaring Fork valley is in the advanced stage of conflict over growth issues. Its winter sports development occurred over the past twenty-five years with a renewed boom since the creation of Snowmass in 1967. Although pressure for winter sports expansion there is still strong, environmental conflict tends to focus on controlling related growth, transmountain diversions of water out of the valley, and pollution control. Since its political leadership and town and county administrators are the most experienced on the Western Slope in responding to rapid growth, it is well into the problem-solving phase of boom response.

The Yampa Valley

We, the unwilling, led by the unqualified
Have been doing the unbelievable, so long with so little,
That we're now attempting the impossible with nothing.
                              —Sign, Town Offices, Hayden, Colorado

The Yampa Valley links Routt and Moffat counties in north-western Colorado. The Yampa basin contains the Yampa coal field and with the Piceance basin and its oil shale deposits, it is the most energy-rich area in the state. The Routt County Mineral and Energy Resources Map identifies the presence of geothermal potential, bituminous and subbituminous near-surface coal, oil, natural gas, uranium, gold, fluorite, lime-stone, volcanics, copper, and oil shale within the region's boundaries. Steamboat Springs, the Routt County seat and a winter sports town, and Craig, the Moffat County seat, railhead and energy boom town, are the valley's population centers. Routt and Moffat are two of the state's larger counties, though, with perhaps 50 percent of their 26,000 inhabitants living in Steamboat Springs and Craig, their rural areas are quite sparsely populated.

The valley has long produced energy. Underground coal mining began in the last century and flourished until 1951. As fossil fuels have risen steadily in value, it has become profitable to mine Yampa coal through stripping and trans-port and by joining with utilities to build mine-mouth generating stations. Yampa coal is there—millions of tons of it—and is desirable for several reasons. Most lies not far below the surface and is relatively inexpensive to mine. It has a low sulfur content, making it desirable for meeting air quality standards. Its BTU content is high compared with other western coal. It is costly to ship, however, and therefore has a competitive advantage over eastern coal only as far as load centers in the Midwest.

Extracting the coal is relatively simple, but the legal and social obstacles to mining it are not. Coal companies lease federal mineral rights, but the coal may lie beneath private land. Seventy-three percent of federal coal in Routt and Moffat lies beneath private surface rights that must be purchased.[2] Ownership rights in the West include surface, mineral, and water rights; and all three must be controlled by the energy industries for successful mining and mine-mouth power generation. The checkerboard pattern of federal mineral grants, in many areas interspersed with those of private agricultural owners who may resist selling their rights, adds further complication. In the Yampa valley, it seems that though some will not sell, the majority will since the land is generally marginal for agriculture.

The Yampa Valley's energy history is written in coal dust. Between Hayden and Steamboat Springs lie the ruins of a once-thriving coal town, Mt. Harris, which as recently as the 1930s had 1,200 inhabitants. The Hayden drugstore still sells postcards showing its broad streets and public buildings, but now all that remains of Mt. Harris are the large trees lining the former avenues, chunks of broken curb concrete, foundation holes, rusting stoves left behind, a disintegrating baby carriage chassis, and, with some imagination, echoes of the shouts of playing children, laughter from taverns, and the alarm whistle and weeping accompanying the great mine explosion of 1942, when forty-two men lost their lives. By 1948, the mines had closed and the town was dying.

As I stood in the ruins of Mt. Harris on a winter afternoon, thinking about a way of life now gone, I was jolted into the present by the sudden roar of the new Hayden generating plant, two miles away, releasing its steam. Then at dusk that same day, I took a lonely trip to the Edna strip mine above Oak Creek where Pittsburgh and Midway Coal, with its 45 cf dragline, makes its 1.2 million tons/year contribution to meeting the nation's energy demands. That massive machine, twenty-four hours a day and six days a week, silently eats away, consuming one-tenth of the electricity in its coal production makes possible, swinging back and forth in the desolate and foreboding landscape. Northwestern Colorado rather reminds

one of the lunar surface even without strip-mining—one
reason why most local people do not oppose stripping.
"You've seen one clump of sagebrush you've seen 'em all."

The Yampa Valley's past and future is bound up with
mining and energy. Before winter sports came to Steamboat
Springs, energy was the economic kingpin of the area. It was
an exploitative past: company towns and the mining industry
were unyielding and oppressive, though less so in the Yampa
than in the southern coal fields of Las Animas and Huerfano
counties. One could argue that there was no fair exchange of
labor for economic and social rewards in the valley's mining
past; the future is ambiguous on this point. Labor seems fairly
compensated now, but the costs of the social and environmental impacts of coal development are as yet unclear. The
people are ambivalent about it: Yes, it will provide jobs for
our young people, but how long will they last? Yes, our
economies will grow, but where are the funds for needed public
services? Yes, the industries are cooperating with us to solve
impact problems, but why are they seeking exemptions from
our local taxes from the legislature? Coal development does
give the region an identity—"puts us on the map," as one
newspaper editor put it—as a national energy-producing area.
Where that identity balances, in the public mind, with being
an "energy sacrifice area," as one Washington bureaucrat
phrased it, remains to be seen.

While new jobs and more money flow into Craig and
Hayden, living costs rise accordingly, leaving those on fixed
incomes far behind. Land values have risen astronomically,
housing is impossible to find, rents are high, educational and
medical facilities are overburdened, and social tension is much
more noticeable in frequency of arrests, marital conflict, and
the like. Local government is not much involved in decisions
on coal development. The present decisional structure effectively excludes it. Decisions are made in Washington and to
a lesser degree by federal and state officials in Denver. The
Bureau of Land Management, U.S. Geological Survey, Federal
Energy Administration, U.S. Forest Service, Federal Power
Commission, State Department of Natural Resources and
Bureau of Mines, and the coal and power industries all make

inputs into coal development decisions that effectively exclude local government in the Yampa Valley.

The lack of local involvement in coal development decisions is also a consequence of the insufficient experience of local government. Karl Deutsch (1963) refers to government as the "steering sector" of society. It gets us where we want to go. To use an automotive metaphor, those in the steering role need maps and experience to steer effectively. In the case of local response to coal development, maps are plans, and the experience is that of dealing with other levels of government and industry that are making decisions that will have both positive and negative impacts on local communities. Moffat County has a decidedly underdeveloped steering capacity: a part-time planner (the previous county planner left for a position with one of the coal companies), no staff to enforce county mining and housing regulations, no staff competent to judge environmental and social impact analyses and to protect the valley's interests in review processes, no staff capable of getting the city and county governments to move in the same direction for mutual self-protection, and no staff to use the county's intervention process to increase its steering capacity. Routt County's steering is better developed but is as yet inadequate to cope effectively with the impact of energy and recreation booms.

To better use Yampa coal on-site, a consortium of Utah International (coal) and several utilities have formed Utilities Group Inc. (UGI) to buy Peabody Coal, which has extensive leases in the Yampa field. For years these industries have also been purchasing water rights in the valley. UGI is developing a complete energy system: millions of tons of coal; water appropriated, diverted from other uses or downstream users; transportation by rail or by transmission lines; and a sparse population.

Impacts on the Yampa Valley

Environmental. Although the Bureau of Land Management's environmental impact analysis (BLM, 1976) estimates the natural and social impacts of the proposed mining, it does not predict the impacts of the total energy system that will emerge. Over time, the constant generation of 3,000 Mw could have a greater effect on air quality deterioration and water consumption and pollution than either mining or plant construction. It requires 14,000 AF/Y of water to generate 1,000 Mw—for cooling and steam alone.

Even with electrostatic precipitators to remove particulate matter and wet scrubbers to remove SO_2, airborne pollution will be considerable; there is little vegetation in such a semi-arid region to absorb residual CO_2. Since by 1990 (BLM, 1976: I-13), an annual production level of 33 million tons of coal is anticipated for the region (much of that to be burned in local power plants) the environmental impact could be severe. The air quality problem alone could conceivably bring the winter sports and energy industries in the valley toe-to-toe.

There is some concern that the proposed strip mining may disturb aquifers and elk and deer migration routes and feeding areas, and that surface runoff from unreclaimed spoil piles and construction of power plants and railroad spurs will pollute waterways.

Social. The social impact of energy development is felt primarily in Craig and Hayden, influenced as they are by both mines and power plants. Craig's population has doubled in the past six years and Hayden's has tripled (Fitch et al., 1975b: Table 2). Adequate planning and financing of such explosive growth is just not possible for these towns even though development has revived them economically. Tax revenue allocation is a serious problem since the counties get the revenue and the towns get the impact—this exacerbates a long-standing lack of coordination between the town and county governments. Trailer parks spring up, municipal services collapse under the weight of new demand, social tension between natives and transient residents increases. The community's dollar income rises but the trade-off imposes dust, noise, housing deterioration, and social hypertension.

Craig is no stranger to boom conditions. Coal, oil and gas, and railroad booms hit Craig in this century as did the economic "levelings" or recessions that followed.[3] These successive levelings have produced some indifference to the current boom with a prevalent attitude that the town will survive—there is a confidence that, as in the past, Craig will have a leveling off, not a "bust." Past booms have also produced a commercial infrastructure in Craig dependent on the infusion of external capital. This infrastructure needs the economic expansion that coal/power development promises. The Craig business community is enthusiastic about the boom with few exceptions, though there appears to be a love-hate attitude toward the extractive industries—business feels dependent on them but fights them all the way.

The opposition evident elsewhere in these communities may spread even to local businessmen, however, as they are forced to confront the costs internalization problem more squarely. Costs internalization occurs when consumers pay the approximate economic, environmental, and social costs of the product they consume. Mine-mouth generation of electricity shipped to distant markets denies costs internalization since the deleterious environmental and social consequences remain largely in the Yampa Valley while the power goes to Fort Collins, Loveland, Paige (Arizona), and many other markets. As yet there has been no technological breakthrough that permits shipping environmental pollution and social disorganization over transmission lines. If Yampa Valley residents feel they are not fairly compensated for their loss of natural resources and their valued way of life and the strain and risks of boom and bust, and think that industries and consumers are not paying a fair price for the energy benefit they derive, there will be increasing dissatisfaction.

The local power to tax can insure at least partial compensation. In fact, Yampa Valley generating plants were "sold" to local governments largely on the basis of the expanded tax base that was anticipated. Tax revenues could soften the impact and expand needed services. There was, therefore, anger and despair last year when a county commissioner learned that the Platte River Power Association, providing eighteen percent of the tax revenues from the Craig stations, had succeeded in gaining from the legislature an exemption from Moffat County taxes. The Salt River Power Authority, part owner of the Craig and Hayden plants, has allegedly petitioned for a similar exemption. It owns 80 percent of the Hayden complex (Fitch et al., 1975b) and could remove overnight a sizable portion of Routt County's tax revenues.

To aggravate this problem, state education equalization funds are allocated to each county on a need basis. When Moffat County's tax valuation rose from $2.8 million in 1975 to $88 million in 1976 as a consequence of the power plant completion, the state reduced its educational allotment to Moffat accordingly. The county lost both its tax revenues and its state funds. Because the coal impact area is so sparsely populated, it has only a weak voice in the legislature.

Conflict over environmental and resource-related issues in the Yampa Valley is beginning. A sense of exploitation by the outside world is slowly developing. More and more of "our" water is being diverted to the Eastern Slope, "our" counties are being used as Denver's playground, "we" give up our natural resources, clean air, and pure water in exchange for higher electric rates. One hears a growing sense of community identity. Two editorial excerpts from the *Hayden Valley Press* of March 11, 1976, reflect citizen concerns.

And now we can't help but wonder if the people in Arizona, who are the prime beneficiaries of Colorado-Ute, are paying the same outrageous electric prices we are—doubtful in our opinion. And the final shaft, we in the Yampa Valley must contend with the Colorado-Ute power plant emission, such as smoke, smog, fly-ash and carbon dioxide and still pay a premium for electrical power. How do you like that one sports fans?

United States Representative James P. Johnson's 130,000-acre Eagles Nest Wilderness Area bill was recently approved by the House Interior Committee and has, for all practical purposes thwarted the Denver Water Board's transmountain water diversion project.

The Wilderness boundaries in the bill will make it impossible for Denver to tap Western Slope water without costly pumping. Needless to say passage of the bill gave the Denver Water Board a bad case of the blahs but Denver Mayor Bill McNichols seems to be taking it worse than anyone. . . . McNichols said, 'The

TABLE 2
Total Expected Coal-related Developments

	1975	1980	1985	1990
Cumulative Tons Coal Produced (millions)	--	71	194	340
Total Number of Mines	9	14	17	21
Number of Power Plants	2	2	3	3
Installed Generating Capacity	1,173	1,173	2,933	2,933
Miles of New Railroads	--	35	40	125
Miles of New Roads	--	20	75	150
Miles of New Powerline	--	75	200	350

Source: Derived from BLM (1976:I-20).

Western Slope will hold onto that water and the Denver Metro area can go dry, as far as he [Johnson] is concerned.' . . . Poor baby. Don't the Mayor's words bring a lump to your throat? We're betting that right now there isn't a dry eye on the Western Slope.

The recreational boom up the river from Hayden and Craig seems somewhat more manageable than the energy explosion. Recreational growth tends to naturally provide more money for impact mitigation than do extractive industries. Environmental impacts may be greater, however, since the impacting populations associated with recreation are much larger and more permanent. Winter sports development is hardly less problematic for local government. Land speculation and poor planning by ski developers in Routt County have left two developments bankrupt and the county with an uncollected $470,000 in back taxes and a physical infrastructure unpaid for.

Future resource-related conflict in the Yampa Valley is likely. If our "change generates conflict" proposition is valid, a look at the projected Yampa coal-related development (Table 2) suggests that the power plants in the valley are likely to generate as much "heat" there as light. Nor will the impact take place only in the valley. As coal is shipped out of the valley, any Colorado community served by a coal-feeder railroad will experience traffic interruption and pollution problems. In Routt County, which has only one highway overpass, an estimated nine unit trains (75 cars each) will move daily each way by 1990. This rail traffic will join an estimated fourteen 130-car trains a day each way in the Front Range north-south corridor, carrying coal from Wyoming fields to Texas. Though the potential for environmental disputes is substantial, the Yampa Valley is still in a preconflict stage. This could change rapidly, however, as the utility tax exemptions and air pollution control hearings raise public awareness.

The Eagle Valley

We need all the help we can get.
                              Dan Koprinikar, Eagle County Commissioner

Were we to write a history of Eagle County, we might well refer to its BV and SV periods—before Vail and since Vail. The development of Vail in the early 1960s might well be the most significant impacting event in the valley's history. Vail is actually in the Gore Valley, but its spillover has impacted the upper Eagle Valley considerably—in anticipation of ski expansion, much of the land in the upper valley has now been bought for speculation or eventual development. Before the development of Vail, the Eagle Valley had some zinc mining in the upper reaches, but stock-raising for beef and wool, and forage cropping were the major economic activities.

Vail is also a benchmark in the evolution of alpine skiing in the Rockies. Skiing as an industry in Colorado began with a rope-tow at Loveland Basin in the early 1940s, accelerated with a double-chair lift at Berthoud in the mid-forties, and took off with the opening of Aspen in 1949. Winter sports, growing steadily since that time, drew much of its momentum from a network of entrepreneurs formed in the Tenth Mountain Division—the ski troops—during World War II. The Tenth trained at Camp Hale at the headwaters of the Eagle River, far above Redcliff. Many of the U.S. Forest Service ski experts and developers of complexes like Vail and Aspen met at Hale and later worked together on ski development.

In 1976, final state approval was given for the development

of a second winter sports area up Beaver Creek north of Avon, financed and designed by Vail Associates. The proposal was more carefully reviewed than any to date in Colorado. Beaver Creek was initially to be the site of the 1976 Winter Olympics alpine events. When the Olympics proposal was rejected by statewide referendum in 1972, Beaver Creek survived as a private venture proposal. Environmental impact questions were raised by environmental activists. How the proposed growth would affect the high upper Eagle Valley and its Mexican-American communities—Minturn, Redcliff, and Gilman—was also a weighty social impact consideration. These towns are at the northern end of a migration route that had brought Mexican-Americans from New Mexico earlier in this century (Knowlton, 1972). Until the ski boom at Vail, these people were able to retain their ethnic identity reasonably well. The pressure from Vail, however, eroded the more traditional lifestyle of upper Eagle Hispanics, and these people have had serious concern about new impact from Beaver Creek.

An additional impacting event in the valley was the construction of the Interstate 70 highway. As a major east-west national artery, it opens up the valley considerably. Its consequences may be as significant as were those of Interstate 91 and 89 for Vermont. The development of Vail and Beaver Creek have positioned the question of growth high on the political agenda in Eagle Valley. Local governments examine growth projections with understandable concern.

Adam's Rib. Development is moving down the Eagle Valley. A third major ski area, Adam's Rib, has been proposed for the mountains south of Eagle, the county seat (Figure 12). If approved, Adam's Rib will increase the visiting skier population by 470,000 by 1985 and the county's permanent population by 4,800. This proposal, which even five years ago would have been approved with little or no opposition, has already generated a healthy environmental dispute. Project approval will depend on where the Eagle Valley comes out on several questions.

1. What precisely is the future potential for winter sports development in the valley and in the state? The ski sites are

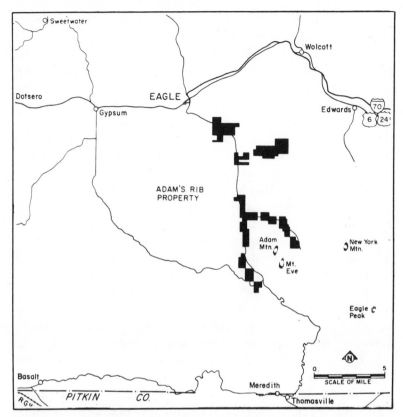

Figure 12. Proposed Adam's Rib recreational area. (Eagle Valley Enterprise, Eagle, Colorado)

there: thirty-four in the White River National Forest alone and ninety in the state as a whole. What will be the future skiing demand? The current demand growth rate hovers around 10 percent annually, and the rationale is that one should build the supply to meet the demand. Of course the supply-demand relationship is reciprocal in that once a supply is established, demand must be generated to use it to capacity. The cause-effect relationship is circular, not linear, and the classical supply-demand rationale seems more than a bit naive as applied to alpine skiing. The large capital investments these winter sports areas represent require heavy use of the facility to return a profit. A very few areas in the state like Aspen and Vail are prospering, most are surviving, a few have "bellied up," as they say in the trade. Can Eagle County rely on straight line projections of a continued increase in skier demand?

2. Can the socioeconomic and environmental impacts of Adam's Rib be accurately predicted? Since U.S. Forest Service land will be involved, an environmental impact analysis must be done. How reliable are such analyses and have they been useful in making similar decisions elsewhere?

3. What will be the costs and benefits of the proposed development for the people of the Eagle Valley? Will the complex be self-supporting and contribute to the county's economic and social health? Will the benefits for local government outweigh the costs? Will the average citizen benefit or will gains accrue to only a few?

4. Can local government handle the projected social impact of Adam's Rib? Both the county government and the town of Eagle will be responsible for increased public services: highway construction and maintenance, subdivision regulation, water and sewer service, public schools, medical facilities, public transportation. Are there sufficient scarce resources such as water and open space to support the additional impact?

5. Can Eagle Valley's ecosystems support the anticipated impact of Adam's Rib without deteriorating? With the impacts of Vail and Beaver Creek, can Adam's Rib be added with a reasonable margin of safety? Will a balance of human and non-human populations in the valley be retained?

As Adam's Rib decisions are made, diverse positions will be taken by different parties in response to such questions. There will be broader participation than in the past in the series of decisions that determine the future of Adam's Rib and, in a very real sense, that of the entire valley.

The Decisional Process. Winter resource decisions in the White River National Forest region are more accessible at the local level than are those concerning coal development elsewhere, and they become more so with time. Unlike the absence of meaningful local participation in the decision to develop Yampa basin coal reserves in Moffat County, local government in Eagle County is invited and in fact forced to participate in decisions on ski area proposals within its jurisdiction. The federal and state governments are now seeking to rationalize the siting of winter sports complexes. The impetus for an involvement of local authorities in ski development decisions comes from the U.S. Forest Service, which has become the injured third party in too many siting battles in Colorado— Haystack Mountain, Marble, and most recently Crested Butte (the Callaway affair). The state, too, wants a more consensual, well-reasoned, and systematic siting procedure that would (1) discourage a developer at an early stage if a site were inappropriate, (2) insure statewide planning for winter resources development, and (3) involve in the decision the communities that would be impacted by it.

Two actions have been taken to insure these changes. First, the U.S. Forest Service in the White River National Forest will not proceed with a development proposal unless the county in question decides that it wants and can handle the related growth. That decision could be made by the county commissioners or by a county-wide referendum, but if local government rejects the proposal, so will the forest service.

Second, the state is formulating a Joint Review Process (JRP) as part of its Winter Resources Management Plan. The lead time necessary for the development of a ski area is now ten years as compared with two or three even five years ago. With more complex technology, increased government regulation, and requisite land and water purchase, a sizable capital investment has already been made when construction begins. Such investment creates a momentum for the project that is difficult to reverse. The JRP would preclude this kind of investment momentum for unacceptable proposals. Were the project feasible, responsible governmental agencies at all levels and opponents of the proposed action would be involved as the review progressed.

The JRP could be an effective conflict resolution device. Each major governmental actor thereby becomes more of an uncommitted third party and less of an advocate. The U.S. Forest Service, through its planning unit approach, designates developable areas, the Colorado winter resources and planning agencies coordinate the review process, the proponent is given a clear idea before major investment whether the proposal has a chance, and the counties and towns concerned are not only involved in the process from the beginning but make the central decision on the proposal. The JRP thus institutionalizes the cross-level consensual decisional process that local and regional officials are seeking, with a "lead agency" designated as responsible for the review, at each level.

The Joint Review Process does not, however, resolve the Adam's Rib issue. The developer has already invested heavily in land, water rights, and planning. The issue is now squarely in the community to be impacted and is being settled there, not without substantial controversy.

Parties to the Dispute. The positions of the parties are by no means clear at this point nor are all the potential parties clearly identifiable. Those that are can be grouped as *primary* or *secondary* according to their degree of interest and involvement in the outcome.

Primary Parties. The key proponents of Adam's Rib are the *developers*, the HBE Corporation of St. Louis, a hospital and bank construction firm, and the Eagle Chamber of Commerce. The major opponent is a citizens' group known as *Concerned Citizens of Eagle County.* The Eagle County commissioners and planning commission will make the decision to grant or refuse a special use permit for Adam's Rib. They could vote to postpone such a decision for further study. The town of Eagle board of trustees and planning commission will decide whether or not to support the proposal since they must cope with much of the Adam's Rib impact in increased annexation, municipal services, and the like.

The U.S. Forest Service will do the environmental impact analysis and will decide on leasing the federal lands for the ski area, but only if the county approves the proposal. Local environmental activists with probable intervention from national organizations such as the Environmental Defense Fund and the Sierra Club will also be active in the decision. No- or slow-growth advocates are now organizing in the valley, and clothing and bumper stickers opposing Adam's Rib are beginning to appear. The local business community, guided by the Eagle Chamber of Commerce, is already active on behalf of growth and Adam's Rib.

State-level actors such as the Division of Wildlife, the Division of Planning, COG Region 12, and in all likelihood the governor himself will inevitably be drawn into the dispute. The Eagle County Livestock Association and the Federal Timber Purchasers Association have a direct economic interest in the decision and may take public positions. The Mexican-American communities in the upper Eagle Valley are concerned about still further development pressure on their towns, but Adam's Rib would probably not have a direct impact that far up the valley unless spillover development from Adam's Rib spreading up and down the valley should collide with that descending from Beaver Creek and force more Beaver Creek pressure into the upper Eagle.

Secondary Parties. Some parties that have both a less direct interest in the decisional outcome and a less clear role in the dispute, may yet become involved at some point. Pitkin County officials may resist the proposed action if it threatens serious development spillover into Pitkin. The Adam's Rib site is near the Pitkin County line and an unimproved road now linking the two counties through a mountain pass might be upgraded and lead growth pressure into an already growth-saturated county. This spillover threat may also activate the Frying Pan Association, residents of the Frying Pan Valley through which development would come. If skier demand should level off in the near future and Adam's Rib be regarded as a competitor of Vail and Beaver Creek in a stable or contracting market, Vail Associates might become more involved in the dispute.

A shadowy actor in this drama is the land and water speculator. Precisely who these individuals and corporations are is unclear at this time, but the speculator seems omnipresent. In the Yampa Valley, coal leases, and land and water rights are bought up quietly if not secretly for later coal and power development. In the Front Range corridor, the advance purchase of rights for both Western and Eastern slope water by municipal water boards is speculation of a sort. There is no Front Range need in the foreseeable future for that water, and it can therefore be traded, sold, or hoarded like any other commodity. In the Four Corners energy impact area, even the Mafia has moved into land and water speculation.

The Issues. The Adam's Rib proposal may well be the central issue in the upcoming November elections. One of the three Eagle County commissioners is running for reelection. He and other local incumbents and challengers will be forced to have opinions if not to take definite positions on growth questions. Several salient Adam's Rib issues are already in sight.

1. *Environmental Impact.* As no environmental analysis will be done unless the county agrees that it wants the growth anticipated from Adam's Rib, there are no data for evaluating likely impact. Initial technical review, however, does predict major Adam's Rib impacts on wildlife and air quality (*EVE*, 1976b). The environmental consequences may not be unlike those anticipated from the Beaver Creek project (USFS, 1976) and could be both positive and negative, as when ski trails interrupt elk movement corridors but also enlarge forage areas for them.

2. *Timing.* Adam's Rib proponents are pushing for an affirmative decision from the county as soon as possible. In view of the long development lead time, capital investment, and inflation, time is money to the developer. Local decision makers, on the other hand, would prefer to evaluate the Beaver Creek impact before committing the valley to still more growth, to wait for approval and implementation of the Joint Review Process and for a more complete sounding of public opinion. *When* the decision is made is likely to be more important initially than *how* it is made.

An affirmative decision on Adam's Rib would hardly terminate the conflict. The county would then have to revise its master plan, rezone itself appropriately, and involve the state through the 1041 land use law—in itself a major point of local-state contention. There is just no easy way through this decision for the county commissioners, the Eagle Town board, or the planning commission and staffs of these two governmental units. Steering through the years to come will be increasingly difficult.

3. *Socioeconomic Impacts.* Here the conflict will revolve around a socioeconomic cost/benefit analysis of the proposed action. What are the probable positive and negative impacts and do the benefits outweigh the costs for Eagle Valley residents? The Technical Working Group of the state Division of Planning produced a revealing report (TWG, 1975) on the potential problems associated with winter resources development, and the Donald and Patterson (1975) study is quite clear on the possible benefits. One view (Dusenbury, 1976) suggests that hypergrowth in ski areas does not pay off for the average citizen and is in fact diseconomic for the community, but there is no thorough study of which we are aware of how the costs and benefits are distributed within a community impacted by winter resource development.

Briefly, some positive impacts might be: economic growth in a presently marginal economy; putting western Eagle County on the map as a four-season recreation area; better public services; and a more culturally diverse and stimulating community. Negative impacts might include: the elimination of agricultural land and production; a vulnerable single-industry and seasonal economy; speculation, bankruptcy, county deficits, and other risks associated with recreational booms;[4] and loss of a rural and small-town way of life.

4. *Public Attitudes.* Should the decision go to public referendum, voter awareness and attitudes will be crucial policy determinants. No unambiguous sounding of public opinion is available. Two surveys (Donald and Patterson, 1975; Roof and Thomassen, 1973) present contradictory results. The former found 44 percent of those interviewed anticipating a positive effect from Adam's Rib development, 34 percent a negative effect, and 14 percent undecided. The Roof and Thomassen study found 65 percent of 233 respondents negative toward Adam's Rib in the area now proposed and 56 percent negative toward it anywhere in the valley. In the case of neither study do we know anything of the reliability or validity of the survey instrument, the accuracy of the sampling procedures, or the competence of the interviewers. This leads us to conclude that a comprehensive and reliable attitude survey is yet to be done. The two-year lapse between the 1973 and 1975 surveys may

explain much of the divergence in their findings. We hardly find support in either set of results for the Donald and Patterson conclusion "that the overall community sentiment is favorable towards Adam's Rib." The fact that it was the conclusion of a proponent-funded study gives it even less reliability.

Settlement of the Dispute. We earlier described the Eagle Valley as an "early conflict" community as concerns environmental disputes. The Eagle County government, the "steering and control" agency in this case, has had some experience in coping with growth and the exertion of local authority in development matters as a consequence of the Vail impact. Its commissioners and planning staff are very active.

An example of the self-protective stance the county government increasingly assumes was its blocking of Rocky Mountain Airways' unilateral decision to shift service from the county airport west of Eagle to an unpaved airstrip at Avon, much closer to Vail and Beaver Creek. The county claims that commercial flights into the strip—especially with the new Dash 7—would be too dangerous, would kill the county airport, and would feed uncontrollable growth. This response reflects a growing willingness of county officials to control outside growth stimulators. Put another way, the county's steering and control capacity is increasing with its growth impact experience. The Eagle Valley has experienced some development bust as well as boom, with 500 condominium units still unsold in the Vail area and two $4 million foreclosures in Eagle-Vail.

My work in the Eagle Valley will involve, first, *clarification* of the conflict for myself and for those directly engaged (e.g., parties, issues, costs and benefits of the proposed action, and the dynamics of the decision as it develops). I will work to objectify the conflict so that disputants can understand it from more than a purely subjective viewpoint. Gaining this broader view is essential for conflicting parties to see the dispute in positive-sum (all can benefit) rather than in zero-sum (some must win while others lose) or negative-sum (all lose) terms.

A second area of focus will be the *mediation* of conflicting objectives in either formal or informal bargaining to produce a settlement acceptable to the community. *Illustration* of conflict resolution methods—techniques and concepts that disputants may find useful later—is another contribution I will try to make. For example, I plan to test the concept of distributional impact analysis. Are there sufficient and appropriate data available in this case (or can we generate them), to give every group of citizens in western Eagle County a fair idea of how Adam's Rib (or any proposed development) will influence their lives, economically, environmentally, socially? If feasible, such an analysis could be useful to citizens, developers, and county officials alike. We might ask: Will the consumer—the skier and the developer—pay the true cost of what they will consume or will much of the cost be borne by the host community? The revised ski permit bill recently introduced by Senator Haskell may encourage costs internalization somewhat because it would require half of the permit revenues to be returned by the U.S. Forest Service directly to the impacted communities.[5]

Let us assume that the making of wise policy, whether it be in Eagle or Denver, involves creative tension. That tension is important because it insures that significant information or some party's interests are not overlooked or ignored in a decision. At a certain level, tension can be creative but it can also easily build beyond that level and create conflict.

The Roaring Fork Valley

Only time water flows uphill is when there's money upstream.
                                                    —Western Slope aphorism

The Roaring Fork Valley is a community in the "advanced conflict" stage. At this writing, there are no less than ten important environmental disputes in high gear there over such actions as: county downzoning to stem growth; the light rail transit system proposal; the campaign to recall Pitkin County commissioners for their antigrowth policies; the Basalt South annexation dispute involving the town of Basalt, Eagle and Pitkin counties, and the developer; Pitkin County opposition to the Twin Forks transmountain diversion; and the Little Annie ski expansion proposal. People in the Roaring Fork Valley and Pitkin County know how to fight over environmental issues and do so with gusto.

Roaring Fork seems also to be the most integral of our three valleys, with regular bus service linking towns in the valley and a growing sense of common destiny. True, the upper valley—Aspen and its environs—and the lower valley are at different stages in environmental consciousness and the valley passes through three different counties (Pitkin, Eagle, and Garfield), but Roaring Fork Valley is still a community.

The valley's economy historically has had both mining and agricultural bases. Gold, silver, coal, and iron ore have been mined in the past century and the latter two are still being mined. In the lower valley, potato farming and stock raising were once major economic activities. Since the development of Aspen skiing, however, the economy has revolved around winter sports and tourism and the production of water. The Roaring Fork is fed by the Frying Pan and Crystal rivers among others and in turn feeds the Colorado. Water is a major element in the valley's scenic grandeur and, therefore, in the valley's warm weather tourist industry. This is one reason why Pitkin County officials are so concerned about maintaining minimum stream flows during the dry months of the summer when transmountain diversion projects place new and heavy demands on Roaring Fork water.

Pitkin County is hypersensitive to growth because it has had so much of it in the past decade—there was a 19 percent population increase in 1974-77. Local government in the upper Roaring Fork is well equipped to manage growth. A joint Aspen/Pitkin planning commission with good training, county commissioners aware of growth problems and committed to strictly controlled and moderate growth, an Aspen town board similarly inclined, and very broad citizen participation in the steering and control processes—all of these produced until recently an efficient growth management and environmental protection program. This was possible because of the close cooperation between the county government and the town of Aspen, the county seat.

Over the past year, segments of the upper valley population have lost confidence in the county commissioners and planning staff—Pitkin County government is thus losing its steering efficiency. One indicator of loss of confidence was a campaign to recall all three commissioners. Ostensibly, the motivation for the recall was the controversial light rail transit issue. Should a light rail system be built to link ski areas and towns or are other options preferable? The underlying issue was the commissioners' downzoning of certain open spaces like Woody Creek. Owners of large tracts were dismayed and incensed to find their land suddenly divisible into no smaller than 160-acre units. Rugged individualism may be as strong a motive as economic gain in the opposition to downzoning as a slow-growth policy. Landowners do not want to be told what they can and cannot do with their land. The large landowners organized and financed the recall campaign but apparently drew on a wider feeling of discontent and powerlessness.

Actually, Pitkin County and the town of Aspen have been rather successful at efforts to insure consensual and participatory government. One device they use is the Citizen Design Caucus, by which policies on specific problems like public transportation are conceptualized and designed largely through citizen study groups. The transit system caucus involved 150 people in an exercise of imagination and cost-benefit analysis that produced a proposal that, for all its citizen participation, has generated lively environmental conflict. The "clean and comprehensive transportation" value collides with "cost effectiveness." One of the trade-off issues not addressed in the dispute thus far is that the electric light rail system will trade clean air in the Roaring Fork for dirty air in the Yampa, since the additional electric power needed will be generated by the Yampa Valley plants.

The county has also recently produced a model land use code that integrates the state 1041 land use requirements with local regulations. It has also developed strict environmental controls governing mineral and fossil fuel extraction. The county's steering capacity is a highly developed one, but events of the past year have generated an unhealthy political tension and interpersonal and intergroup hostility that already jeopardize sound environmental growth policy in the county. The protection of Roaring Fork water is one responsibility that has gone unmet as a consequence of political dissensus in the county.

Water-related Conflict. Water conflict on the Roaring Fork reflects in its diversity the range of water-related disputes throughout the state. We must explore that larger setting to understand where the Roaring Fork fits in. Water is a scarce and nonrenewable resource in any given year, and conflict over it grows more and more common. Energy growth and urban growth are the two major demands on Colorado water. The Western States Water Council predicts that the federal energy policy that plans oil shale refining, coal conversion, and electric power generation in the West will require up to three million additional acre feet per year by 1990 for those energy purposes. Colorado should produce 387,000 AF/Y as its share (*BDC*, 1975). With very little unappropriated water left in Colorado, most of the additional needs will be diverted from current users. Energy industry users will conflict with Front Range municipal water boards who predict a population boom in the West with Denver at its center. As the local folk wisdom says, water flows toward money, and the Denver Water Board is prepared to pay up to $5,000 per acre foot for its urban growth goals.

Water conflict has its deepest roots in the beneficial use principle on which Colorado water law is based: water must go to the one who uses it. Colorado water law is stuck with a nineteenth century consumption ethic for dealing with a twenty-first century conservation problem. To complicate environmental protection, "beneficial use" is narrowly defined. Users must be human, and they can use water for domestic, agricultural, industrial, and recreational purposes in that order. Nonhuman populations have no right to water in Colorado nor do humans acting in their behalf. Colorado Senate Bill 97 (1974) permits the state to appropriate water for maintaining minimum stream flows, but it has access only to unappropriated water and cannot preempt a senior user's rights. If the Roaring Fork waters are fully appropriated, the users can dry up the river (they have done so in the past). One of the sharpest environmental conflicts of the future will involve the maximum beneficial use doctrine supported by water law, and the minimum stream flow demand rooted in the conservation ethic. The Colorado Water Conservation Board (CWCB), given the junior right to maintain minimum stream flows, does have an important weapon in that any junior right on a stream can protest a senior action to make a use change. If the Denver Water Board buys senior water rights on the Roaring Fork, and acts to divert the water from agricultural to municipal use, the CWCB can protest and block the action, maintaining the minimum stream flow in that manner.

Courts are only one arena for water conflict, which is increasingly a political and social struggle. The Placita Dam dispute in western Pitkin County over the construction of a diversion dam was resolved with no legal action but with considerable political activity and interpersonal confrontation.

Water Allocation. Water allocation policy is made by governmental agencies interpreting water law and resolving disputes over it. The Colorado Water Conservation Board and the Colorado Water Conservation Division of the Department of Natural Resources (through its eight divisions in the state) allocate and adjudicate water use. Each division has a water court with judges, master referees, and ordinary referees. Each court decides how much water in any one river basin or stream goes to which of the four categories ranked with the following right priority: (1) municipal/domestic, (2) agricultural, (3) industrial, and (4) recreational. Within each category the court allocates water on the basis of the priority number of each use, while the water commissioners enforce the allocation given each user. Division engineers usually mediate and settle allocation disputes out of court.

If a waterway is fully appropriated (i.e., all normal water flow to which the state is entitled is being used every year), whether a user has a senior or a junior right determines who gets water first in years when less than normal flow cuts some users out. Use priority in a water dispute always takes precedence over right priority. For example, the City of Thornton (a domestic/municipal right has priority over all other categories) cannot condemn the rights of the Farmers' Irrigation Company, which has a lower right priority but a higher time priority since it has been using that water for agricultural irrigation for many decades. Thus, Front Range municipal water districts must go to the Western Slope to find and divert unappropriated water. However, Thornton is currently testing the use priority principle by condemning Farmers' Irrigation agricultural water for its future urban growth. How the courts decide in this case will have the most serious implications for agricultural production anywhere in the state. If a municipal water district can find unappropriated water, it files for a conditional use right, implying its intent to use the water in the future. That right is junior to those of present users and can be used only by impounding water during the early spring runoff season (when agriculture does not need it) to store for later use.

In-state allocation is sufficiently complex but Colorado water flows out of state as well. River basin compacts among Colorado and downstream states and Mexico allocate the total annual flow along the entire length of any river. On the Yampa River alone, by compact at least 500,000 AF/Y must flow past the Maybell gauging station annually on its way to downstream users—users protected by similar stations on rivers all over the basin. As Colorado uses more of its "surplus" water for energy production, urban growth, and recreational development, interstate and international conflict will increase in the same proportions.

Enter the federal reservation doctrine into this already overcrowded resource-scarce allocation system. Many of the Colorado headwaters are on federal lands. The federal government claims it is not subject to state water laws and that its water right decree for all federal lands should date from the nineteenth century, when they were first reserved. This would give it prior claim to all waters originating and flowing through federal land—a right senior to and preemptive of the rights of all present users.

The federal position was expressed this month by Walter Kiechel, Jr., deputy assistant U.S. attorney general: "The water upon, within and adjacent to the public domain lands is as much a natural resource pertaining thereto as is the timber thereon and the minerals therein. The right to use that water was and is one of the whole bundle of rights acquired by the United States when it acquired ownership of the lands. The reserved right is not lost by any period of non-use, it always being superior to the rights on the same stream system which went into effect after the date of the creation of the reservation." (*BDC*, 1975)

The anticipation of a federal raid on Colorado water, with current users having to defend rights against federal claims, impels those users to press with even greater vigor and determination to appropriate and use as much water as quickly as possible to strengthen their rights. This is certainly one motive behind the impoundment policy of the CRWCD. The federal government generates additional water-related disputes through legislation like the Wild and Scenic Rivers Act (twelve Colorado rivers are to be thus designated) and the creation of wilderness areas, the consequences of which impinge on timber harvesting, water diversion, ski development, and other economic uses of public lands.

Impoundment and Diversion. Damming streams and storing water has both positive and negative impacts. First, it creates water rights by increasing the water available each year by as much as the capacity of the reservoir. In addition to creating new rights, stored water can be used throughout the year for industry, municipal use, and recreation, not just during the runoff season, and therefore protects users against bad years. Water storage is particularly necessary for energy industries needing a year-round supply. Flood control is an additional potential benefit.

There are considerable negative impacts as well. Dams, particularly of the earthen type used frequently on the Western Slope, can be a hazard to downstream areas, as recently illustrated by the Teton Dam failure. While impoundment creates usable water, the net water gain is less than reservoir capacity since impoundment permits evaporation over a large surface area that does not occur as a waterway flows naturally.

The impact of impoundment on wildlife can be considerable

since valleys above dams are flooded and downstream flow is altered. Evening out that flow may be beneficial for storage consumers but may eliminate fish downstream. The above-dam flooding may impact human populations as well. The town of Dillon was inundated by the Dillon Reservoir. The projected Narrows Dam, which will displace 850 persons in northeastern Colorado, has become one of the state's sharpest environmental disputes.

Aesthetic change is another possible consequence of impoundment. Whether the change causes aesthetic enhancement or deterioration in a valley is often a controversial issue. The confrontation of the Crystal Valley Environmental Protection Association (CVEPA) with the CRWCD was fueled in large part by the CVEPA conviction that a dam would adversely affect the valley's natural beauty. Diversion structures carrying the water over (or under) the Continental Divide—tunnels, pumping stations, sluiceways—can also have an impact on social and natural environments.

Each positive and negative impact draws additional combatants into the water conflict arena. They range from the individual consumer family and wildlife species to Mexico and the federal government.

Actors and Dyads in Water Conflict. Let us introduce the concept of the conflict dyad—a concept not universally applicable since many water disputes involve more than two parties. In allocation, impoundment, and diversion disputes state may confront state. The Colorado Water Conservation Board (CWCB), whose primary responsibility is to protect and pursue the water interests of the state of Colorado, may confront its counterparts in any other state using water originating in Colorado. In addition, the CWCB attempts to keep peace among major in-state users, most of whom are represented in the Colorado Water Congress.

Watershed may conflict with watershed, as in Western Slope versus Eastern Slope over transmountain diversion. The most likely disputants in a watershed conflict dyad are the CRWCD and the Denver Water Board (DWB). While the CRWCD was formed to "protect and put to beneficial use the water of the

Colorado River and its tributaries to which the state is entitled under compacts," its primary concern is the advocacy of Western Slope water interests. It is the primary water policy body for the upper Colorado River basin, with a board of fifteen directors representing fifteen districts in fifteen Western Slope counties.

Since the CRWDC is a basin-specific agency as well as the major Western watershed advocate, it engages in basin versus basin disputes as well. It might, for example, conflict with Arkansas River basin interests over a transmountain diversion such as the Frying Pan–Arkansas Project that directly affects the Roaring Fork Valley.

Wherever impoundment is at issue, the U.S. Bureau of Reclamation (BuRec) may be a party to the dispute since it finances and builds most of the dams in the state. We should note here that one of the interests of bureaucratic organizations involved in water disputes has to be the maintenance and expansion of their own influence. The CRWCD exists to keep as much Colorado River water in-state as possible, and the more successful it is, the more influential it becomes. There is nothing sinister about this underlying motive: it is in the nature of bureaucratic institutions.

Water rights conflict may pit one municipal water board against another. Thus are the Denver and Colorado Springs water authorities competing for Eagle River water in the Iron Mountain impoundment case. To win, the latter will ally itself with CRWCD. Such an alliance insures that part of the disputed water will go to Western Slope users whereas the Denver Water Board would divert the entire amount. In another dispute, like the Twin Forks diversion involving Roaring Fork water, the CRWCD and Colorado Springs, allies in the Iron Mountain dispute, may oppose one another.

A water conflict dyad may be comprised of a river basin authority and residents of an impacted valley. The CRWCD-CVEPA dispute in the Crystal Valley is a case in point. CVEPA refused to let "its" water be impounded and diverted elsewhere in the basin. In another dispute, CRWCD may be fighting for CVEPA against diversion of Crystal River water to Pueblo. Other water conflict levels and dyadic possibilities include:

individual against individual at the local level; state versus federal interests; and nation-state in conflict with nation-state as with the United States versus Mexico and Canada. A water conflict dyad can be intra- or cross-level and can be transformed into multiparty combinations as the dispute progresses.

The outcome of a dispute at any one level involving any particular dyad may influence conflict at any other level, and not necessarily as logic might lead one to expect. By way of illustration, the Twin Forks diversion project places Pitkin County on the Roaring Fork in opposition to Eastern Slope cities like Colorado Springs. The former wishes to keep water on the Western Slope, the latter to divert it across the Continental Divide for Front Range use. Water diverted from the headwaters of the Roaring Fork is quite pure, and its withdrawal augments the salinity of the Colorado, which increases as the river flows toward Mexico. Understandably, Mexico might prefer to have Pitkin County triumph, that is, until it learns that if the water remains on the Western Slope, it will be used for irrigation, power generation, and urban consumption and then returned to the river contributing possibly more salts than diversion creates by withdrawal. Would Mexico prefer salinity by omission or commission? That would be a topic for discussion in international negotiations that are certain to heat up with time—heat related to whether Pitkin or Colorado Springs is victorious. Such future lower-level outcomes may be influenced as well by international decisions on salinity and volume. The systemic nature of the "water culture" becomes ever more apparent as one realizes that the destiny of the small rancher and individual elk in the Roaring Fork Valley is inextricably linked to that of the Mexican peasant several thousand miles downstream through a despairingly complex conflict management process.

A common thread running through these conflict combinations is that of proprietary interest. At each level, the concept of "our water" has a different point of reference. When Eastern Slopers speak of it, the primary referent seems to be the state of Colorado or the municipal water board. A Western Slope resident more often means by "our water" Western Slope water. River valley residents generally mean by the term the water in their river. There does seem to be a sort of aquitorial imperative operating that has each community or region responding to threat to what it perceives as its water. In fact, aquitoriality seems stronger than territoriality in these parts. Like the land, a volume of water can only support so many users at a certain level of well-being—but without land, water is still valuable; without water, land generally is not.

Supply Augmentation. One method of reducing conflict over a finite resource is to expand the supply. Two approaches, weather modification and water mining, are already increasing Colorado's water supply. Unfortunately, each will create new conflicts to replace those they might eliminate. BuRec plans large-scale cloud seeding in its Winter Aerographic Snowpack Augmentation (WOSA) program in the Colorado Rockies (Schneider and Mesirow, 1976:223). Although WOSA may increase the annual snowpack and subsequent water supply, its unintended consequences will certainly disturb environmental activists, because of its serious implications for the alpine ecosystems; Western Slope stockmen, for its effect on stock raising; and the state highway department, because of its consequences for avalanche and winter driving hazards. The winter sports industry might be ambivalent—there will be more snow for earlier and later skiing but more difficulty in getting skiers to it if driving and flying conditions deteriorate.

Water augmentation can occur below ground as well. Large deposits of trapped water or ground water basins have been discovered, particularly under Colorado's eastern plains. They are underlying aquifers, immobile and nonrenewable. They can be mined just as any other subterranean resource. Who is entitled to them? Do those entitled to them have mineral or water rights? Renewable water is also mined by deep well drilling. Mining such groundwater, however, may deplete the surface water, bringing well users into conflict with surface water users and requiring an additional set of conflict-managing regulations.

Water Pollution. In this section we have concentrated on water quantity as a source of environmental conflict. As pressure to use water increases, so will pressure to have it returned to the water cycle in usable condition. As the 1983 Environmental Protection Agency water quality deadline approaches, the region will experience increased intercity conflict as pollution from upstream towns prohibits downstream towns from achieving the set standard. Here, technological innovation may reduce conflict, as the natural filtration method of tertiary sewage treatment becomes more common.

Water Conflict in the Roaring Fork Basin. The Roaring Fork and its tributary valleys have their share of the water conflict in Colorado. Pitkin County is fighting to keep what water it still has, central as it is to the valley's tourism and agriculture. Three contemporary disputes will suggest the range of possibilities for water conflict management.

West Divide–Placita. The CRWCD proposed to divert water from the headwaters of the Crystal River to another part of the basin either by constructing a dam at Placita or by some other method. The project generated lively opposition among valley residents, many of whom organized the Crystal Valley Environmental Protection Association. Personalization and polarization of the dispute occurred, the leaders of both organizations vilified one another, and CVEPA threatened a referendum to provide elected rather than appointed water district representatives. Finally, CRWCD withdrew its diversion proposal in favor of another plan not affecting the Crystal. The dispute has been characterized by a maximum of miscommunication, interpersonal hostility, rigidity of positions, and mirror images (i.e., each party sees the other reflecting the opposite of his own virtues and good intentions). The conflict also illustrated perfectly the aquitorial principle referred to earlier. The leaders of both CVEPA and CRWCD were convinced they were acting in the best interests of "our water"— and they were, but within different geographical parameters. The leaders of CVEPA were also apparently unaware of initial flexibility in CRWCD commitment to a headwaters diversion—a flexibility that eroded as positions hardened with time and mutual animosity.

Frying Pan–Arkansas–Twin Forks. The Frying Pan–Arkansas involves a massive diversion of water from the Frying Pan

River, a tributary of the Roaring Fork, eastward across the Continental Divide into the Arkansas River. The program is not yet completed, and its Twin Forks project will divert still more valley water to the Eastern Slope. Pitkin County, in its suit to block the diversion, argues that current diversion is agricultural and seasonal and that new diversion is for year-round municipal use. It would reduce stream flow in the valley and would stimulate Front Range urbanization. Since the Roaring Fork is already over-appropriated, further diversion would increase the probability that the stream would dry up in dry years and adversely affect fish and wildlife, and Roaring Fork tourism.

Salvation Ditch. The Roaring Fork, according to water law, has no minimum stream flow protection. The county could insure minimum flow by (1) purchasing senior rights from other users (it cannot compete, however, with Denver's $5,000 per acre-foot capability); (2) having the water law changed—though the eastern-oriented legislature is not likely to oblige; or (3) arranging a trade-off with water rights holders not using all of their entitlement. One possibility within the third approach is the following: the Salvation Ditch Company (even the name implies the importance of water) uses only 40 percent of its entitled water and has an antiquated and inefficient water distribution system. Pitkin County could build them a good system in exchange for their unused water, thus insuring minimum stream flow. This eminently sensible solution founders, unfortunately, on the hostility and mistrust currently directed at the antigrowth county administration. Major stockholders in Salvation Ditch include the Woody Creek landowners who are very hostile to current growth control policies. No trade-off is possible in such a climate.

Environmental Peacemaking Skills

Colorado may present some of the more spectacular problems in environmental conflict management, but they are not unlike environmental disputes in other parts of the nation. Regulation of conflicts like these will become more and more urgent as industrial and development pressures on natural environments grow and social environments become increasingly influenced by crowding and pollution. Conflict regulation skills must focus on both hot-response dispute settlement and more effective citizen participation in planning. Environmental dispute settlement should facilitate sound environmental policymaking. Hot-response intervention by outside conciliators is often necessary, but perhaps more important is the design of organizational structures and procedures that bring advocacy roles together in the decisional process—to make certain that the confrontation of interests inevitable in any environmental policy decision takes place in creative ways.

We can anticipate the fields of resource, environmental, and international conflict regulation overlapping more and more with time. Resource allocation and environmental degradation are the international conflict foci of the near future. We had better be prepared to respond to them.

7. Postscript

Keeping conflict relatively nonviolent and within reasonable bounds is of paramount concern in social relations. So too is the invention of new methods of facilitating peaceful change that maximize social justice. In this book, I have explored a set of multiple perspectives on conflict and its regulation. Conflict shows itself to the careful observer as a multifaceted process. Each aspect of it gives us clues to the method of regulation to be used: (1) its degree of symmetry; (2) the level at which it occurs, from interpersonal to international; (3) the mixture of violent and nonviolent techniques used; (4) the relative importance of interests, values, and affective factors in the conflict; and so forth.

I have furthermore urged teachers and students of conflict regulation to combine intellectual and experiential learning modes, study and practice, in developing their skills. Each without the other is insufficient. Readers have had to stretch the conventional concept of conflict management to include the conflict regulation modes I have discussed that rest on empowerment and nonviolent action. I would maintain, however, that the development of nonviolent action and empowerment strategies as means of waging conflict are as essential to peacemaking as the more conventional means of mediation and judicial settlement.

Applying Knowledge

I have argued in this book for the application of what we

already know to the management of real world conflict. There
are now available conflict regulation models that we should
be clarifying, refining, and testing out with practitioners in
actual conflict situations. As conflict forecasting improves, we
should be developing the peacemaking tools for the most likely
categories of future conflict, and training a corps of social
scientists, teachers, mediators, and citizen activists to use these
tools.

Conflicts concerning the oceans and seabed, environmental
pollution, resource utilization, and political, racial, and cultural self-determination will require thousands of skilled
intervenors. Conflict over resource control will increasingly
separate the rich from the poor nations, and the rich from the
poor within nations. There will continue to be ideological
or dissensual conflict in which there is no agreement on goals
and objectives. The variety of conflict requires an equally
diverse set of conflict regulation techniques and persons skilled
in their use.

Peace and conflict research is still far from its maturity. In
fact, one could thus describe the whole of social science. As
Kuhn (1962) observes, the earlier stages of scientific development witness an extraordinary degree of competition among
diverse paradigms and explanatory views. Over time, this disagreement gives way to the acceptance of certain paradigms
and the discarding of others. Even after basic consensus is
reached, there may be innovative breaks or revolutions that
involve what Kuhn calls "shifts of vision" that send the
discipline off in entirely new directions as a particular world
view long dominant in the discipline is questioned. In international studies, for example, the nation-state paradigm is
currently being challenged by the global system model. Research and teaching emphases within a discipline may change
accordingly. As we move toward a global systemic view in
international studies, for example, corollary perspectives like
conflict regulation and transnational relations may increase in
currency because they deal directly with problems that war
and violent conflict pose for the survival of the world as a
system.

A Final Word on Nonviolent Action

At first glance, it would seem that university students would find training in negotiation and third-party intervention more useful than training in the type of nonviolent action I discussed in the later chapters of this book. This may not be the case. A concentration of governmental power such as has occurred in the United States and elsewhere in the past decade may well continue and require in the future massive nonviolent resistance to unwise or repressive policies. One could argue convincingly that had students in the 1960s been trained in both negotiation and nonviolent resistance, the changes sought by student protesters could have been achieved with less rancor and bloodshed.

The way in which university students around the world are currently building a movement of generally peaceful protest against the proliferation of nuclear weapons and nuclear power suggests that nonviolent action is becoming institutionalized as a conflict management technique. Walker (1973) estimates that 25,000 persons in the United States alone were trained in nonviolent direct action in the period 1967-72. With the nonviolent campaigns of more recent years, that number has likely doubled.

In this book I have included methods of nonviolent protest as useful skills in conflict regulation, skills of political action with which every member of a democratic society should be familiar. The time may not be too far off when citizen participation in policymaking through nonviolent direct action will be as acceptable, if not as common, as voting and lobbying.

List of Organizations Engaged in Conflict Regulation Training, Education, and Research

American Arbitration
  Association
Robert Coulson, President
140 West 51st Street
New York, New York 10020

American Friends Service
  Committee
Peace Education Division
Community Relations Division
International Division
1501 Cherry Street
Philadelphia, Pennsylvania
  19102

Board of Church and Society
Reverend John Adams
United Methodist Church
Washington, D.C.

Center for Conflict Resolution
731 State Street
Madison, Wisconsin 53703

Community Relations Service
Dispute Settlement Section
Department of Justice
Washington, D.C.

Environmental Mediation
  Program

Gerald Cormick, Director
University of Washington
Seattle, Washington

Friends Peace Committee
Stephanie Judson, Coordinator
Nonviolence and Children
  Program
1515 Cherry Street
Philadelphia, Pennsylvania
  19102

Hostage Negotiating Team
Frank Bowles
New York City Police
  Department
New York, New York

Institute for Mediation and
  Conflict Resolution
George Nicolau, Vice President
49 East 68th Street
New York, New York 10021

International Peace Academy
Indar Jit Rikhye, Chairman
777 United Nations Plaza
New York, New York 10017

National Center for Dispute
  Settlement of the American

Arbitration Association
Alfred E. Cowles, Director
1212 16th Street, N.W.
Washington, D.C. 20036

Program in Conflict, Resources
and the Environment
Paul Wehr, Department of
Sociology
University of Colorado
Boulder, Colorado 80309

Rocky Mountain Center on
Environment
1115 Grant Street
Denver, Colorado

Shanti Sena (Peace Brigade)
Narayan Desai, Director
Sarva Seva Sangh Prakashan
Rajghat
Varanasi, India

Southern Christian Leadership
Conference
334 Auburn Avenue, N.E.
Atlanta, Georgia 30303

Training/Action Affinity
Group
Movement for a New Society
4819 Springfield Avenue
Philadelphia, Pennsylvania
19142

United Nations Institute for
Training and Research
(UNITAR)
801 United Nations Plaza
New York, New York 10017

Urban Center
James Laue, Director
University of Missouri
St. Louis, Missouri

North American Academic Centers for Conflict Regulation Training, Education, and Research

Teaching, Research, and Training Programs

Alternative Futures Program, University of Hawaii

Associated Mennonite Biblical Seminaries, Elkhart, Indiana

Beloit College, Cullister Center for International Studies, Beloit, Wisconsin

Bethel College, Peace Studies, North Newton, Kansas

Center for Conflict Resolution, University of Wisconsin, Madison

Center for International Studies, Massachusetts Institute of Technology

Center for International Studies, University of Minnesota

Center for Peace Studies, University of Akron

Center for Peace Studies, Georgetown University

Center for Peaceful Change, Kent State University

Center for Teaching about Peace and War, Wayne State University

Center for World Order Studies, University of Iowa

Center of International Studies, Princeton University

Conflict and Peace Studies Program, University of Colorado

Conflict and Peace Studies Program, Harvard University

Conrad Grebel College, Peace Studies, University of Waterloo, Canada

Department of History, Wittenberg University, Springfield, Ohio

Global Survival Studies, University of Massachusetts

Goshen College, Goshen, Indiana

Graduate School Committee on Conflict Studies, University of Washington

Graduate School of International Studies, University of Denver

Gustavus Adolphus College, St. Peter, Minnesota

Honors and Experimental Programs, College of William and Mary

Institute for Education in Peace and Justice, St. Louis

International Peace Academy, New York City
Mankato State College, Peace Studies Program, Mankato, Minnesota
Nonviolence Studies Program, Syracuse University
OSU Peace Education Resource Group, Oregon State University
Pacem in Terris Institute, Manhattan College
Peace and Conflict Studies Program, University of Pittsburgh
Peace Science Curriculum Council, William Patterson College of
    New Jersey
Peace Studies Committee, University of Missouri
Peace Studies Institute, University of Dayton
Peace Studies Institute, Manchester College
Peace Studies Program, Colgate University
Peace Studies Program, Earlham College
Program for the Study of Peace and War, Boston College
Program in Nonviolence, University of Notre Dame
Program of Studies in Peace and Human Development, St. Joseph's
    College
Program on Peace Studies, Cornell University
School of International Affairs, Carleton University, Canada
School of International Service, The American University
Studies in International Conflict and Integration, Stanford Uni-
    versity
Studies of Conflict and Peace Program, University of North Carolina
War and Peace Studies Program, Richmond College
World Issues Program, School of International Training, Brattle-
    boro, Vermont
World Order Program, University of Texas

Research Centers

Bureau of Social Science Research, Washington, D.C.
Canadian Peace Research Institute, Oakville, Ontario
Computer Institute for Social Science Research, University of
    Michigan
Institute for Policy Studies, Washington, D.C.
Institute of Behavioral Science, University of Colorado
Mershon Center, Ohio State University
Peace Research Laboratory, St. Louis, Missouri
Rule of Law Research Center, Duke University
World Data Analysis Program, Yale University

APPENDIX C:
Family Past–Imaging Exercise

War between nations and smaller social units, and structural violence issuing from exploitation of one group or class by another, have been central characteristics of human society for millenia. Tracing your geneology back two (grandparents), three, or four generations, select a branch of your forebears, locate it geographically, culturally, socially, and occupationally in its time. If migration is involved, indicate it. Write a four-page, double-spaced scenario of the ways in which the wars, civil strife, and structural violence of that period and region might have affected your family, positively or negatively. You should not invent conflict and violence. Some periods were relatively peaceful (e.g., Europe between the Napoleonic and Franco-Prussian wars). However, do not forget the processes and effects of any structural violence of the period as you image.

Research Required

1. Tracing your family history back several generations, to include, where possible (a) oral history gained from key members (particularly elderly members) whose knowledge might reach back two or three generations; and (b) family historical documents, memorabilia, and the like.
2. Library research on the particular historical period and geographical area concerned. Special interest in (a) social, political, and economic structures that existed and your family's position in same; and (b) collective violence events such as wars, riots, revolutionary activity, and government repression.
3. Class Discussion: in plenary and in small groups students may share insights gained through the exercise, as well as particularly significant events in their respective family histories.

Objectives

1. Skills development in personal history research
2. Skills development in conceptualizing the past-present relationship
3. Knowledge of conflict and violence characteristic of a particular geographical region in a particular historical period
4. Awareness of the cumulative impact of conflict and violence on one's personal life and of the existence of the past and its impact on our present and future states

Useful Sources

Darlington, C. D., *The Evolution of Man and Society*
Garland Library of War and Peace
Glass and Eversley, *Population in History*
Mumford, Lewis, *The City in History*
Russett, Bruce, *World Handbook of Political and Social Indicators*
Toynbee, Arnold, *A Study of History*
Wright, Quincy, *A Study of War*

Conflict Waging and Regulation Styles Exercise

Most of us are rather unaware of how we deal with conflict and regulate it in the various settings within which we operate (e.g., family, community, university).

1. What are your own styles of conflicting and regulating conflict?
2. How did you develop them? Are they learned or do they have more to do with incidental variables such as mood of the moment or your opponent's style?
3. Are you consistent in them or do they vary from situation to situation?
4. What determinants are there of your styles (e.g., body chemistry, personality type, conditions of stress, parental modeling, mass media impact)?
5. How many response styles to conflict situations (e.g., avoidance, confrontation, displacement, conciliatory, subservient) can you identify among friends and acquaintances?

APPENDIX E:
Personal Conflict Impact Essay

Produce a five-page essay in which you discuss the role of conflict and conflict regulation in your personal life experience. Some questions you will be responding to are:

1. With whom have you been most in conflict at various points in your life?
2. Over what issues?
3. How did conflictful behavior affect you?
4. How do members of your family and your family as a group deal with conflict?
5. What devices or skills have you developed to regulate and resolve conflict?
6. Have you had direct, personal exposure to violence and in what forms?
7. How do you view conflict? As unhealthy? Natural?

Objective of Assignment

To help you reflect on the influence of the often unconscious process of conflict and conflict resolution in your own life experience.

Parker High School Scenario

This is an exercise in preparing for multilateral negotiations in a crisis situation. The parties are: (a) the all-white student council, (b) the newly formed black student union, and (c) the faculty. If negotiations occur, the principal will be played by an NCDS/AAA instructor who will serve as convenor-conciliator.

The primary objective of this simulation is *not* to enter into collective negotiations and to arrive at an accommodation, but to *prepare* for multilateral joint negotiations. Emphasis will be placed upon internal team bargaining; identification and priority ranking of issues; development of primary, secondary, subsequent, last offer, and fall back positions; documentation of case presentation; anticipation of other parties' positions.

Parker High School is an urban school recently affected by a city-wide school desegregation federal court order. Current student population totals 823: 530 white students, 293 black students. September was a fairly normal month although several minor fights occurred between black and white students. Most of these incidents occurred in the corridors during class passing periods.

Two weeks ago the all-white faculty convinced the school's principal to implement a comprehensive "Accumulative Demerit Discipline Code" and to reduce class passing time from five minutes to three minutes. The new code contains the following provisions:

Fighting	10 demerits	
Tardiness to School	5	,,
Loitering	5	,,
Failure to Identify	5	,,
Tardiness to Class	3	,,
Running in Corridors	3	,,

Defiance of Faculty	3 demerits
Minor Misbehavior	3 "
Smoking	3 "
Swearing	8 "
Eating in Class	2 "
Silent Impudence	1 "

When a faculty member believes a student has violated a rule, she/he simply completes and submits a form to the Central Office, usually without the student's knowledge. Any student who accumulates 10 demerits is automatically suspended for three to twenty days, at the discretion of the principal.

Most students are opposed to this code, but black students are more vocal in their objections. Since the code was implemented sixty-three separate students have been suspended for reasons other than fighting. Fifty-four of these students are black. Most of the demerits distributed are specifically or indirectly related to tardiness to class or running in the corridors. Most students seem to be in agreement that the three-minute class passing allowance is unrealistic—particularly passing to and from the men's gym and locker rooms located in an adjacent building. The principal and most of the faculty maintain the three-minute passing time is ample and is necessary if racial incidents between students are to be reduced and controlled. Some faculty members, however, agree with students who claim the code has increased student tensions and that the school is ready to "blow."

The twelve-member student council, elected last June by the previous all-white student body, has planned to discuss the code, but the primary purpose of planning social events has taken most of their time. Plans for the Harvest Dance and Touchdown Banquet are already behind last year's schedule.

Yesterday a majority of the black students spontaneously met in the auditorium. This event was provoked when it was rumored that the students waiting on the school steps, out of the rain, for their buses were going to each receive appropriate demerits for loitering, defiance, minor misbehavior, silent impudence, and in some cases for smoking and swearing. These students hurriedly formed a black student union and elected a six-member Executive Board that demanded to meet with the principal, who refused. The principal passed word through members of the Police Tactical Force, whom he called to the building, that (a) he would not allow separate or ethnic organizations in his school, (b) the black student union would not be recognized, (c) it had no base for broad school representation or support, and (d) had no justification for "contrived concerns."

Issue	Primary Position	Secondary Position	Last Offer Position	Fall Back
1.				
2.				
3.				

Figure 13. Sample negotiation preparation sheet.

When students arrived for school today, fifty police officers were stationed in the school while another twenty officers were assigned outside around the grounds. All students were screened through a metal detector and book bags were searched. All students are angry at police presence. At the end of the second period the white students went to the auditorium to discuss the matter while black students went to the unused cafeteria for a similar meeting. The principal said, "I've had it!" and called several faculty leaders to the library for a special meeting. Police have been ordered to maintain their positions and not to interfere unless violence occurs or until the principal orders the building cleared.

It is now 10:15 AM. Word has been given that upon orderly dismissal of school at the regular 12:15 PM time, the principal will meet with four members of the student council, four members of the black student union, and four members of the faculty senate. The parties have agreed to these conditions.

Your trainer will indicate whether you are a member of the student council, the black student union, or the faculty senate. In light of the scenario and in anticipation of the other groups' demands, develop your negotiation preparation sheet (Figure 13). Use your newly acquired skills in consensus for internal team bargaining as you identify issues, rank order their priority, develop positions and strategies, and choose a spokesperson. The NCDS/AAA instructor will provide additional information and direction as she/he deems necessary.

Sheet A: For Student Council Only

The student council is all white. Twelve members were elected last June, prior to the desegregation court order.

You do not like the court order because many of your friends are subject to forced bussing to other schools, usually into primarily black neighborhoods. "Blacks seem so different from us. You never know what they are thinking" is a prevailing attitude. Nonetheless, you see an opportunity for real student involvement in school policy decision making rather than the council being merely a social organization. This will mean some concessions to black concerns. A student smoking area is a real priority and would win wide popularity from almost all students.

You all wonder whether or not you will be replaced in another full school election for a new student council if such is called by the principal.

Remember, all black students arrive at Parker School by 7:45 AM via buses and that the cafeteria is not yet in use. White students arrive leisurely by 8:15 AM, just before the late bell.

Sheet B: For Black Student Union Only

You don't like forced bussing any better than whites do. Many of your neighborhood friends have been sent to other schools. You catch your bus about 7:00 AM and arrive at Parker at 7:45 AM—often without breakfast or a cigarette. White students arrive leisurely before 8:15 AM—just before the late bell. The cafeteria has yet to be opened due to some undisclosed reason—except for coffee/donut/smoke breaks for the faculty and administration.

You feel the whole system is discriminatory against black students. The disciplinary code and demerit system have led you to think double standards and inconsistencies by white teachers and administrators favor white students.

You want a significant "piece of the action" in a student government; adjustments and provisions allowing blacks to participate in after-school activities without transportation hassles; and black adults in the school until black teachers and administrators are hired.

Sheet C: For Faculty Senate Only

You want to teach—that's all! Teach as you always have before the court ordered bussing program. It was you and your representatives who influenced the principal to adopt the disciplinary code. But you put the blame on him—after all, it was merely a proposal that he adopted.

You realize there is no turning back to an era of "no code."

Although you won't admit it to either students or to the principal, you do realize some teachers are inconsistent, prejudicial, and/or play a "got you" numbers game with students they don't like. How can you make midcourse corrections in the code? What can you delete or add?

Don't forget the rest of the scenario. Also note that black students arrive on buses at 7:45 AM while white students casually arrive by 8:15 AM, just in time for the late bell. Note also that the cafeteria has not been opened this year for student use, but only for faculty and administrators.

Ranking Conflict Behaviors

Joan has nearly reached the end of her rope. School was cancelled and she has been irritated by her children all day. Her environmental action group (which had to meet at her house since she couldn't get a sitter) had a long and frustrating afternoon meeting.

Tom has been looking forward all day to relaxing at home and having a leisurely drink with Joan. His subordinates have been remarkably inept in carrying out an important assignment, and he has been blamed. One of his best friends at work is being fired, and now he is considering quitting his job as well. He arrives at home, looks around at the noise and disorderliness, and snaps at Joan: "With nothing else to do all day long, I can't understand how you can be such a sloppy housekeeper!"

Assume that you are Joan, and rank the following responses in order of your preference for them, marking your most preferred response as 1, etc.

_____ "Well, why don't we clean up together if it makes you so uptight?" (negotiation)

_____ "I'd be neater if you acted more like a real father and took the kids off my hands every once in a while." (issue proliferation)

_____ "Did you have a hard day at the office, dear?" (placating)

_____ (Say nothing; assume it will all blow over.) (avoidance)

_____ "I get angry when you accuse me unfairly; I've had at least as rough a day as you have. I think it's time we discussed sharing household responsibilities more." (confrontation, expression of feelings)

_____ "If that's the nicest thing you can say, I'm leaving! I'll be next door at Sharon's until you cool off." (ventilation and withdrawal)

_____ "Give me another ten minutes and it will be all cleaned up." (submission)

_____ "Timmy! Will you get off that floor and wash your filthy hands before dinner!" (displacement)

Instructor's Note: The exercise is to be done by students without their seeing the types of responses given in parentheses. The response types are then introduced as the exercise is processed. In the processing, each response is discussed in terms of conflict origins, conflict resolving potential, mental health, etc. Students explain why they ranked each response as they did and what determined their overall ranking.

Future Imaging/Role Invention Exercise

An essential part of the process of creating the future is the ability to image (1) what the future might be like given current forecasts, and (2) what we would prefer it to be like. Using relevant sources of forecasting data on environmental deterioration, peace/war prospects, technological innovation, and other dimensions of likely change, write a four page double-spaced typewritten scenario of your life in 1990, centering on imaging a conflict management role for yourself in the several webs of relationships of which you will be a part (e.g., family, occupation, citizen of some type of polity). Keep in mind that creative conflict management may or may not involve short-term resolution.

Objectives

1. Developing skills of imaging alternative future states of society and the world and acting upon the present to create the future.
2. Initiating or furthering the ability to conceive a realistic personal role for conflict management in both the present and the future.
3. Familiarizing yourself with current futures literature.

Useful Sources

Ehrlich and Ehrlich, *Population, Resources and Environment* (2nd edition)
Irades, *Social Forecasting*
Jungk and Galtung, *Mankind 2000*
Kahn and Weiner, *The Year 2000*

Kostelanetz, *Social Speculations: Visions for Our Time*
McHale, *The Future of the Future*
Polak, *Image of the Future*
Toffler, *Future Shock*

International Conflict Resolution Exercise

However one views the globe and its various present and future problems, conflict has an undeniable prominence within that problem set. Conflict resolution between nation-states should be a process that involves citizen awareness and participation as well as professional negotiation and conciliation carried on by diplomats and national policymakers. One important capacity for citizens who anticipate active involvement in international conflict resolution is the skill of transcending a purely or predominantly national perspective on interstate conflict. Each of you has received a map of the world centered about one of several regions of the world (see Figures 14 and 15). Using relevant sources of information, identify a major interstate or intergroup conflict now occurring in your assigned region. Analyze it and suggest alternative, complementary but realistic strategies for resolving it creatively (in four double-spaced typed pages). These may include direct negotiations, third-party intervention, introduction of peacekeeping forces, exchange of nationals of the states involved, nonviolent direct action, and the like.

Useful Sources

AFSC, *Search for Peace in the Middle East*
Bailey, Sidney, *Peaceful Settlement of Disputes*
Bloomfield and Leiss, *The Control of Local Conflict*
Burton, John, *Conflict and Communication*
Doob, Leonard, *Resolving Conflict in Africa*
Fisher, Roger, *International Conflict for Beginners*
Harbottle, Michael, *The Impartial Soldier*
Randle, Robert, *The Origins of Peace*
Rikhye et al., *The Thin Blue Line*

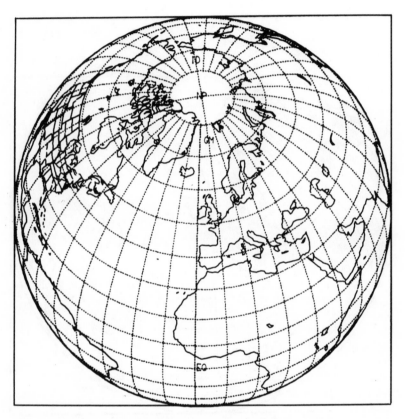

Figure 14. Dublin-centered map for international conflict resolution exercise. (Produced by Graphic Software Systems, Computing Facility, National Center for Atmospheric Research, Boulder, Colorado)

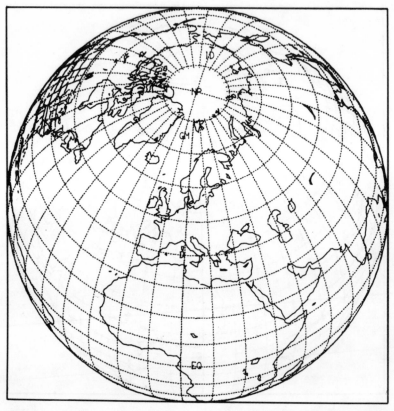

Figure 15. Moscow-centered map for international conflict resolution exercise. (Produced by Graphic Software Systems, Computing Facility, National Center for Atmospheric Research, Boulder, Colorado)

Bomb Shelter Exercise

Pretend that a nuclear bomb has been dropped and ten people are left in a bomb shelter. There is only enough food and oxygen for seven people to live until the fallout has dropped to a safe level. These seven people will have to create a new society. Your group must decide unanimously which three people must go. You have forty minutes to reach a unanimous decision on the problem. Each person in the group plays one of the ten roles.

1. A seventy-year-old minister
2. A pregnant woman
3. Her hysterical husband
4. A laboratory scientist
5. An electrician
6. A famous writer
7. A female vocalist
8. A professional athlete
9. An armed policeman
10. A high school girl

At the end, each group will report on its decision, naming the three persons who have to leave the bomb shelter and giving reasons for that decision.

Instructor's Note: Class is divided into groups of ten, each person being designated in one of the roles. Roles that do not have any sex or age specified may be designated to persons of any age or of either sex. Simulation is preceded by relevant readings and films. This exercise is most effective when linked with participants' preplay reading of Tom Stonier's "What Would It Really Be Like?" in *Breakthrough to Peace* (New York: New Directions, 1962). Other preliminary reading might include John Hersey's *Hiroshima* and Robert Jay Lifton's *Death in Life: Survivors of Hiroshima*. Also films such as *The War Game* might be used to heighten the sense of reality. Simulation is followed by a plenary discussion of values in conflict and how such conflicts are resolved.

Attica Negotiation Analysis

Following the viewing of the film *Attica* and reading the official report *Attica*, the following questions will stimulate reflection and analysis.

1. What requisites for successful negotiation were absent from the Attica context?

   a. Mutual trust

   b. Credibility of negotiating parties (e.g., ability to deliver, past experience at Auburn prison, negotiating style of major actors)

   c. Immediate setting conducive to bargaining (e.g., neutral ground, no press coverage, no deadlines)

   d. Careful timing (e.g., Oswald's precipitous concessions)

   e. Accurate self-evaluation of strength by negotiators

   f. Clearly-defined roles for major actors in conflict (e.g., negotiators, advocates, mediators, observers, communication facilitators)

   g. Accurate communication (e.g., rumor control, clear understanding of ultimatums, importance of subcultural differences in communication style and imagery, Oswald's release of statement)

   h. Negotiating mechanisms and experience (e.g., iconoclastic negotiations, systematic representation of both sides—who got left out?, rules observed by negotiators)

   i. Atmosphere of realism to minimize nonrealistic conflict and to allow achievement of the goals of the negotiating parties

2. Was the Rockefeller role important in the outcome? Why?

   a. Implementation—trust in ability and intention

b. Credibility—intervenor of great stature
c. Intervention from higher level

3. How important were symbolic acts and events in determining the failure of negotiations? (e.g., tearing up the injunction, death of Quinn, refusal of governor to go to Attica.)

Community Peacekeeping Exercise

All communities have problems that—as they become evident to community members—tend to generate conflict and reinforce divisions already present. Few communities have learned how to regulate such conflict, to strengthen the potential bonds that can work for the common good and community growth. Some sort of road map is needed to assist citizens of our towns and cities in learning community problem solving and peacemaking skills. One important assumption is that conflict can be productive of growth. If citizens know how to conflict creatively, they can in the process discover old and new bases for cooperative effort and tolerance among disparate groups in the community.

I suggest here a simple "road map" that might help communities find their way through seeming insoluble disputes. The map suggests certain questions a community might ask itself and some specific techniques it might use to regulate conflicts and solve problems as they are identified.

1. What problems are generating the conflict?

   a. Scarce resources (e.g., insufficient job opportunities for some)
   b. Insufficient information about all segments of the community
   c. Inadequate political participation of certain segments
   d. Underdeveloped political decision-making structure

One means for defining specific problems and solutions would be the creation of study teams to gather adequate data about the problems and prepare solutions requiring the cooperative action of the total community. Communities can learn from one another too.

2. What divisions aggravate these problems?

    a. Lifestyle and value differences
    b. Economic status and interests
    c. Length of presence in the community
    d. Divergent goals of groups (e.g., quiet retirement vs. dynamic growth)

A community must know where these divisions are before it can regulate them. An analysis of value and goal divergence is one possible response. This would identify both divergent and convergent or overarching values/goals—the source of conflict and the potential for conflict regulation. An essential part of this value/goal clarification process is the identification of areas of high-potential and low-potential for peacemaking. Citizens would work immediately in the high-potential sphere while agreeing to set aside the other indefinitely. One technique here might be the establishment of culture-sharing groups or sessions whereby different ethnic and social segments of a community explain and rationalize dissimilar values and behavior for one another. This can build tolerance and understanding of different cultural perspectives and lifestyles.

3. How effective is the community at communicating?

    a. In-group versus across-group communication
    b. Distortion of information in the community
    c. Establish mechanisms to facilitate information sharing

The question of who talks to whom in a community is essential for peacemaking. One goal should be to make communication as accurate and as widely shared as possible. Such community inventions as rumor control centers, analytical diagrams of the community as a network of communication channels, a community newspaper, an information exchange like a town bulletin board, and subnetworks of telephones to maximize sharing across the conflict groups are possible devices.

4. Are there "bridging" persons and institutions?

    a. Existing organizations as arenas where sharing could occur
    b. Individuals trusted by most or all groups in conflict
    c. "Outsiders" whose intervention might be useful

A community must not only identify such potential peacemakers but also must protect their bridging and catalytic roles from the polarization process that so often occurs.

5. How might the conflict environment be modified?

   a. Create visible symbols of community (e.g., community center building, library) to become centers for public social events that pair families across subgroup lines.
   b. Reduce the sense of intracommunity threat by innovations (e.g., economic cooperatives) that build on rather than eliminate existing businesses.
   c. Identify threats external to the community against which members can unite.
   d. Develop the community's capacity for empathy.
   e. Develop the community's capacity for visioning its future in relation to its members' needs and those of the "outside world."

Small-group discussions could be useful here in which techniques like background/identity sharing, future visioning through scenario exercises, and innovation brainstorming might be used. A costing analysis of community conflict might also be tried—by which groups assess the relative costs of conflict and the benefits of peacemaking for the community as a whole. Focusing the discussion on planning for the future is an effective approach.

Glossary

Arbitration   A dispute settlement technique that involves a third-party arbitrator whose judgement is accepted as the basis for the settlement.

Bargaining/Negotiation   A dispute settlement with face-to-face interaction of the antagonists, who win gains and make concessions to achieve agreement.

Behavioral violence   Violence resulting from overt conflict and societal deviance, like wars, mob violence, random street crime, and police brutality.

Civilian defense   A national defense strategy based on civilian unarmed resistance to an invading or occupying force.

Communication facilitation   A third-party intervention technique in which channels of constructive communication are opened between antagonists, distorted or inaccurate information is minimized, and possibilities for conciliation are enhanced.

Deterrence   A process by which threat and counterthreat by antagonists to do injury to each other deters both from doing so. Reciprocity and credibility are basic ingredients of the process.

Empowerment   A dispute settlement technique involving the introduction of third parties who help weaker parties to strengthen themselves sufficiently to bargain effectively with opponents and bring about changes in intolerable situations.

Escalatory Spiral   A dynamic of conflict that has each party responding to a hostile act from the other with an even more hostile one.

Interposition The placement of third-party actors between disputants or their territories to moderate or terminate their conflict.

Mediation Introduction of a third party into a dispute who acts as an intermediary and brings the conflicting parties together in bargaining or some other form of negotiation.

Negative-sum conflict A conflict in which each antagonist loses more than he gains in the conflict. The result is that both are worse off than they were before the conflict.

Nonviolent action The application of nonviolent resistance or protest techniques focused at a particular problem, injustice, or attack. Such techniques range from strikes to civil disobedience.

Positive-sum conflict A conflict in which each antagonist, through settlement, gains more than he loses. A game in which each player wins, though not necessarily in equal degrees.

Notes

Chapter 1

1. Asbjorn Eide, "Dialogue and Confrontation in Europe," *Journal of Conflict Resolution* 16, no. 4 (December 1972).

Chapter 2

1. Burton maintains, in response to this point, that his approach does not change the values or attitudes of those participating directly in controlled communication experiments, but does lead them to a point where they can entertain new options around which a settlement can be built. This openness to new options can, he feels, be shared to some degree with others in the governments involved.

Chapter 3

1. Observation noted in a taped interview (January 1974) with J. B. Kripalani, a former leader in the Gandhian movement.
2. In a taped interview, January 1974.

Chapter 4

1. Denmark (Boserup and Mack, 1975) and Sweden (Roberts, 1972) have both commissioned feasibility studies of civilian defense as a possible alternative or supplement to present defense policies.
2. From a copy of Hitler's personal communication to Wehrmacht forces at the outset of *Weserubung*. Here and elsewhere in this chapter, translations from the German and Norwegian sources are the author's.
3. The central communications importance of the "strategic

208   *Notes*

middle-level" personnel in an organization that Karl Deutsch has referred to (*Nerves of Government*, 1966 [paperback edition], p. 154) is underscored by the role of these second-level leaders. Because of their intermediary positions in the voluntary associations they had access to unequalled communicative capability. Their position was crucial vertically—they were the link between the top and the rank and file—and horizontally—where they were permitted sufficient communication to effectively organize large numbers.

4. Physicians played a major role in the development of KK and other protest groups. This seems strange in view of their conservative position in the Norwegian society and polity. Malm suggests it may have been the threat to a privileged, autonomous position by the "New Order" that elicited a stiff negative reaction. Another factor was the occupiers' early attempt to take over the hospitals—an effort that produced the Gjessing case and alienation of the medical profession to nazification.

5. Most of the information on constructing the system and how it operated was gained in personal interviews with Ole Jacob Malm, Arne Okkenhaug, Tor Schonsberg, Per Alveberg, Kare Norum, Olav Drivnes, and others deeply involved in KK activity.

6. For a more detailed account of "negative tactics" used by the Nazis in Norway, see Lyng (1948).

7. From the diary of schoolmaster Olav Drivnes, February 24, 1942.

8. *Ibid.*, March 1, 1942.

9. A total of 42,000 Norwegians had made their way to Sweden by such routes by the end of the war (Grimnes, 1969:301).

10. Information from discussions with Tor Schonsberg.

11. Information from discussions with Per Alveberg, a member of the KK press committee.

12. The best historical account of this response is Magne Skodvin's "Det Store Fremstot" in Steen, *Norges Krig*, vol. 2.

Chapter 6

1. Pets conflict immediately with wildlife in remote areas and also bring humans into conflict (e.g., stock raisers vs. condominium owners).

2. Bureau of Land Management Maps NW 3 and NW 9.

3. The region still produces large quantities of oil (22 million barrels in 1973) and natural gas (54,590,250 cf in 1973) (BLM, 1976: I-43).

4. Ski resorts are economically delicate operations. Diversification is the key to survival. Vail prospers not from its skiers but through

its real estate developments in the environs. Aspen prospers through its winter sports investments in other parts of the world. Steamboat Springs, Breckenridge, Keystone, and Crested Butte all survive because they were developed or absorbed by out-of-state conglomerates able to finance that survival from their more profitable companies.

5. Garrett Hardin (1972:122) suggests, only partly tongue-in-cheek, some methods for internalizing social and environmental costs of an economic activity: (1) that a city's sewage outfall pipe be required by law to be *upstream* from its water supply intake; (2) that the effluent from industrial smokestacks be piped into the homes of the management; (3) that governments sell "licenses to pollute." Were this principle applied in the Eagle Valley, the flue on every Vail fireplace would lead at least some of the smoke back into the appropriate living room.

Bibliography

Preface

Beitz, Charles, and A. Michael Washburn
  1974 *Creating the Future: A Guide to Living and Working for Social Change.* New York: Bantam.
Boulding, Elise, and J. Robert Passmore
  1979 *Bibliography on World Conflict and Peace,* Boulder, Colorado: Westview Press (forthcoming).
Brock, Peter
  1968 *Pacifism in the United States.* Princeton, N.J.: Princeton University Press.
        An excellent study of the growth of pacifist ideology and social movements in the United States.
Curle, Adam
  1971 *Making Peace.* New York: Barnes and Noble.
        An unusually perceptive analysis of peacemaking as a process by which oppression is recognized and eliminated by the oppressed.
Galtung, Johan
  1965 "Institutionalized Conflict Resolution." *Journal of Peace Research*, no. 4.
  1969 "Violence, Peace and Peace Research." *Journal of Peace Research*, no. 3.
Haavelsrud, M.
  1974 *Education for Peace: Reflection and Action.* Surrey, England: IPC Science and Technology Press.
Lynd, Staughton, ed.
  1966 *Nonviolence in America.* New York: Bobbs-Merrill.
Randle, Robert
  1973 *The Origins of Peace.* New York: The Free Press.

Sharp, Gene
    1973   *The Politics of Nonviolent Action.* Boston: Porter Sargent.
         The definitive book to date on the historical development
         and variety of uses of nonviolent direct action in social and
         political conflict.

Chapter 1: Conflict Analysis

Adorno, T. W., et al.
    1969   *The Authoritarian Personality.* New York: Norton.
Alger, Chadwick
    1975   "Foreign Policies of United States Publics." Columbus,
         Ohio: Mershon Center, Ohio State University. Mimeo.
Alinsky, Saul
    1971   *Rules for Radicals.* New York: Random House.
Angell, Robert
    1969   *Peace on the March.* New York: Van Nostrand–Reinhold.
         Based on research showing the development of nongovern-
         mental exchange of ideas, personnel, and institutions across
         national boundaries.
Ardrey, Robert
    1966   *The Territorial Imperative.* New York: Dell.
Baran, P., and P. Sweezy
    1968   *Monopoly Capital: An Essay on the American Economic
         and Social Order.* New York: Monthly Review Press.
         A Marxist analysis of the structure of the United States
         economy and its role in the global economy.
Bernard, Jessie
    1957   "The Sociological Study of Conflict," *The Nature of Con-
         flict,* 33-117. Paris: International Sociological Association,
         UNESCO.
Bondurant, Joan
    1965   *Conquest of Violence.* Berkeley: University of California
         Press.
         The most incisive analysis of Gandhi as political theorist
         and tactician I have read. Her description of the satyagraha
         campaign is especially helpful.
Bonoma, Thomas, and Thomas Milburn, eds.
    1977   "Social Conflict." Special issue, *Journal of Social Issues*
         33, no. 1.
Boulding, Elise
    1972   "The Child as Shaper of the Future." *Peace and Change* 1,
         no. 1 (Fall):11-17.

An interesting analysis of the socialization process in American society and the types of perspectives on the world, attitudes towards relations with others, and self-concepts this process produces in children. The paper suggests to society's failure to integrate "emotional and spiritual—intuitive capacities with cognitive learning" inhibits learning and stunts the capacity for imagining alternatives.

Boulding, Kenneth
  1962   *Conflict and Defense.* New York: Harper & Row.
         An economist's view of the processes of conflict, competition, and cooperation in society. One of the basic works in the development of modern theory of conflict and conflict regulation.

Bourdieu, Pierre
  1962   *The Algerians.* Boston: Beacon Press.
         An ethnologist describes the social structures and collective behavior in several traditional societies in Algeria. Particularly good on the impact of modernization—cultural diffusion—on these societies.

Burgess, Guy
  1973   "The Zandar Crisis Simulation." Available from Guy Burgess, Department of Sociology, University of Colorado, Boulder, Colorado.
         One of the best international conflict simulations I have used.

Burton, John
  1969   *Conflict and Communication.* New York: Oxford University Press.
         Burton presents the process of controlled communication as one technique of intervening in disputes to achieve settlement. The book details an experiment carried out in London with representatives of two warring states: Indonesia and Malaysia. A fine example of both applied and experimental social science.

  1972   *World Society.* London: Cambridge University Press.

Coleman, James S.
  1957   *Community Conflict.* New York: Free Press.
         A classic in conflict theory literature, though too brief and in need of revision. This book sets the lines of development for microanalysis of conflict and suggests the importance of understanding it as a dynamic and controllable social process.

Coser, Lewis
   1956   *The Functions of Social Conflict.* New York: Free Press.
          Presents revised propositions based on the theory of Georg
          Simmel that suggest how conflict can be functional in social
          and international relations.
Curle, Adam
   1971   *Making Peace.* New York: Barnes and Noble.
Dahrendorf, Ralf
   1958   "Toward a Theory of Social Conflict." *Journal of Conflict
          Resolution* 11, no. 2.
   1959   *Class and Class Conflict in Industrial Society.* Palo Alto,
          California: Stanford University Press.
          Lays out a theory of social conflict rooted in interest groups
          and their struggle for access to authority in society. He uses
          both coercion/conflict and integration theories.
Dolci, Danilo
   1970   *Report from Palermo.* New York: Viking.
Dollard, John, et al.
   1939   *Frustration and Aggression.* New Haven: Yale University
          Press.
Dougall, Lucy
   1973   *War-Peace Film Guide.* World Without War Publications,
          7245 South Merrill Avenue, Chicago, Illinois 60649.
          An excellent guide to visual media appropriate for use in
          courses dealing with war and peace, and violence problems.
Eckhardt, William
   1972   *Compassion: Toward a Science of Value.* Oakville, Ontario:
          CPRI Press.
Eide, Asbjorn
   1972   "Dialogue and Confrontation in Europe." *Journal of Con-
          flict Resolution* 16, no. 4 (December).
Falk, R., and S. Mendlovitz
   1966   *The Strategy of World Order.* New York: Institute for World
          Order.
          This book lays out the World Order Studies approach and
          leads toward a view of peace development based on the
          cooperative solution of the global problems of overpopula-
          tion, war, poverty, ecological imbalance, and injustice.
Freire, Paulo
   1971   *Pedagogy of the Oppressed.* New York: Seabury.
Freud, Sigmund (John Rickman, ed.)
   1953   *Civilization, War and Death.* New York: Hillary-
          Humanities.

Galtung, Johan
  1969 "Violence, Peace and Peace Research." *Journal of Peace Research,* no. 3.
  1970 "Feudal Systems, Structural Violence and the Structural Theory of Revolutions." *Proceedings of the IPRA Third Conference.* Assen, Netherlands: Van Gorcum.
  1975 "Non-Territorial Actors and the Problem of Peace." *On the Creation of a Just World Order,* S. Mendlovitz, ed. New York: Free Press.

Gamson, William
  1972 *SIMSOC.* New York: Free Press.
      A valuable simulation of social relations, power, authority, and social exchange. A good tool for use in preparing students for the study of conflict and conflict regulation.
  1975 *The Strategy of Social Protest.* Homewood, Ill.: Dorsey Press.
      An interesting analysis of the careers of fifty-three challenge groups that, since 1800, have succeeded or failed in permanently impacting the nature and direction of American society, with explanations of why they did so.

Gorney, Roderic
  1973 *The Human Agenda.* New York: Bantam.

Guetzkow, Harold, et al.
  1963 *Simulation in International Relations.* Englewood Cliffs, N.J.: Prentice-Hall.
      A comprehensive treatment of the use of simulation and gaming in the teaching of international relations.

Gurr, T., and H. Graham
  1970 *The History of Violence in America.* New York: Bantam.
      The official report of the National Commission on the Causes and Prevention of Violence. The best analysis yet of violence as a major determinant and consequence of United States national development.

Halberstam, David
  1972 *The Best and the Brightest.* New York: Random House.
      Halberstam, a most astute observer of the U.S. involvement in the Vietnam war, examines the backgrounds, motives, perceptions, and misperceptions of the prime makers of U.S. Southeast Asia policy. McGeorge Bundy and Robert McNamara are two of the major actors in this study.

Hanson, D. J.
  1968 "The Idea of Conflict in Western Thought." *International Review of History and Political Science,* no. 5.

Heirich, Max
    1971   *The Spiral of Conflict: Berkeley 1964.* New York: Columbia
           University Press.
           A sociological analysis of the confrontation of the Free
           Speech Movement with university officials. An interesting
           use of the concept of spiraling and an excellent study of a
           case of missed opportunities for conflict regulation.
Himes, Joseph
    1966   "The Functions of Racial Conflict." *Social Forces* 45.
International Peace Research Association
    1970   *Proceedings of the IPRA Third Conference.* Assen, Nether-
           lands: Van Gorcum.
Johnson, Chalmers
    1966   *Revolutionary Change.* Boston: Little, Brown and Co.
           Characterizes political revolution as a response to dis-
           equilibrium within a social system that loses legitimacy
           because conditions are out of synchronization with estab-
           lished values.
Judge, Anthony
    1972   "The World Network of Organizations." *International
           Associations,* no. 1.
Kelman, Herbert, ed.
    1965   *International Behavior: A Social Psychological Analysis.*
           New York: Holt, Rinehart and Winston.
           An excellent collection of articles by behavioral scientists
           applying behavioral concepts to problems of conflict and
           miscommunication among nation-states.
Kissinger, Henry
    1964   *World Restored: The Politics of Conservatism in a Revolu-
           tionary Age.* New York: Grossett & Dunlap.
           Gives more than a glimpse into the political orientation
           and future visions of its author. The theory contained
           therein was reflected in Kissinger's foreign policy.
Klineberg, Otto
    1964   *The Human Dimension in International Relations.* New
           York: Holt, Rinehart and Winston.
Knorr, K.
    1966   *On the Uses of Military Power in the Nuclear Age.* Prince-
           ton, N.J.: Princeton University Press.
Kolko, Gabriel
    1962   *Wealth and Power in America: An Analysis of Social Class
           and Income Distribution.* New York: Praeger Publishing.

Kriesberg, Louis
  1972 "International Nongovernmental Organizations and Trans-
       national Integration," *International Associations, no. 11.*
  1973 *The Sociology of Social Conflict.* Englewood Cliffs, N.J.:
       Prentice-Hall.
       A valuable textbook on conflict theory, dynamics, and ter-
       mination. It is the only comprehensive integrative work I
       am aware of in the field. Good foundation reading.
Laue, James, and Gerald Cormick
  1974 "The Ethics of Social Intervention: Community Crisis
       Intervention Programs." St. Louis, Mo.: Community Crisis
       Intervention Center, Washington University. Mimeo.
       This paper outlines the premises and techniques of crisis
       intervention. A major concept is that of empowerment of
       the weak conflict party through the intervention of a team,
       some of whom work at strengthening weaker parties for
       negotiation.
Leakey, Richard
  1977 *Origins.* New York: Dutton.
Lewin, Kurt
  1948 *Resolving Social Conflicts.* New York: Harper and Row.
Lorenz, Konrad
  1969 *On Aggression.* New York: Bantam.
       Lorenz posits the innate origins of fighting among humans
       by drawing close analogies between human and lower
       animal behavior.
Lynd, Staughton, ed.
  1966 *Nonviolence in America.* New York: Bobbs-Merrill.
       A good collection of essays, tracts, diary entries, and other
       literature by major figures in the development of nonviolent
       thought and action in the United States. It supports the
       proposition that nonviolence is as American as cherry pie.
Mack, R., and R. Snyder
  1957 "The Analysis of Social Conflict: Toward an Overview and
       Synthesis." *Journal of Conflict Resolution,* 1, no. 2.
Marcuse, Herbert
  1968 *Reason and Revolution.* New York: Humanities Press.
Marx, Karl
  n.d. *Capital.* New York: Modern Library.
Mendlovitz, Saul, ed.
  1975 *On the Creation of a Just World Order.* New York: Free
       Press.

A collection of very interesting essays by distinguished members of the World Order Models Project. Authors include Mazrui (Uganda), Kothari (India), Galtung (Norway), Sakomoto (Japan), Falk (USA), and Lin (China).

Milgram, Stanley
1963   "Behavioral Study of Obedience." *Journal of Abnormal and Social Psychology* 67, no. 4.

Mills, C. Wright
1959   *The Power Elite.* New York: Oxford University Press.

Montague, Ashley, ed.
1968   *Man and Aggression.* New York: Oxford University Press.
A collection of essays critical of the Lorenzian theories of the innate fighting instinct in human behavior.

Morgenthau, Hans
1967   *Politics Among Nations.* New York: Knopf.
The "bible" of international political theory. It spells out the balance of power theory, which is accepted by the majority of both scholars and foreign policymakers— though it is increasingly challenged by a changing global system and new theories to explain the change.

Myrdal, Gunnar
1962   *An American Dilemma.* Revised edition. New York: Harper & Row.
Fascinating foreign perspective on American race relations written in the 1940s. A classic analysis of not only the conflict between races but the contradiction of explicit values and actual practice with regard to racial discrimination. Given the striking lack of historical perspective among the current population of university students, this book should be required reading in many courses.

North, Robert, et al.
1963   *Content Analysis: A Handbook with Applications for the Study of International Crisis.* Evanston, Ill.: Northwestern University Press.
Probably the best work done on content analysis as a promising method of social science. A major portion of the book is devoted to research on the origins of World War I, analyzed through content analysis of documents of that period.

Nye, Joseph, and Robert Keohane
1971   *Transnational Relations and World Politics.* Cambridge,

Mass.: Harvard University Press.
The most comprehensive book to date on the development of transnational exchange and its impact on politics between nations.

Oberschall, Anthony
1973   *Social Conflict and Social Movements.* Englewood Cliffs, N.J.: Prentice-Hall.

Parsons, Talcott
1951   *The Social System.* New York: Free Press.

Rapoport, Anatol
1961   *Fights, Games and Debates.* Ann Arbor: University of Michigan Press.
A classic book on the application of game theory to the analysis and resolution of disputes.

Senghaas, Dieter
1973   "Conflict Formations in Contemporary International Society." *Journal of Peace Research,* no. 3.

Shirts, Gary
n.d.   *Starpower.* LaJolla, Calif.: Western Behavioral Institute.

Singer, J. David
1969   "The Global System and Its Sub-Systems: A Developmental View." *Linkage Politics,* J. Rosenau, ed. New York: Free Press.
1972   "The Correlates of War Project: Interim Report and Rationale." *World Politics* 24, no. 2 (January):243-270.

Smelser, Neil
1962   *Theory of Collective Behavior.* New York: Free Press.

Snyder, Richard C., et al., eds.
1962   *Foreign Policy Decision Making.* New York: Free Press.
Affords multiple perspectives on decision-making analysis, a major methodological tool in the policy sciences. Behaviorists analyze decisions through identifying various factors influencing the selection of one policy option over others.

Sorel, Georges
1967   *Reflections on Violence.* New York: Collier.

Stagner, Ross, ed.
1967   *The Dimensions of Human Conflict.* Detroit: Wayne State University Press.

Storr, Anthony
1968   *Human Aggression.* New York: Atheneum.

Tinbergen, N.
   1968   "On War and Peace in Animals and Man," *Science* 160
          (June 28).
White, Ralph K.
   1970   *Nobody Wanted War: Misperception in Vietnam and Other
          Wars.* New York: Doubleday Anchor.
          A good treatment of the irrational processes that operate
          in sending nations into war.
Wright, Quincy
   1965   *A Study of War.* Chicago: University of Chicago Press.
          A monumental application of social scientific methodology
          to analyze the incidence, causes, and consequences of war
          as a sociopolitical institution.
Young, Oran
   1969   *Politics of Force: Bargaining during International Crises.*
          Princeton, N.J.: Princeton University Press.
Zimbardo, Philip
   1969   *The Cognitive Control of Motivation: The Consequences
          of Choice and Dissonance.* Glenview, Ill.: Scott Foresman.

Chapter 2: Conflict Regulation: Models and Techniques

Adelman, Leonard, et al.
   1974   "A Case History of the Application of Social Judgment
          Theory to Policy Formulation." *Program of Research on
          Human Judgment and Social Interaction, Report No. 173.*
          Boulder, Colo.: Institute of Behavioral Science, University
          of Colorado. Mimeo.
American Friends Service Committee (AFSC)
   1970   *Search for Peace in the Middle East.* New York: Hill and
          Wang.
          An even-handed analysis of the Arab-Israeli conflict. A
          product of a Quaker conciliation and research mission to
          the Middle East. Suggests a workable strategy for peace-
          making in the area.
Bach, G., and H. Goldberg
   1974   *Creative Aggression.* New York: Doubleday.
Bach, G., and P. Wyden
   1969   *The Intimate Enemy.* New York: Morrow.
Bailey, Sidney
   1970   *Peaceful Settlement of Disputes.* New York: UNITAR.
Bain, H., N. Howard, and T. L. Saaty
   1971   "Using the Analysis of Options Technique to Analyze a

Community Conflict." *Journal of Conflict Resolution* 15, no. 2.

Balke, Walter, et al.
1973 "An Alternate Approach to Labor-Management Relations." *Administrative Science Quarterly* 18, no. 3 (September).

Bandura, Albert
1973 *Aggression: A Social Learning Analysis.* Englewood Cliffs, N.J.: Prentice-Hall.

Bard, Morton
1969 "Family Intervention Police Teams as a Community Mental Health Resource." *Journal of Criminal Law* 60, no. 2.
An imaginative training program for police dealing with intrafamily conflict in New York City.

1971 "Police Family Crisis Intervention and Conflict Management." New York: Urban Research Graduate Center of the City University of New York. Mimeo.

Bartos, Otomar
1974 *Process and Outcome of Negotiations.* New York: Columbia University Press.
Bartos, through controlled experiments in which subjects use different payoff matrices, tests the validity of two categories of negotiation models: (1) the predictive and (2) the normative. A major finding is that hard-line negotiation strategies pay off better than conciliatory ones.

Berman, Maureen, and Joseph Johnson, eds.
1977 *Unofficial Diplomats.* New York: Columbia University Press.
Studies of nongovernmental organizations involved in international peacekeeping.

Blake, R. R., H. A. Shepard, and J. S. Mouton
1964 *Managing Intergroup Conflict in Industry.* Houston: Gulf Publishing.

Blake, R. R., and J. S. Mouton
1970 "The Fifth Achievement." *Journal of Applied Behavioral Science* 6(4).

Bondurant, Joan
1965 *Conquest of Violence.* Berkeley: University of California Press.

Boulding, Elise
1974 "The Child and Nonviolent Social Change." *Handbook on Peace Education,* Christoph Wulf, ed. Oslo: International

Peace Research Association (Education Committee). Pp. 101-132.

Boulding, Elise, and Robert Kahn, eds.
  1964   *Power and Conflict in Organizations.* New York: Basic Books.

Boulding, Kenneth
  1962   *Conflict and Defense.* New York: Harper & Row.
  1968   *Beyond Economics: Essays on Society, Religion and Ethics.* Ann Arbor: University of Michigan Press.

Burton, John
  1969   *Conflict and Communication.* New York: Oxford University Press.

Butterworth, Robert, and Margaret Scranton
  1976   *Managing Interstate Conflict, 1945-74.* Pittsburgh: University Center for International Studies.

Carpenter, Susan
  1977   *A Repertoire of Peacemaking Skills,* Institute for World Order, New York, New York.

Chai, Nam-Yearl
  1974   "International Law in the Korea-Japan Conflict Management of 1965."
         Paper presented to the International Studies Association, St. Louis, Missouri. March.

Chesler, Mark
  1969   "Shared Power and Student Decision Making in Secondary Schools." University of Michigan: Educational Change Team.

Coleman, James S.
  1957   *Community Conflict.* New York: Free Press.

Cormick, Gerald, and James Laue
  1974   "Third Party Intervention in Community Disputes: A Review of the Experience to Date." St. Louis: Social Science Institute, Washington University. September. Mimeo.

Cormick, Gerald, and Jane McCarthy
  1974   "Environmental Mediation: Flood Control, Recreation and Development in the Snoqualmie River Valley." St. Louis: Social Science Institute, Washington University. December. Mimeo.

Coser, Lewis
  1956   *The Functions of Social Conflict.* New York: Free Press.

Council on Environmental Quality
  1970   *Annual Report.* Washington, D.C.: U.S. Government Printing Office.

Curle, Adam
 1971 *Making Peace.* New York: Barnes and Noble.
Dahrendorf, Ralf
 1959 *Class and Class Conflict in Industrial Society.* Stanford,
   Calif.: Stanford University Press.
Davies, Peter
 1973 *The Truth about Kent State.* New York: Farrar, Straus,
   Giroux.
   A lucid analysis of what actually happened during the Kent
   State crisis, who might have been responsible for the
   disaster, and what might be done to insure justice in the
   case. Very critical of authorities handling the crisis.
Deutsch, Morton
 1973 *The Resolution of Conflict.* New Haven: Yale University
   Press.
Desai, Narayan
 1972 *Toward a Nonviolent Revolution.* Varanasi, India: Sarva
   Seva Sangh Prakashan.
   The head of the Indian Peace Brigade (Shanti Sena) de-
   scribes the roots and operation of the organization and its
   rural and urban peacemaking/development teams throughout India.
Doob, Leonard, et al.
 1970 *Resolving Conflict in Africa: The Fermeda Workshop.* New
   Haven: Yale University Press.
   An experiment in peacemaking through group process.
   Representatives of hostile states—in this case Kenya and
   Somalia and other interested African nations—met for an
   extended period in a controlled environment to improve
   communication and move toward settlement of issues.
Doob, Leonard, and William Foltz
 1973 "The Belfast Workshop: An Application of Group Tech-
   niques to a Destructive Conflict." *Journal of Conflict
   Resolution* 17, no. 3 (September).
Douglas, Ann
 1962 *Industrial Peacemaking.* New York: Columbia University
   Press.
   A study of labor-management negotiation processes and
   outcomes.
Druckman, Daniel
 1971 *Human Factors in International Negotiations.* New York:
   Academy for Educational Development.
Dubois, Rachel, and Mew-Soong Li

1971   *Reducing Social Tension and Conflict: Through the Group Conversation Method.* New York: Association Press.
        Practical manual for both lay persons and professional group workers that shows how the unique group conversation process can be applied in diverse settings where social tension or conflict threatens or exists.

Duke, Richard
  n.d.   "Impasse." Environmental simulation exercise designed for UNESCO (Paris) sponsored conference. Ann Arbor, Mich.: University of Michigan.

Erikson, Erik
  1969   *Gandhi's Truth.* New York: Norton.
          A beautifully written psychohistory of the growth of Gandhi, his political philosophy, and his satyagraha movement. It presents Gandhi as a sociopolitical innovator and a person rather than a saint. Refreshing.

Etzioni, Amitai
  1964   "On Self-Encapsulating Conflict." *Journal of Conflict Resolution* 8, no. 3 (September).
  1967   "The Kennedy Experiment." *Western Political Quarterly* 20, pp. 361-380.

Etzioni, Amitai, and Martin Wenglinsky, eds.
  1970   *War and Its Prevention.* New York: Harper & Row.
          One of the best collections of readings on war and international conflict reduction to emerge from sociology.

Evan, W., and J. A. McDougall
  1967   "Interorganizational Conflict: A Labor-Management Bargaining Experiment." *Journal of Conflict Resolution* 6, no. 1 (December).

Falk, Richard
  1968   *Legal Order in a Violent World.* Princeton, N.J.: Princeton University Press.

Fisher, Roger
  1969   *International Conflict for Beginners.* New York: Harper & Row.
          An interesting and entertaining book by an international law professor on conflict resolution among nation states. His focus is on training national leaders to be rational and systematic about negotiation, both tacit and formal.

Fisher, Ronald
  1972   "Third-Party Consultation: A Method for the Study and Resolution of Conflict." *Journal of Conflict Resolution* 16, no. 1 (March).

Fitch, Russell, et al.
  1975 "Socioeconomic Impacts and Federal Assistance in Energy
       Development Impacted Communities in Colorado." Den-
       ver, Colorado: Committee on Socioeconomic Impacts of
       Natural Resource Development, Mountain Plains Federal
       Regional Council. May. Mimeo.
Ford Foundation
  1974 *A Time to Choose.* Cambridge, Mass.: Ballinger.
Freeman, David, JoAnne Tremaine,
and Patti Madson
  1977 "The Natural Resource Decision-Maker and the Problem
       of Analyzing Social Well-Being—Employing a Sociology of
       Conflict Approach." *Journal of Environmental Manage-
       ment* (Summer).
Frost, Joyce, and William Wilmot
  1978 *Interpersonal Conflict.* Dubuque, Ia.: William C. Brown.
Galtung, Johan
  1969 "On the Meaning of Nonviolence." *Journal of Peace Re-
       search* 3.
Gordon, Thomas
  1970 *Parent Effectiveness Training.* New York: Wyden Press.
       A manual for parents (and children) for resolving family
       conflicts and improving parent-child relations. Some very
       interesting and workable strategies for family peacemaking
       including active listening, modification of environment,
       and enlarging areas of acceptable behavior.
Guetzkow, Harold, et al.
  1963 *Simulation in International Relations.* Englewood Cliffs,
       N.J.: Prentice-Hall.
Haas, Ernst, Joseph Nye, and Robert Butterworth
  1972 *The Resolution of International Conflict.* Morristown,
       N.J.: General Learning Press.
Hammond, Kenneth
  1965 "New Directions in Research on Conflict Resolution."
       Journal of Social Issues 21, no. 3.
Hammond, Kenneth, and Leonard Adelman
  1976 "Science, Values, and Human Judgment," *Science* 194:
       389-396.
Hare, A. Paul
  1968 "Nonviolent Action From a Social-Psychological Perspec-
       tive." *Sociological Inquiry* 138, no. 1.
       Presents case studies of nonviolent action within the frame-
       work of exchange and interactionist theory.

Himes, Joseph
  1966 "The Functions of Racial Conflict." *Social Forces* 45.
Ikle, Fred
  1971 *Every War Must End.* New York: Columbia University
         Press.
         The author gives welcome attention to the means by which
         wars are concluded through negotiation, peace treaty, etc.
Institute for Social Research (ISR)
  1970 *Training Teachers for New Responses to Intergenerational
         and Interracial Conflict.* Ann Arbor: University of Michi-
         gan.
International Labor Office
  1973 *Conciliation in Industrial Disputes.* Geneva: International
         Labor Office.
International Peace Academy (IPA)
  1971 *International Peace Academy Helsinki Project.* July. New
         York: IPA.
         IPA's summer peacekeeping seminars for international
         military officers and civil servants.
Jackson, Elmore
  1952 *Meeting of Minds: A Way to Peace through Mediation.* New
         York: McGraw-Hill.
         Somewhat dated but still useful description and analysis of
         the conciliation process within the United Nations.
Jandt, Fred
  1973 *Conflict Resolution Through Communication.* New York:
         Harper & Row.
         Quite useful book of readings with one or two interesting
         simulations.
Judson, Stephanie, ed.
  1977 *A Manual on Nonviolence and Children.* Philadelphia:
         Friends Peace Committee.
Keniston, Kenneth
  1968 *The Young Radicals.* New York: Harcourt Brace Jovano-
         vich.
         Based on extended interviews with radical student leaders
         of the mid-sixties. This study reveals much of the motiva-
         tion behind the deviant behavior of young political activists.
Kissinger, Henry
  1969 *Nuclear Weapons and Foreign Policy.* New York: Norton.
Kriesberg, Louis
  1973 *The Sociology of Social Conflict.* Englewood Cliffs, N.J.:
         Prentice-Hall.

Lakey, George, and Martin Oppenheimer
1965 *A Manual for Direct Action.* Chicago: Quadrangle.
A very helpful exposition of basic nonviolent direct action
strategy and tactics. Good for initial nonviolent training
sessions.
Laue, James, and Gerald Cormick.
1974 "The Ethics of Social Intervention: Community Crisis
Intervention Programs." St. Louis, Mo.: Community Crisis
Intervention Center, Washington University. Mimeo.
Lewin, Kurt, ed.
1948 *Resolving Social Conflicts.* New York: Harper & Row.
Likert, Rensis, and Jane Gibson Likert
1976 *New Ways of Managing Conflict.* New York: McGraw-
Hill.
Lord, William, Leonard Adelman, Paul Wehr, et al.
1978 *Conflict Management in Federal Water Resource Planning.*
Boulder: Institute of Behavioral Science, University of
Colorado.
Morgan, William
1972 "Faculty Mediation of Student War Protests." *Student Pro-
test in America.* Foster and Long, eds. Clifton, N.J.:
Morrow.
Moskos, Charles
1976 *Peace Soldiers: The Sociology of a United Nations Military
Force.* Chicago: University of Chicago Press.
National Center for Dispute Settlement
1974 "A Report Concerning the Involvement of the NCDS in
the Massachusetts Correctional Institution." Washington,
D.C.: NCDS. Mimeo.
New York City Police Department (NYCPD)
1969 "Police Response to Family Disputes." New York City:
Mimeo.
Training manual for police training course.
New York State Special Commission on Attica
(NYSSCA)
1972 *Attica.* New York: Bantam.
The official report of the Attica uprising, the response of
the state, and the abortive attempt at negotiated settlement.
A well written and fair account.
Nicolau, George
1973 "Training in Community Conflict Resolution Skills." New
York: Institute for Mediation and Conflict Resolution.
Mimeo.

Noton, Mitchell, et al.
  1974   "The Systems Analysis of Conflict," *Futures* 6, no. 2 (April): 114-132.
Nye, Joseph S.
  1971   *Peace in Parts: Integration and Conflict in Regional Organizations.* Boston: Little, Brown and Co.
Pechota, V.
  1971   "Complementary Structures of Third-Party Settlement of International Disputes." New York: UNITAR.
Pfeiffer, J. W., and J. Jones, eds.
  1973   *Handbook of Structured Experiences for Human Relations Training.* LaJolla, Calif.: University Associates. Four volumes.
Pirages, Dennis
  1975   *Managing Political Conflict.* New York: Praeger Publishing.
Platt, John
  1972   "Beyond Freedom and Dignity: A Revolutionary Manifesto," *Center Magazine* 5 (March-April).
Randle, Robert
  1973   *The Origins of Peace.* New York: The Free Press.
         One of the very few studies of how wars are terminated.
Rikhye, Indar, Michael Harbottle, and Bjorn Egge
  1974   *The Thin Blue Line: International Peacekeeping and Its Future.* New Haven: Yale University Press.
         The definitive work to date on the use of United Nations armed forces to intervene as a neutral force in armed conflict. A very important contribution.
Roberts, Adam
  1972   *Total Defence and Civil Resistance: Problems of Sweden's Security Policy.* Stockholm: Research Institute of Swedish National Defence.
         A report commissioned by the Swedish Defence Ministry for use in considering new national defense strategies based more on civilian unarmed reistance.
Rubin, Jeffrey, and Bert Brown
  1975   *The Social Psychology of Bargaining and Negotiation.* New York: Academic Press.
Schelling, Thomas
  1963   *Strategy of Conflict.* New York: Oxford University Press.
Schonborn, Karl
  1975   *Dealing with Violence.* Springfield, Ill.: Charles C. Thomas.

Sharp, Gene
1973 *Politics of Nonviolent Action.* Boston: Porter Sargent.
Sherif, Muzafer
1966 *In Common Predicament: Social Psychology of Intergroup Conflict and Cooperation.* Boston: Houghton Mifflin.
Shirts, Gary
n.d. "Starpower." Western Behavioral Institute: La Jolla, California.
A game illustrating the dynamics of power concentration and conflict over power.
Smith, Clagett
1966 "A Comparative Analysis of Some Conditions and Consequences of Intra-Organizational Conflict." *Administrative Science Quarterly,* no. 10.
Sorokin, Pitirim
1957 *Social and Cultural Dynamics.* Boston: Porter Sargent.
Stonier, Tom
1962 "What Would It Really Be Like?" *Breakthrough to Peace.* New York: New Directions (333 Sixth Avenue).
A biologist describes the likely consequences of a twenty-megaton nuclear air blast over Manhattan Island.
Straus, Donald
1975 "Data Validation." Paper presented at Conference on Coastal Zone Management, Asilomar, California. May 30. Mimeo.
Available from American Arbitration Association, New York.
United Nations Institute for Training and Research (UNITAR)
1970 *Social Psychological Techniques and the Peaceful Settlement of International Disputes.* New York: UNITAR.
1973 "UNITAR Specialized Course on Procedures for Settlement of Disputes." New York: UNITAR.
Document for restricted circulation.
Walker, Daniel
1969 *Rights in Conflict: Convention Week in Chicago, August 25-29, 1968.* New York: Dutton.
The official report of the commission investigating the 1968 Chicago political demonstrations and police riot at the time of the Democratic National Convention.
Walton, Richard
1969 *Interpersonal Peacemaking.* Reading, Mass.: Addison-Wesley.

Warren, Roland
  1964   "The Conflict Intersystem and the Change Agent." *Journal of Conflict Resolution* 8, no. 3 (September).
         An analysis of the author's role as a Quaker intermediary attempting to effect greater communication and concilia- tion between East and West German policymakers.
Wehr, Paul, and Robert DeHaan
  1978   "Conflict Education: A New Direction in Higher Learn- ing." *Design for Nonviolent Change*, Charny, I., ed. Boulder, Co.: Westview Press.
Wehr, Paul, and A. Michael Washburn
  1976   *Peace and World Order Systems: Teaching and Research.* Beverly Hills, Calif.: Sage Publications.
White, Gilbert
  1974   "The Role of Scientific Information in Anticipation and Prevention of Environmental Disputes." Paper delivered to the Conference on Adjustment and Avoidance of Environ- mental Disputes, Bellagio, Italy. July 19-23. Boulder, Co.: Institute of Behavioral Science, University of Colorado.
Williams, Robin
  1947   *The Reduction of Intergroup Tensions: A Survey of Re- search on Problems of Ethnic, Racial and Religious Group Relations.* New York: Social Science Research Council.
Willrich, Mason
  1975   *Perspective on the Non-Proliferation Treaty Review Con- ference.* Muscatine, Ia.: Stanley Foundation.
Yarrow, C. H.
  1978   *Quaker Experiences in International Conciliation.* New Haven, Conn.: Yale University Press.
Young, Oran
  1967   *Intermediaries: Third Parties in International Crises.* Princeton, N.J.: Princeton University Press.
  1969   *Politics of Force: Bargaining During International Crises.* Princeton, N.J.: Princeton University Press.
  1972   "Intermediaries: Additional Thoughts on Third Parties." *Journal of Conflict Resolution* 16, no. 1 (March).

Chapter 3: Self-Limiting Conflict: The Gandhian Style

Abrams, G., and F. Schmidt
  1972   *Learning Peace: A Resource Unit.* Philadelphia: Jane Addams Peace Association.
         The best resources and ideas book for secondary school

peace education yet produced. Particularly strong on active learning techniques.

Bartos, Otomar
1974   *Process and Outcome of Negotiations.* New York: Columbia University Press.

Bondurant, Joan
1965   *Conquest of Violence.* Berkeley: University of California Press.

Boulding, Elise
1974   "The Child and Nonviolent Social Change." *Handbook on Peace Education,* Wulf, ed. Oslo: International Peace Research Association, International Peace Research Institute.

Bourdieu, Pierre
1962   *The Algerians.* Boston: Beacon Press.

Coleman, James S.
1957   *Community Conflict.* New York: Free Press.

Hare, A. Paul
1968   "Nonviolent Action from a Social-Psychological Perspective." *Sociological Inquiry* 38, no. 1.

Hare, A. Paul, and Herbert Blumberg, eds.
1977   *Liberation without Violence: A Third Party Approach.* London, Rex Collings.

King, Martin Luther, Jr.
1961   *Stride Toward Freedom.* New York: Ballantine.
       King's account of the Montgomery bus boycott, the first organized massive resistance to a racial injustice in modern U.S. history. Well written and a classic that should be required reading in all social studies courses.

Klitgaard, Robert
1971   "Gandhi's Non-Violence as a Tactic." *Journal of Peace Research* 2:143-152.

Kriesberg, Louis
1973   *Sociology of Social Conflict.* Englewood Cliffs, N.J.: Prentice-Hall.

Mangione, Jerre
1972   *The World Around Danilo Dolci.* New York: Harper & Row.
       A sympathetic treatment of Danilo Dolci, leader of a Sicilian rural development movement against Mafia repression. Nonviolent direct action and innovative social/economic development programs are made interdependent, in much the same way as in Gandhian satyagraha.

Matthiessen, P.
   1970   *Sal Si Puedes.* New York: Delta.
          An account of the Cesar Chavez United Farmworkers move-
          ment, one of the major nonviolent movements in the Ameri-
          can experience.
Muste, A. J.
   1940   *Nonviolence in an Aggressive World,* New York: Harper
          & Row.
Naess, Arne
   1958   "Systematization of Gandhian Ethics of Conflict Resolu-
          tion." *Journal of Conflict Resolution* 2, no. 2.
Nesbitt, William
   1973   *Teaching Youth about Conflict and War.* Washington,
          D.C.: National Council for the Social Studies.
          A good source book for secondary school teachers.
Nute, B. R.
   1974   *Helder Camara's Latin America.* London: Friends Peace
          and International Relations Committee.
          A brief account of the nonviolent action and resistance
          movement led by Archbishop Dom Helder Camara in Brazil
          and throughout Latin America.
Oberschall, Anthony
   1973   *Social Conflict and Social Movements.* Englewood Cliffs,
          N.J.: Prentice-Hall.
Quaker Action Group
   1970   *Resistance in Latin America.* Philadelphia: American
          Friends Service Committee.
          Analyses of historical nonviolent resistance movements in
          Latin America.
Sharp, Gene
   1970   "The Origins of Gandhi's Nonviolent Militancy." *Harvard
          Political Review* 2, no. 1 (May).
   1973   *Politics of Nonviolent Action.* Boston: Porter Sargent.
Shure, G., R. Meeker, and E. Hansford
   1965   "The Effectiveness of Pacifist Strategies in Bargaining
          Games." *Journal of Conflict Resolution* 9, no. 1.
Tolley, Howard
   1973   *Children and War: Political Socialization to International
          Conflict.* New York: Columbia University, Columbia
          Teachers College Press.
Walker, Charles
   1973   *Training for Nonviolent Action.* Monograph Series on
          Nonviolent Action, no. 11. Haverford, Pa.: Haverford
          College.

Wehr, Paul
  1968   "A Southern Sit-In." *Nonviolent Direct Action*, Hare and Blumberg, eds. Washington, D.C.: Corpus. Pp. 100-106.

Chapter 4: Self-limiting Conflict: The Norwegian Resistance

Aanerud, Jon
  1963   *Fellesprogrammet.* MA Thesis. Oslo, Norway: Oslo University. Mimeo.
Boserup. A., and A. Mack
  1975   *War Without Weapons.* New York: Schocken.
          A feasibility study of civilian defense commissioned by the Danish government. It reviews the history and theory of nonviolent direct action and assesses its capability for redirection of Danish defense policy.
Coser, Lewis
  1956   *Functions of Social Conflict.* New York: Free Press.
Department of Peace and Conflict Research
  1972   "Nonmilitary Forms of Struggle." University of Uppsala, Uppsala, Sweden. Mimeo.
          Research proposal to explore the use of nonviolent strategy and tactics in various types of repressive situations such as colonial domination and external aggression.
Desai, Narayan
  1972   *Toward a Nonviolent Revolution.* Varanasi, India: Sarva Seva Sangh Prakashan.
Deutsch, Karl
  1963   *Nerves of Government.* New York: Free Press.
Drivnes, Olav
  1942   Personal Diaries.
Ebert, Theodore
  1969   "Civilian Resistance in Czechoslovakia: Implications of the August Campaign." *The World Today* 25, no. 1 (February).
Grimnes, Ole Kristian
  1969   *Et Flyktningesamfunn Vokser Fram: Nordmenn I Sverige 1940-45.* Oslo, Norway: Aschehoug.
Hansen, B. J.
  1946   "Referat Fra Motet hos dr. Bjorn Helland Hansen." Norwegian National Archives. Mimeo. February 1.
Heirich, Max
  1971   *The Spiral of Conflict: Berkeley, 1964.* New York: Columbia University Press.

Kelman, Herbert
  1968 *A Time to Speak: On Human Values and Social Research.*
        San Francisco: Jossey-Bass.
Lakey, George, and Martin Oppenheimer
  1965 *A Manual for Direct Action.* Chicago: Quadrangle.
Lid, Ingvald
  1962 *Det Norske Postmannslag 1934-1959.* Oslo: Mallingske.
Lyng, John
  1948 *Forraederiets Epoke.* Oslo: Steensballes.
Malm, Ole Jacob
  1945 "Orientering pa Landsmotet for den Sivile Hjemmeledelses
        Kontaktpunkter." Norwegian National Archives. Mimeo.
Olson, T., and L. Shivers
  1970 *Training for Nonviolent Action.* London: War Resisters
        International.
Parsons, Talcott
  1961 "Some Considerations on the Theory of Social Change."
        Rural Sociology, no. 26 (September).
Riste, O., and B. Nokleby
  1970 *Norway 1940-45: The Resistance Movement.* Oslo: Tanum.
Roberts, Adam, ed.
  1969 *Civilian Resistance as a National Defence.* Baltimore:
        Penguin.
        A collection of essays on the feasibility, advantages, and
        disadvantages of nonviolent civilian resistance as a national
        defense policy.
Roberts, Adam
  1972 *Total Defence and Civil Resistance: Problems of Sweden's
        Security Policy.* Stockholm: Research Institute of Swedish
        National Defence.
Rose, Arnold
  1968 "The Ecological Influential: A Leadership Type." *Sociology and Social Research* 52, no. 2.
Sharp, Gene
  1973 *The Politics of Nonviolent Action.* Boston: Porter Sargent.
Skodvin, Magne
  1950 "Det Store Fremstot." *Norges Krig,* vol. 2, Steen, ed. Oslo:
        Gyldendal.
Steen, Sverre, ed.
  1950 *Norges Krig.* Vols. 2 and 3. Oslo: Gyldendal.
Wehr, Paul
  1978 "Nonviolent Resistance to Occupation: Norway and
        Czechoslovakia." *Creative Conflict in Society.* Bruyn, S.,
        and P. Wayman, eds., New York: Irvington Publish-
        ers.

Wright, Myrtle
  1974   *Norwegian Diary 1940-45.* London: Goodwin Press.
Wyller, T. C.
  1958   *Nyordning Og Motstand.* Oslo: Universitets Forlaget.
Zietlow, C., and B. Yaffe
  1971   "Spring Action Training Manuals." Washington, D.C.: People's Coalition for Peace and Justice.

Chapter 5: Self-limiting Conflict:
The Rocky Flats National Action

Boulder Daily Camera (BDC)
  1978   "Army Nerve Gas Inventory Planned." February 15.
Carlton, David, and Carlos Schaerf
  1975   *International Terrorism and World Security.* London: Crown Helm.
Comptroller General of the United States (CGUS)
  1977   *Safety and Transportation Safeguards at the Rocky Flats Nuclear Weapons Plant.* Unclassified digest of a classified report. Washington, D.C. January 11.
Coover, V., E. Deacon, C. Esser, and C. Moore
  1977   *Resource Manual for a Living Revolution.* Philadelphia: New Society Press.
Denver Post (DP)
  1977   "Agents Seize $300,000 Loot, Suspects." July 28, p. 1.
Flood, Michael
  1976   "Nuclear Sabotage." *Bulletin of the Atomic Scientists* (October), pp. 29-36.
Gamson, William
  1975   *Strategy of Social Protest.* Homewood, Ill.: Dorsey.
Goffman, Erving
  1959   *Presentation of Self in Everyday Life.* New York: Doubleday.
Hamilton, Lawrence
  1978   "The Ecology of Terrorism." Unpublished Ph.D. dissertation. Department of Sociology, University of Colorado at Boulder.
Hare, A. Paul, and Herbert Blumberg, eds.
  1977   *Liberation without Violence: A Third Party Approach.* London: Rex Collings.
Hayes, Denis
  1977   *Rays of Hope: The Transition to a Post-Petroleum World.* New York: Norton.

Hyams, E.
  1975   *Terrorists and Terrorism.* London: J. M. Dent.
Jenkins, Brian
  1977   "The Potential for Nuclear Terrorism." Unpublished paper
         presented at the Conference on Nuclear Arms Proliferation
         and Nuclear Terrorism, Arms Control Association, Wash-
         ington, D.C., May 8.
Jessel, Margaret
  1977   "An Analysis of Security and Safeguards of Nuclear Ma-
         terials Within the Transportation Process." Unpublished
         paper, Institute of Behavioral Science, University of
         Colorado, Boulder. December.
Lamm-Wirth Task Force on Rocky Flats (LWTFRF)
  1975   *Final Report.* Office of the Governor, Denver, Colorado.
         October 1.
Lind, Ian
  1976   "Hazards of Nuclear Weapons Presence on Oahu, with
         Recommendations for Action: A Report to Governor
         George Ariyoshi." American Friends Service Committee,
         2426 Oahu Avenue, Honolulu, Hawaii 16822. May 21.
MacCannell, Dean
  1973   "Nonviolent Action as Theater: A Dramaturgical Analysis
         of 146 Demonstrations." No. 10, Monograph Series on Non-
         violent Action, Center for Nonviolent Conflict Resolution,
         Haverford College, Haverford, Pennsylvania 19041.
Oberschall, Anthony
  1973   *Social Conflict and Social Movements.* Englewood Cliffs,
         N.J.: Prentice-Hall.
Partridge, Kathryn
  1977   "Nukes? No Thanks." Unpublished paper, Department of
         Sociology, University of Colorado at Boulder. December.
Rocky Flats Action Group (RFAG)
  1977   *Local Hazard, Global Threat.* Denver: American Friends
         Service Committee.
Rocky Mountain News (RMN)
  1978   "Tooele Civilian Pleads Guilty to Nerve Gas Loss Cover-
         Up." February 19.
Sivard, Ruth
  1977   *World Military and Social Expenditures: 1977.* Leesburg,
         Virginia: WMSE Publications.
Smelser, Neil
  1962   *Theory of Collective Behavior.* New York: Free Press.

United States Energy Research and Development Administration
  1977   *Draft Environmental Impact Statement: Rocky Flats Plant Site.* Vols. 1 and 2, ERDA-1545-D. September.
Wehr, Paul, and Susan Carpenter, eds.
  1976   *Nuclear Energy and Public Health and Welfare in Colorado.* Denver: American Friends Service Committee. 65 pp.
Willrich, Mason, and Theodore Taylor
  1974   *Nuclear Theft: Risks and Safeguards.* Cambridge, Mass.: Ballinger.

Chapter 6: Regulating Environmental Conflict

Anthropological Quarterly
  1968   "Dam Anthropology: River Basin Research." Special Issue. Vol. 41, no. 3 (July).
Boulder Daily Camera (BDC)
  1975   "State Could Be Squeezed in Middle of 'Water War.'" February 11.
Burch, William, Jr.
  1971   *Daydreams and Nightmares: A Sociological Essay on the Environment.* New York: Harper & Row.
Bureau of Land Management (BLM)
  1976   "Northwest Colorado Coal: Draft Environmental Statement." Denver, Colorado. May.
Coleman, James S.
  1957   *Community Conflict.* New York: Free Press.
Cormick, Gerald, and Jane McCarthy
  1974   "Environmental Mediation: Flood Control, Recreation and Development in the Snoqualmie River Valley." St. Louis: Social Science Institute, Washington University. December.
Department of the Interior
  1976   "New Federal Coal Leasing Policy to Be Implemented Under Controlled Conditions." January 26.
Deutsch, Karl
  1974   "On the Interaction of Ecological and Political Systems: Some Potential Contributions of the Social Sciences to the Study of Man and His Environment." *Social Science Information* 13 (December). International Social Science Council. Paris: Mouton.
Donald, Dennis and Jefferson Patterson
  1975   "An Analysis of Western Eagle County." Denver, Colorado: Bickert, Browne, Coddington and Associates.

Dusenbury, Adele
  1976 "Growth Brought Riches to Some, Not all, and Walter Paepke's Dream Has Faded." *Aspen Times.* April 1.
Eagle Valley Enterprise (EVE)
  1976a "County Accepts 'Mediation' Help for Pending Environmental Conflicts." May 27, p. 6.
  1976b "Tech Review Cites Adam's Rib Impacts." June 10.
  1976c "Adam's Rib: How Does It Fit?" Special Supplement. June 17.
Exxon Corporation
  1975 *Energy Outlook 1976-1990.*
Fitch Russell, et al.
  1975a "A Listing of Proposed, Planned or Under-Construction Energy Projects in Federal Region VIII." Denver, Colorado: Mountain-Plains Federal Regional Council. August.
  1975b "Socioeconomic Impacts and Federal Assistance in Energy Development Impacted Communities in Federal Region VIII." Denver, Colorado: Mountain-Plains Federal Regional Council. July.
Foundation for Urban and Neighborhood Development (FUND)
  1975 "Social-Cultural Impact Study of the Upper Eagle Valley." Denver, Co. June.
Gilmore, John
  1976 "Boom Towns May Hinder Energy Resource Development." *Sci nce* 191 (February).
Gilmore, J., and M. Duff
  1974 "The Evolving Political Economy of Pitkin County: Growth Management by Consensus in a Boom Community." Denver Research Institute, University of Denver.
Goeldner, C., et al.
  1972 "Economic Impact of Power Plant Installations: Routt and Moffat Counties." Business Research Division, Graduate School of Business Administration, University of Colorado, Boulder.
Hammond, Kenneth, et al.
  1975 "Social Judgment Theory: Applications in Policy Formation." *Human Judgment and Decision Processes: Applications in Problem Settings.* Kaplan and Schwartz, eds. New York: Academic Press.
Hammond, Kenneth, and Leonard Adelman
  1976 "Science, Values, and Human Judgment." *Science* 194: 389-396.

Hardin, Garrett
1972 *Exploring New Ethics for Survival.* New York: Macmillan.
Ives, Jack, and Ann Stites
1975 "Impact of Human Activities on Mountain and Tundra Ecosystems." INSTAAR Special Publication, University of Colorado, Boulder. May.
Knowlton, Clark
1972 "Culture Conflict and Natural Resources." *Social Behavior, Natural Resources and the Environment,* Burch et al., New York: Harper & Row.
Lamm-Wirth Task Force on Rocky Flats (LWTFRF)
1975 *Final Report.* Office of the Governor, Denver, Colorado. October 1.
Lord, William, et al.
1975 "Fish and Wildlife Implications of Upper Missouri Basin Water Allocation." Monograph 22, Program on Technology, Environment and Man, Institute of Behavioral Science, University of Colorado, Boulder.
Meier, Richard
1974 *Planning for an Urban World,* Cambridge, Mass.: MIT Press.
Mesarovic, Mihajlo, and Eduard Pestel
1974 *Mankind at the Turning Point.* New York: Dutton.
Monarchi, David, and Charles Rahe.
n.d. "A Study of the Social and Economic Needs Created by the Proposed Craig Power Installation." Business Research Division, Graduate School of Business Administration, University of Colorado, Boulder.
Natural Resources Journal
1976 "Symposium on Public Participation in Resource Decision Making." Special Issue. Vol. 16, no. 1 (January).
Northern Great Plains Resources Program (NGPRP)
1975 "Effects of Coal Development in the Northern Great Plains." Denver, Colorado.
Office of the Governor
1974 "Impact: An Assessment of the Impact of Oil Shale Development." Colorado Planning and Management Region 11, Denver, Colorado. December.
Radesovich, G., and D. Hamburg
1976 *Colorado Water Laws: A Compilation of Statutes, Regulations, Compacts and Selected Cases.* Colorado State University, Fort Collins.

Roof, Richard, and Per Thomassen
    1973   "A Survey Testing the Attitudes of Town of Eagle Residents
           Toward the Proposed Adam's Rib Ski Area and Other
           Community Growth Issues." Graduate School of Business
           Administration, University of Colorado, Boulder. Fall.
Schneider, Stephen, and Lynne Mesirow
    1976   *The Genesis Strategy: Climate and Global Survival.* New
           York: Plenum.
Technical Working Group (TWG)
    1975   "Glossary: Areas of Concern Related to Intensive Winter
           Recreation Development." Division of Planning, Colorado
           Department of Local Affairs, Denver. August.
U.S. Forest Service (USFS)
    1976   "Environmental Analysis Report: Beaver Creek Winter
           Sports Site and Year Around Recreational Area." White
           River National Forest, Glenwood Springs, Colorado.
Wehr, Paul
    1979   "Environmental Conflict Management: Problem, Theory
           and Method." *Research in Social Movements, Conflict and
           Change.* Kriesberg, ed. Greenwich, Conn.: JAI Press.
Wehr, Paul, and Susan Carpenter, eds.
    1976   "Nuclear Energy and Public Health and Welfare in
           Colorado." American Friends Service Committee, Denver,
           Colorado.
Wolpert, Julian
    1976   "Regressive Siting of Public Facilities." *Natural Resources
           Journal* 16, no. 1 (January).

Postscript
Kuhn, Thomas
    1962   *The Structure of Scientific Revolutions.* Chicago: Univer-
           sity of Chicago Press.

Listing of Peace Research Journals and Newsletters
Bulletin of Peace Proposals. Universitetsforlaget, Box 307, Blindern,
    Oslo 3, Norway. Published quarterly.
Cooperation and Conflict. Universitetsforlaget, P. O. Box 142,
    Boston, Mass. 02113.
Defense Monitor. Center for Defense Information, 201 Massachusetts
    Avenue, N.E., Washington, D.C. 20002.

Economic Development and Cultural Change. University of Chicago Press, 5801 Ellis Avenue, Chicago, Illinois 60637. Published quarterly.

Instant Research on Peace & Violence. Tampere Peace Research Institute, Tammelanpuistok 58 B V, 33 100 Tampere 10, Finland. Published quarterly.

International Associations. Union of International Associations, 1 rue aux Laines, 1000 Brussels, Belgium. Published monthly.

International Interactions: A Transitional Multidisciplinary Journal. Gordon and Breach Science Publishers, 440 Park Avenue South, New York, N.Y. 10016. Four issues per volume.

International Journal of Group Tensions. International Organization for the Study of Group Tensions, Inc., 7 West 96th Street, New York, N.Y. 10025. Published quarterly.

International Organization. Sponsored by the World Peace Foundation and the University of Wisconsin, Journals Department, University of Wisconsin Press, Box 1379, Madison, Wisconsin 53701. Published quarterly.

International Peace Research Newsletter. Editor, Raimo Väyrynen, International Peace Research Association (IPRA), Secretariat, P.O. Box 70, 33101 Tampere 10, Finland. North American Subscription Office: IPRA Newsletter, Institute of Behavioral Science, University of Colorado, Boulder, Colorado 80309. Issued approximately six times a year.

International Peace Studies Newsletter. Center for Peace Studies, University of Akron, Akron, Ohio 44325. Published quarterly.

International Studies Quarterly. Official Journal of the International Studies Association; Sage Publications, Inc., 275 South Beverly Drive, Beverly Hills, California 90212.

IPRA Studies in Peace Research: Proceedings of the International Peace Research Association Conferences. Vol. I-IV (1965-1971) available from Van Gorcum Publisher, Assen, Netherlands; Vol. V: PRIO, P.O. Box 5052, Oslo 3, Norway; and Vol. VI: IPRA Secretariat, Tampere, Finland.

Journal of Conflict Resolution. Sage Publications, P. O. Box 776, Beverly Hills, California 90212. Published quarterly.

Journal of Peace Research. Universitetsforlaget, P.O. Box 307, Blindern, Oslo 3, Norway or P.O. Box 142, Boston, Massachusetts 02113. Published quarterly.

Journal of World Education. Association of World Colleges & Universities, 3 Harbor Hill Drive, Huntington, New York 11743. Published quarterly.

Peace and Change: A Journal of Peace Research. Managing Editor, Han-shen Lin, Sonoma State College, 1801 East Cotati Avenue, Rohnert Park, California 94928.

Peace Research. Canadian Peace Research Institute, 119 Thomas Street, Oakville, Ontario, Canada. Published monthly; current issues available free to any interested person or institution.

Peace Research Abstracts Journal. Canadian Peace Research Institute, 119 Thomas Street, Oakville, Ontario, Canada. Published monthly.

Peace Research in Japan. Edited by the Japan Peace Research Group, c/o Prof. Takeshi Ishida, Institute of Social Science, University of Tokyo, Hongo 7-3-1, Bunkyo-ku, Tokyo, Japan.

Peace Research Reviews. Canadian Peace Research Institute, 119 Thomas Street, Oakville, Ontario, Canada. Published six issues per volume.

Peace Science Society (International) Papers. Walter Isard, Peace Science Society, Department of Regional Science, University of Pennsylvania, Philadelphia, Pennsylvania 19104.

Index